THE GODS WHO FELL FROM THE SKY

To my Mom and Dad, my breathtaking Penny, and my children
Heartfelt thanks to my sister-in-law Heather

THE GODS WHO FELL FROM THE SKY

A memoir of my adventurous life

Dick Mawson

PORCUPINE PRESS

Johannesburg, South Africa

© Richard Mawson 2014
ISBN: 978-1-920609-48-1
Published by Porcupine Press
PO Box 2756
Pinegowrie, 2123
South Africa
info@porcupinepress.co.za
www.porcupinepress.co.za

Cover designed by Wim Rheeder: wim@wimrheeder.co.za
Set in 11 point on 15 point, Minion Pro
Printed by Mega Digital in Cape Town, South Africa

Contents

Author's note

I was born on 18 February 1942 at home in Maghull, a stone's throw from Aintree, home of the English Grand National as well as the British Grand Prix in the 1950s. Perhaps these two facts – being born so close to a famous Grand Prix circuit and coming into the world during the darkest days of a World War – prefigured the risks and adventures that have characterised my life. I have been involved in racing on land and water, and I served in the Rhodesian military. I have lost a limb and yet I continue to build racing cars and enjoy the company of my young granddaughters. I have thoroughly enjoyed my life. That is why I have decided to share it with others. My story began in typically spectacular fashion. But I was too young to remember the earliest adventures. I have therefore used something my mother wrote. In this way I acknowledge her major influence in my life. For the rest, I relate my story from memories of the various incidents and phases that have given shape to my journey.

Prologue

This prologue is an edited version of Dorothy Mawson's document *Mayday Mayday* which she wrote for her sons, and a version of which was published in a Rhodesian magazine 20 years after the Mawson family had settled in southern Africa.

*M*Y *husband was a coal merchant and a senior NCO with the home guard on an anti-aircraft battery at the Liverpool docks during the war. Once peace returned to Europe and the world, however, we decided that there would be more opportunity in a new land. So we took our two young sons – Richard (4) and Clive (2) – and went to Africa. I have never regretted this adventurous move, although it was characterised by several significant coincidences and nearly began in disaster.*

Our house and coal business in Liverpool were sold almost immediately they were put on the market, and before I had time to catch my breath we were on our way to London to procure a passage to South Africa.

Back in 1946, it seemed impossible to book any sort of passage to South Africa without long delays. After spending a futile week in London, we were on the verge of giving up when we heard about a MTB (Motor Torpedo Boat) which was being converted for passenger use in Portsmouth. Arriving there, we were transported to the docks where the craft was under refit. After an hour of viewing the facilities available on the boat, we left and caught the train back to London. George, my husband, was quiet all the way back, but he did not tell me at the time the misgivings he had about taking his family on a journey of some six thousand miles across three oceans to South Africa in a plywood boat. By the time we reached London, he had decided that the boat journey would be too great a risk for his beloved family.

On our arrival at our London hotel, a message awaited us: Would we contact a travel agency we had seen earlier in the week? So, arrangements were made for us to be there the next morning where we were offered various alternative passages, none of which suited us. We were just about to leave the travel agency when we were called back. Were we interested in a private charter?

A small Avro Anson aircraft (twin-engine and used by the RAF during the war) was available, the cost of which would be shared with a prominent businessman who was also having the same difficulties regarding travel as we were having. With the optimism of youth, a meeting was arranged for the next day at the offices of CL Air Surveys in Cromwell Rd, where we met with Lt Col Lloyd. We immediately liked the proposed charter and took up the option.

We returned to Liverpool to finalise our departure and to bid farewell to friends and family who mattered to us. My brother Alf had given us a lift to the train station and at last we were on the move with what we felt was some real direction in our lives. Reading a newspaper George had bought at Lime Street Station before catching the London express, a report on the second page caught his eye. A chartered MTB, which had left from Portsmouth a few days earlier, had floundered in the Bay of Biscay with the loss of all on board. He wondered if perhaps it was the same one we had looked at.

Our adventure that nearly ended in tragedy started on the 25th of June 1946. The Anson was waiting for us on the tarmac at Gatwick where we met our pilot, navigator and our travelling companion for the first time. The formalities taken care of, we took off about midday and landed at Le Bourget for a late lunch and then on to Marseilles 'Mariguane' Airport for the night stop. The fuel capacity of our plane necessitated having to make frequent stops for refuelling, and for the passengers to partake of any refreshment available. Hotel accommodation also had to be arranged for the coming night stop.

We spent our first night at a comfortable little French inn in Marseilles and, bearing in mind a dawn start was planned for the next *morning, we retired early. Taking off around seven after a flight plan had been filed, we flew over Sardinia, which looked picturesque nestled in the middle of the Mediterranean. The sea was the most beautiful shade of blue, which turned to a brilliant turquoise as we landed in Tunis for lunch. Then on to Tripoli, where we were sent on by the Yanks to Castle Benito, landing just after four in the afternoon. An army barracks was our accommodation for the second night.*

Our son Richard was fascinated by the camel trains leaving for their long journey across the desert, but being intimidated by the size of the camels, he kept his distance and a tight hold of my hand. To bed early for a dawn start again the next morning.

A stop at Benito for lunch and on to Eli Adem near Benghazi for fuel. We saw lots of burnt-out planes in the desert around Benghazi, and flew on to Cairo where we landed at Abmaza Airport.

We stayed at the Heliopolis Palace, which was spacious and cool after our hot and dusty trip. With the children bathed and asleep, we went down for dinner, served outside on a marble terrace with millions of stars and a crescent moon hanging overhead. It was a magical night, and as we were not leaving until the following afternoon, our pilot suggested a trip to Cairo the following morning.

After breakfast we boarded a tram, which proved to be hair-raising. The passengers swarmed aboard and hung on to every conceivable inch like flies on flypaper. The driver of the tram hurled us down the hills at breakneck speed, the tram bell ringing constantly in our ears as pedestrians dived for cover in all directions.

Groppis Ice Cream Parlour was a must for visitors to Cairo. Being a favourite with the tourists, the ice cream was superb and cooled us down considerably. Our sightseeing over and given our hair-raising ride into town, we decided to take a taxi back, which was an eye-opener in itself. I don't know which was the lesser of the two evils and was thankful the driver had a good horn. We were eager to be on our way, so we packed and caught a taxi to the airport for an afternoon flight to Luxor.

Unlike the aircraft of today, we did not reach a very high altitude, so passing over the desert we could see the camel trains criss-crossing below. The burnt-out wrecks of planes and tanks brought home the realities of the war, which had been fought so recently on the desert below us.

We stopped for the night at Luxor on the banks of the Nile, with the pyramids in the distance. We had arrived late and were seated at dinner with the manager of BOAC, Mr Frank Edge, who was fascinated to hear about our journey so far. I did not get a very good night's sleep as the ceiling was alive with sand lizards.

We left at eight-thirty the next morning for Wadi Halfa where we landed for fuel and lunch – but it was too hot to eat. It had been 150 years since the area had last had good rains and everything looked very parched.

Khartoum was the next stop, where we stayed in the Grand Hotel. Despite huge fans whirling all over the hotel, the heat was intense. Our early arrival allowed us time to visit a small zoo, a welcome change for two small boys unaccustomed to the tiny cabin of a small plane.

Off early the next morning, we arrived at Malakao on Lake Victoria for lunch where a flying boat landed just in front of us. The trip was very bumpy, and the worst part of the journey so far. The terrain below us was horrible desolate desert country which changed dramatically to green swamps as we approached our night stop.

We couldn't land at Nairobi so we put down at Kisumu and booked into its only hotel, where we met our friends from the flying boat. It was very hot and we saw lots of elephants as we passed over the swamps as we were preparing to land.

An early start from Kisumu, and we headed to Juba for more fuel and a lousy sandwich. It was very pretty, green and fertile country as we flew over Kenya with Mt Kilimanjaro looming skywards in the distance that seemed to dwarf our tiny plane. We had not long ago crossed the equator and the heat in the tiny cabin was stifling, but it was breathtaking to see a snow-capped mountain so close to the equator. We had at *last left the desert behind. It turned very cold as we left for Tabora and then on to Mybeya in Tanganyika. We had been travelling for seven days and it was now 1 July.*

Flying over the Serengeti in our little Anson, herds of wildebeest were massing in their millions as they prepared for their annual migration to pastures anew. We watched this spectacle in awe and fascination from the air above. Nowhere in the world is there a movement of animals as immense as the wildebeest migration in Africa; over two million animals migrate from the Serengeti National Park in Tanzania to the greener pastures of the Masai Mara National Reserve in Kenya from July to October. The recent experience of seeing Kilimanjaro's snow-capped summit so close to the equator was still fresh in our minds, as we watched the herds congregate below us. I believe we were some of the first ever to see this unique spectacle from the air.

In Tanganyika we were accommodated in chalets and warned not to move around outside, as leopards frequently came down from the hills. Thankfully, we left the following morning early without incident, not realising that by nightfall, we would be placed in a very precarious situation.

It was the intention of the pilot to refuel at Fort Jameson, in then Northern Rhodesia, which we should have reached by midday and in time for lunch.

Flying low, we were now in thick bush country and could see many herds of elephant roaming around the scrub and wallowing in the rivers. We had been in the air for some hours now and lunch hour was nearly over. I heard our navigator tapping out a message on the Morse key.

Suddenly, George gripped my arm and whispered, 'We're in trouble, lass, I have just heard the May Day call going out'. Before I realised the implication of this remark, the door of the cockpit opened and our navigator appeared.

'I have been trying to contact Fort Jameson for some time now, but no reply,' he said. 'We are out of fuel and have to make a forced landing,'

confirming what my husband had heard going out on the radio. The navigator looked around the cabin and continued talking, asking us to strap the children in tightly within our seat belts and pad around them with clothing and blankets.

There was no time to think about what could happen as we attended to the children. We felt the plane bank and drop. It had been used in the war and for whatever reason, had two sirens attached under the wings; these were switched on, creating a frightful noise inside our tiny cabin.

We were busy trying to comfort and secure our two little boys as the African bush loomed ever closer. I felt a prayer would not be out of place and I recited the Lord's Prayer. The ground rushed towards us at a terrifying speed as I went about protecting our two precious children from impact.

We were heading for a dry riverbed when our very observant pilot spotted a small clearing off to the left covered with elephant grass. He immediately lifted the nose and banked the aircraft away from the riverbed, dropping expertly into the ten-foot tall elephant grass covering the clearing.

Thank God! As well as heartfelt thanks to a very good pilot who was able to expertly guide the plane in safely. The tall elephant grass took off a little speed before the wheels contacted rather heavily with the African earth. Looking out of the window, all I could see was the propeller on the left of the plane chopping the grass, which was flying up and over the cabin, accompanied by clouds of dust. The plane must have hit an ant bear hole (an ant bear is a small African animal with a long snout that feasts on termites) as we felt it drop, and the propeller folded back over the engine cowl after striking the ground. We finally came to a very jerky halt. The silence was profound for a few moments. The door to the cockpit opened, and a very apprehensive crew looked out and saw that their five passengers were all in one piece.

George scratched through Richard's bag before going to the door with the navigator. They walked along the wing and jumped down and around to the front of the aircraft, and when they came back after their inspection, I noticed that George had one of Richard's toy guns stuck in his waistband. I burst out laughing.

'What were you planning to do with that?' I chortled. Of course I didn't get a reply.

George asked the pilot why the sirens were switched on and it was explained to him that they would attract the attention of any persons within a ten-mile zone of our crash site.

'All they did was scare the daylights out of any wildlife hereabout,' replied George. 'There's not a human being within fifty miles of here,' he continued. But how wrong he was!

We were now faced with a big problem. We had landed in the heart of the Luangwa Valley in the district of Jumbe, a very big game area, close to the border with the Belgian Congo. The aeroplane was shattered, we had no food or water and most important, no guns or ammunition to fend off any attack by wild animals.

The inspection of the Anson had shown cracked wings and a badly damaged propeller. As we were sorting everything out inside the aircraft, suddenly I saw the tall grass waving, and in a few minutes, we were surrounded by natives. The plane's sirens must have attracted all and sundry from miles around. Terrible thoughts of cannibals crossed my mind. George made a grab for Richard's toy gun, which he had returned to its bag and went to stand in the open door of the aircraft.

My fears proved to be unfounded, when from the back of the crowd of milling African locals, one pushed forward and announced, 'Me Augustine! Mission boy, I speak English'. Greatly relieved, our pilot asked, 'Where might we get help?'

He replied that there was a mission in the hills forty miles away, but in the meantime he would fetch the chief, whose name was Nikanya. The chief must have also heard the sirens as he and his entourage arrived a short while later. We ascertained through Augustine, acting as interpreter for the chief, that there was a white padre reportedly at a local village about thirty-five miles away to whom he would send a message immediately. We took photographs of them all around the aircraft, which pleased them greatly, and with their help, we rigged up an outside aerial and made contact with flight control centre at Salisbury airport.

Salisbury informed us that a rescue operation was being set up and help would be arriving in the form of an air drop as well as a foot operation from Fort Jameson. We could only give them a vague idea of our location, which was approximately eighty-six miles Northwest of Fort Jameson. The village reference given to us by Augustine was Katemo, which was the name of the small kopje (hill) just above the village.

Augustine had suggested we trek to his village where his family would be pleased to house us, which left me with the distinct feeling that as far as hotel star ratings went, we would be lucky for a twinkle. No five stars where we were headed. He also suggested that the nkosi (male chief/my husband), nkosikas (female chief/me), and the picannins (our children) follow him. A runner was sent off to the village and a convoy of excited Africans followed, carrying our luggage.

It was late afternoon and we were trekking through thick forest, the ground strewn with mopane leaves, the favourite diet of elephants. Bearing in mind the vast number of elephants we had seen before crash landing, I was very apprehensive of possible herds, but subdued my fears as nobody else seemed particularly worried.

On our way to the village upon walking across the dry riverbed we would have landed on, our pilot noted and commented that the sand was very loosely packed with deep ruts running across it. If we had landed on it, the probability would have been that the aircraft would have dug in and flipped tail over nose, almost certainly resulting in a number of fatalities. I had been praying fervently as we were about to crash, and there was no doubt in my mind who had guided us to our safe landing site.

We came out into thick bush terrain and the Africans who accompanied us were carrying the children on their backs. I remember in particular the Head Man leaving our party to erect a small grass enclosure where food and water was provided for these important and strange visitors. The local people, many of whom had never seen a white person before, peered through every chink in an attempt to see us.

It was early evening and we were all quite exhausted after walking for hours over the rough terrain, which had taken its toll on our feet. The few miles to the village seemed interminable, and it was to our great relief when we spotted many small fires lighting up the darkness. When we finally arrived at Augustine's kraal (village of round huts), we were immediately surrounded by the inhabitants and a big 'indaba' (meeting) took place to agree on the etiquette that should be shown to these 'Gods who had fallen from the sky,' or to translate into their language these 'Amilungu Anagwa Kumwamba'.

Those who know Africa will be aware that an indaba can last days. Eventually though, we were conducted to a native-built thatched hut. The sole amenities inside were two low native-made beds with no mattresses but a kind of interwoven animal-hide thong. This was a luxury that was usually reserved for people of note. Apparently, we were people of note.

After our crash landing and the long trek through the jungle, we were all on the point of collapse, but some effort had to be made. A decision to bring with me three tins of Ostermilk, a small pan and a packet of tea, proved to be a Godsend, as I was able at least to give the children a nourishing drink.

Having no blankets, we had to use whatever clothing we had with us to bed them down on one of the thong beds. The other members of our group were discussing the best way of affecting a rescue in the event that we could not be found. This proved to be pointless, and we could only hope that the coordinates we had given to Salisbury were close enough for the rescue party to locate us.

Dawn comes early to the African bush and the inhabitants, human and otherwise, are up with first light. Young Richard took one look around at the foreign-looking habitation and said, 'Let's go home, Mom. I don't like this hotel'. That was easier said than done, and we were only too thankful that we had not provided a meal for some carnivorous animal on our recent trek to this small community.

While the men folk were debating how to get us back to 'civilisation,' as we knew it, I had more domestic issues to deal with, i.e. facilities for bathing, food and washing, to say nothing of the language difficulty. The nearby 'spruit' (stream) was our water supply and the children splashed happily in it, surrounded by an admiring group of local piccanins. My washing was accomplished by rubbing and battering clothes against the large stones in this small stream; my blue wool Jaeger suit was never quite the same again.

The following day we spotted planes flying grid pattern to the west of us. They were flying low and had the roundels of the RAF on their wings and on the sides of the fuselages. But they were too far away to locate us. Powder compacts were quite large in those days, and I opened mine with its large mirror and flashed it in the direction of the searching planes, catching the sun's rays in the mirror. An instant response resulted. All three planes turned towards us and a message was dropped: 'Stay where you are! We have got your location'.

The next day the planes flew right to us and two sacks of supplies were dropped by parachute and picked up by locals from the village. We were provided with six blankets, which were more than welcome as it had been bitterly cold the previous night. Also in the parachute drop was a loaf of bread, bully beef, Oxo, Bovril, raisins and a 303 rifle, but with no magazine or ammunition. Instead of this token weapon, I would have preferred butter, tea and sugar, which we could have done with.

George made a grab for the rifle and announced, 'Don't worry, Dot. We'll be safe now we have this'. The absurdity of the situation struck me as very funny. A rifle with no ammunition and a balanced diet of Oxo, bully beef and Bovril, combined with a trek through some sixty miles of uncharted jungle. Home had never been like this.

The runner, who had been sent off to the Catholic Mission in the

Hills, returned three days later during the late afternoon with Father Robertson. We made a huge fuss of him as he was the first white man we had seen since the crash.

He told us that the rescue operation was under way from Fort Jameson and that he had sent word via a runner as to our location. Bernard Hesson, the Chief of Police for Northern Rhodesia, and John Sugg, District Commissioner, were on their way with two trucks, but they were having to cut a road through the bush, building bridges from cut-down trees and four-gallon paraffin tins. Father Robertson told us we had found the only possible spot to crash land within a fifty-mile radius.

A few days later John Sugg and Bernard Hesson arrived with a number of 'askaris' (police recruits). They had been unable to reach us with the trucks and had had to leave them about six miles away. Finally, after nine days in the bush, we set off on foot to find the trucks after saying goodbye to our hosts. The whole village turned out to send us on our way.

We walked through dense bush in such intense heat that I thought we would have to give up. Just as we were reaching exhaustion, we were delighted to see two trucks under the shade of some trees. After a short break for tea, we continued in the trucks through some extremely demanding terrain, down steep slopes and up escarpments. In one very steep place, the truck slid back three times. A hundred or so local natives turned out from a nearby village to push them up the slopes and hold them from slipping over the edge going down the slopes, a feat involving several hours.

How those chaps drove in the dark around those winding tracks still amazes me. Most of the time, we were in first or second gear with a top speed of eight miles per hour. At about nine that evening a halt was made for a meal. We were very hungry. Eating in the bush is a fine art when properly done with the headlights of the trucks left on and grass mats spread on the ground. We were introduced for the first time to the popular 'braai' (barbecue), a lovely meal, finished off with a brandy, water or tea.

The trucks were packed and we continued on again over almost impossible terrain for many more hours, until we arrived at Moore's Mission after a day and a half travelling. Sugg went to one of the bungalows to wake up the priest he knew (a Mr Heritage), who emerged not very ecclesiastically garbed and remarking that it 'was bloody cold'.

We were given accommodation at the Mission, which was very comfortable considering the preceding eleven nights in the bush. After trying to sleep on a thong bed at the village, I was beginning to feel like a zebra – so my night's rest at the Mission was sheer bliss. The next morning, after a good soak in a hot bath for me and the kids, a leisurely breakfast, and a walk around the mission station, it was time to say goodbye and to thank our new found friends for their hospitality.

We departed for Fort Jameson, which lay fifty miles away, that afternoon, arriving in the early evening. Accommodation had been arranged at the Rangley's Hotel and after a hot bath and a good meal, it was early to bed in an attempt to recover from what had been a very arduous journey. It was Friday, 12 July, and we were looking forward to a relaxing weekend. We were advised to stay close to the hotel as leopards came down from the hills at night and one had recently attacked a man and his dog outside the Knowles Hotel a few blocks away.

Our arrival had caused quite a stir among the residents, who were mainly tobacco farmers, and on discussing our future plans regarding settling in South Africa, we were advised to look at Salisbury in Southern Rhodesia. After several days' rest, we flew to Salisbury in a Rapide, piloted by Jed Spencer. We were so impressed with what we had seen of Rhodesia that we decided to settle in this new and rapidly growing country. Fate had taken a hand: our forced landing caused us to change our plans.

Chapter one
A ploughing accident

DAD was booking us all into the Grand Hotel in Salisbury when he collapsed. A doctor by the name of Pockroy was called and diagnosed him as having cerebral malaria, which is a disease transferred by the bite of an infected mosquito as it sucks blood from a human body. There are less serious forms of malaria, but the cerebral type can immediately be life threatening.

Dad slipped in and out of a coma; when his temperature reached danger level, Mom would sponge him down to alleviate the worst of the temperature. Dr Pockroy treated him with lumbar puncture injections directly into the spinal cord. As Dad lay on his stomach to receive these extremely painful injections, he attempted to relieve the pain by holding on to the solid cast-iron bedstead – and he ended up bending it! This treatment as well as Mom's nursing worked and put him on the road to recovery. Dad shed a lot of weight and was very weak for a good six months afterwards.

Throughout the rest of his life, he was constantly plagued by headaches and fevers. Dr Pockroy became our family doctor and he and his son after him tended the medical needs of the Mawson family for the next forty years.

Despite our harrowing adventure and my dad's near fatal illness, my parents decided Rhodesia was the perfect place for our little family to put down roots.

Salisbury was a modern city compared to what we were used to in England, and small by comparison, but it was clean and tidy, and both black and white residents were friendly and accommodating. We purchased the Avoca Restaurant in Salisbury, which was part of a busy block of shops situated about a hundred yards from the main post office and two city blocks from the centre of town. It had a hundred seats, was open for breakfast, lunch and dinner, and served tea and coffee. The restaurant had lots of potential for improvement, and for a start we renamed it, 'The New England'.

My mother ran the restaurant by herself until my father was well enough to help her. Mum was a terrific cook and worked tirelessly to improve the viability and popularity of the business, and it wasn't long before customers were queuing at the door to reserve a table. She served good North-of-England food: hotpot, plenty of roasts, vegetables, delicious gravies, and I'll never forget the Yorkshire puddings along with fish and chips, treacle and apple tarts.

Mom was a very pretty lady and clever intellectually, having been offered a chance to go to university in her younger days. In 1926 this offer was no mean feat for a woman as, back then, women were considered inferior. My brother and I were enrolled in Treetops, a Salisbury nursery school, where we learnt our reading, writing and arithmetic and all about this new country of ours.

Quite by chance, my parents saw an advert for the lease on a hotel named 'Whitehall' in the avenues opposite the Causeway Post Office. Whitehall had twenty rooms and a large dining room and kitchen. When Mom and Dad went to see it, they liked what they saw and made a commitment to take on the lease. 'The New England' was put on the market and sold almost immediately, as by now it was the most popular restaurant in town.

Leaving behind a successful restaurant did not faze Mom. She soon had the new venture running at maximum capacity. The dining room at 'The Whitehall' became as popular as 'The New England' ever was and was always well booked for lunch and dinner, thanks once again to Mom's cooking.

Friday or Saturday evenings became her buffet evenings with a dance band, a beetle drive and even horse racing with a game called Totopoly. Sometimes, she would organise fancy dress evenings accompanied by the most lavish buffet ever seen in the Rhodesian capital. Her evenings were the talk of the town and were sold out almost as soon as the tickets went on sale.

Dad decided to buy a farm, which would not only supply the hotel with fresh produce, but would keep him out of mischief by giving him something constructive to do. A suitable location was found out on Mtoko Road, twelve miles from town, in the area known as Umwinsedale. All but the last mile and a half of roads to the farm were fully tarred. In the next few months, this eighteen-acre tract of virgin bush land with nothing on it would become our home.

Within a year Dad had built access roads, established six fields with irrigation channels and contour ridging, and built two water reservoirs to supply water to the irrigation channels for the crops in the fields. He added a borehole, a lift pump enclosed in its own weatherproof shed, and a 'rondavel' (round walled dwelling with thatched roof) for us all to stay in while working at the farm. This structure offered protection from the fierce African sun during the midday heat. Dad built storerooms for grain and feeds, chicken runs and, most importantly, a three-bedroom house for the family.

All the bricks used in the buildings were made and fired on the farm; sand came from the Umwinsedale River, and stone from granite outcrops located at the kopje (a small hill) on the farm itself.

My father was a true pioneer and a remarkable man. In England he had been a racing mechanic working on Stan Higson's motorbike in the late 1930s. This machine had raced at Birkdale Sands as well as many other venues in and around Lancashire, and had won numerous trophies. Dad had his own coal supply business, owned his own home, and was a successful entrepreneur in Maghull, while Mom was an everyday housewife looking after the family.

On the farm, he taught himself to make bricks and with them he built numerous structures, including our new home, which included a swimming pool for the family thrown in along the way. My father was a clever self-taught man who had a tremendous influence in my life. He was a good-looking man around five-foot-eight-inches, well-built and immensely strong. He was fair-haired with two sons who resembled him in many aspects – but with a lot of Mom's character in us at the same time.

The farm was responsible for the birth of 'Rhodesian Farm Products,' which would become one of the largest suppliers of vegetables and poultry to the Salisbury market. A large room was built with infrared lamps to house the chicks and keep them warm until they became big enough to be put into the main pens. From the farm, the hotel was supplied with not only vegetables, but fresh eggs and poultry as well.

Once Dad had finished all he had to do around the farm, he found himself at a loose end. Ever the entrepreneur, he bought a DKW truck, fitted it out and went on the road selling his farm products.

After two years, a new four-story hotel was planned, which was Mom's baby. She busied herself with planners and architects to create a modern establishment with sixty bedrooms. She was also supplying Dad with cold meats and preserves from home to sell on the vans. At the same time, she was supervising the building of the new hotel as well as seeing to the furnishings and fittings for sixty rooms. This astonishing workload did not seem to deter her in the slightest. In fact, I think she thrived on it. Once the new hotel was up and running, Mom made the jams and preserves, along with hams and cold meats from her kitchens there, which made her life a lot easier. She was, to say the least, a busy little bee. So was Dad. He took on and trained an African driver to take over his route, freeing himself up to build another truck to operate in a different part of town.

The new hotel had some distinguished visitors in its first year of opening. The King of England along with his Queen and daughters,

Elizabeth and Margaret, were to visit Rhodesia. Of all the countries that stood by England in the war with Germany, this little country of ours had the largest contingent of soldiers per capita than any other in the Commonwealth. Rhodesian soldiers, black and white, had distinguished themselves above and beyond the call of duty in that war. The King and his family visited us to say thank you for our efforts. Some of the royal party stayed in our hotel: ladies in waiting, butlers and secretaries. Mom received a letter from our Prime Minister thanking her once the royal party had departed.

The indigenous people of Rhodesia were Iron-Age pastoralists who had over nearly two thousand years migrated south from Africa's densely populated north-western areas below the Sahara. Their wealth lay in their sons and in the number of cattle in their herds. Daughters were only useful at a marriageable age, when a lobola (the bride price) could be asked for them. Payment was made in so many head of cattle, depending on the desirability of the young lady concerned.

My mind somewhat reluctantly moves on from this peaceful, uncomplicated rural setting inhabited by simple people with few wants apart from the basic necessities of life. Their lives were peaceful and unhurried, revolving around the pasturing of their cattle, collecting wood on which to cook their food of porridge, meat and home-grown vegetables. They knew nothing of bank accounts, mortgage rates, the price of petrol, the cost of water and electricity, or the competitive culture of the civilized world.

The nearest school which concentrated mainly on the older black children was Chishawasha Mission, some eight miles distant. This was a long walk to undertake there and back every day, especially for the little ones. With the littlies in mind, Mom set up a school on the farm with the help of Father Myerscoegh, a father at the nearby seminary which supplied one of their nuns as the teacher. Mom and Dad supplied everything else for the school. Every morning on his way into town, Dad gave most of the older children, who were pupils at Chishawasha

Mission, a lift in his farm truck. In return, they would help out on the farm during the harvests.

In town, Dad always parked the van at the end of the Rezende Street Bus Terminal, and all the ladies queuing for buses would buy their vegetables, eggs, cold meats and preserves from him. He built up such a clientèle, that he eventually leased one of the shops being erected alongside the bus station at the time. He continued to use the business name Rhodesian Farm Products, and it wasn't long before he was making a fortune.

The year was 1952, I was ten, and Salisbury was growing in leaps and bounds. New European immigrants flocked into this African jewel, investing heavily in this rapidly-growing breadbasket of Africa. We were on our way to becoming the largest exporter of beef in the world. Our tobacco was the world's best, and overseas buyers heatedly bid for it on the tobacco floors. Production soared as new farms were carved out of the bush. Rhodesia was among the top gold producers of the world, and had the largest reserves of chrome in the world. All these products brought in valuable foreign currency.

Salisbury had three movie houses – the Palace, the Victory and Prince's – which showed all the up-to-date films. Overseas artists, like Cliff Richard and the Shadows, Pat Boone, and The Everly Brothers visited, so we weren't completely out of touch. Farm life in Rhodesia was similar to what it was all over the world; there was always plenty to do. Our work force on the farm and in the hotel was all African, so we had plenty of contact with the local population.

By this time I was eleven years old, in standard four at school, and excelling academically as well as in sport. School work was getting serious as high school was a year away. Nevertheless, I found time to enjoy my fair share of female admirers. Extra-curricular activities included a role in the nativity play with me playing a starring role as the innkeeper. I was sure Hollywood contracts were on the cards. To top it off, I was in love with the girl who played Mary and she with me.

I would have played the role of a lamb or the shepherd's crook to get a part in that play.

School sports days were another passion. I was an enthusiastic athlete. Apart from being a member of both the football and cricket teams, I had also qualified for the long jump event. The preliminaries were scheduled for the Wednesday before the sports day. Having already obtained second place in the high jump, which was unexpected, I was now ready to obliterate the opposition in the long jump. I knew I had made a good jump. I had landed well and rolled forward as instructed, the jump was almost perfect in its execution. It proved to be good enough for first place in the standard four category. I was feeling very pleased with myself. As Mom drove us back to the farm after the event, I couldn't help feeling a sense of pride in the afternoon's performance. Little did I know that I would never long jump or high jump competitively again. Something was about to happen that would change my life forever.

When I got home, I changed out of my sports clothes, threw on my old school pants along with a T-shirt and slops (slip-on shoes) and went into the fields. The tractor had just come to a stop in the lower field, and I could see a huge cloud of dust rolling over it. As I walked down the track to the lower field, I was lost in positive thoughts of the sports day.

Our tractor driver, known as Four Corner, had parked by the old water tree (an African tree usually found close to an underground water source) and was taking a break for tea. I told him I would take over as my dad had taught me to drive the tractor soon after its acquisition. I had only been ploughing for a few minutes when, suddenly, the front wheels dropped down an ant bear hole. The tractor bounced to one side, and the sudden jolt threw me from the seat – and into the path of the plough discs.

I was winded and felt my body roll over as one of the discs struck my right leg, severing it above the ankle. I didn't know where my left leg was and could only presume that it was in the air somewhere above the discs. Thank God! It all happened so fast and I felt no pain! I sat up, surprised to see ragged flesh and a bone sticking out of the bloody mess. This was all that remained of my lower right leg. I had the presence of mind to remove the belt I was wearing to use as a tourniquet.

Four Corner raced towards me, his eyes growing huge as he realised the severity of my injury. He shouted for my father, who was in the next field, and at the same time jumped on to the tractor, bringing it to a halt.

My father came running towards me and stopped dead in his tracks when he saw my condition. His exclamation of, 'Oh, my God!' and the look of horror on his face frightened the life out of me. He turned away and ran towards our car, a Morris Isis station wagon, which was two hundred yards away. My mom was splitting some seedlings on a table next to the car, so Dad bundled her into the car and drove back towards me.

The belt had stopped the flow of blood, and I remember sitting on the ground watching everything happen as if it were in slow motion. Dad braked the car, opened the door and got out, all in one seamless motion. He scooped me up and put me on the seat between himself and Mom, whose face said it all. Her exclamation of, 'Oh, God, please no,' didn't help either. As we accelerated away from the farm, I remember cuddling into Mom. I had felt no pain, but I do remember feeling very tired.

As I looked down at the ragged stump with blood oozing from it, I wondered what had happened to my shoe, as there was just a bone with no ankle or foot. The hospital was fourteen miles away, and Dad was driving at breakneck speed to get us there. Waves of tiredness swept over me. I could have gone to sleep with ease, but each time I nodded off, I would snap awake thinking, 'If I fall asleep, I am going to die'. This thought repeated with each wave of tiredness. It so firmly embedded itself in my eleven-year-old brain that I managed to stay wide awake as we sped into town. A police BSA Gold Flash (a British motorcycle used by our police force) had come alongside the car. Dad, 'the lunatic driver,' had been observed going through red lights and stop signs with headlights on and horn blaring away.

Once he had managed to relay to the officer that I was badly hurt, the officer's response was to pull in front of our car to clear traffic for a speedier run to the hospital. We pulled up outside emergency and Mom ran in, returning almost immediately with a doctor, some nurses and a trolley.

I can remember feeling very tired but that little voice inside me kept telling me I would die if I fell asleep. I was determined to stay awake. Fortunately, fate dealt me an ace as Mr Nangle, the top orthopaedic surgeon in Rhodesia and South Africa at the time, and his assistant, Mr Standish Whyte, were standing in Emergency looking at X-rays of an accident victim who had a badly broken leg. As I was wheeled in, Mr Nangle took one look at me, barked out a few orders and hurried off to scrub up.

I remember feeling ashamed as the nurse prepared me for theatre, as sometime during the accident I had messed my trousers. She assured me that this happened all the time in accidents, and I was not to worry. I just hoped she was telling the truth.

Once I was on the operating table, the anaesthetist attempted to put me to sleep but with little success. The brain is such a powerful organ, and I had convinced myself that if I slept I would die, so the sodium pentothal was having little or no effect on me.

In a desperate attempt to calm and soothe me, Mom was called into the theatre to speak to me, which she did, and Mr Nangle backed her up with positive assurances. There was so much bombardment going on: needles, drips, blood, machines, nurses, surgeons, assurances; my thoughts were scrambled, and I suppose I was in shock and probably more than a little frightened. I finally dropped off with my mother's promise that she would be there when I awoke, and Mr Nangle's voice assuring me that I was in the best of all possible hands. He told me later in life that he was inwardly cursing as every moment that slipped by brought me closer to death.

The next thing I remember was the murmur of voices and the feeling that I had been run over by fifty tractors, all at the same time, never mind just one. I can also remember feeling pain for the first time since the accident. As things came into focus, I saw Mom, Dad and Mr Nangle at the foot of the bed. A large cradle had been placed over my right leg below the waist. Mr Nangle leaned over the cradle and asked if I was in pain. I nodded and burst into tears, as the whole of my right side below the waist was throbbing and bloody sore. I was frightened and confused and could remember very little of my ordeal. He turned to my father, 'That's a good sign'.

Mom was by my side, comforting me. I can remember feeling tired and bilious. I dumped a good amount of vomit in a bowl and felt much better for it. I believe I slept for twenty-four hours and awoke feeling weak and groggy; in place of the pain there was a throbbing ache akin to toothache. Mom was there when I awoke, and she told me that I had lost my right leg, although this piece of news didn't particularly register with me as being too serious.

I didn't remember much of the accident, but I could clearly recall the journey into town. I remember seeing my blood washing from side to side in the passenger well of the car. When I asked Mom if they had put it back inside me, she had smiled and answered that she had given blood for me as the hospital had not had enough of my own blood type in stock, given the amount that had spilled on the soil of Africa. I felt quite contented at having been 'topped up' in this way, as I was sure I could not have had much left by the time we reached the hospital.

I slipped in and out of sleep during the next few days, and was awakened every two hours for injections. After each day the ache got less and less. All the nurses in the hospital had heard of the 'little boy' who had nearly died after a nasty farm accident, and they treated me like a celebrity. As I improved, I would race around the corridors of the hospital in my wheelchair. The staff brought me generous amounts of drinks and sweets, leaving them on the table next to my bed. It was always loaded with goodies; I was very spoilt and everyone made a great fuss of me.

Five weeks later I was sent home to recuperate. The first present given to me was a five-week-old wire-haired fox terrier that I named Champ because he had a pedigree longer than my arm, and we became inseparable from that day forward. My second present was a book called *Reach for the Sky*, the biography of Squadron Leader Douglas Bader, who had lost both legs in an aircraft crash prior to WWII. He had talked the RAF into letting him fly once more, thereby achieving the goals he had set for himself. He flew a Spitfire during the Battle of Britain; later he was shot down over Germany and sent to the high security Colditz Castle from which he constantly tried to escape.

It still did not seem to have registered with me that I had lost a limb and that I would not be able to run the four-minute mile or win the long-jump again. I continued to view the situation as a minor mishap in my life and still believed there was nothing I wouldn't be able to do. I knew I could feel my missing toes and wriggle them around, so I reasoned they must be there somewhere. It seemed irrelevant that I could no longer see them. I had then, and still retain, a very positive outlook on life.

As an eleven-year-old, I had little, if any, concept of what life would be like with one leg. I used to tell my Mom that my new leg was being made and as soon as the stump hardened and the swelling had gone down, I would be out and about like I had been before. I promised her I would walk to her unaided one day.

I know from talking to her later in life that she had gained a lot of respect for me, as young as I was, because of my attitude, which had impressed so many people. Little did I realise at that time how insurmountable some mountains would seem, especially in my younger years, as I battled to level the playing field between me and my peers.

Mom took me to the municipal pool, where I joined Otters Swimming Club to build up the muscles in my right leg. I spent five afternoons a week training with the club and soon became a familiar figure around the pool. The self-consciousness I originally felt seemed to dissipate as I became more proficient. I swam in a couple of competitions against a rival swimming club and in my best finish came sixth. With no right foot, my speed was down some twenty-five percent. With no way of rectifying the problem, I lost interest in the competitive side of swimming, but I have always enjoyed the social aspect of it.

About four months after the accident, Dad and I set out for Johannesburg, South Africa, where I was to be measured and fitted with a leg. I was very excited and informed Mom that the next time she saw me I would be running and walking.

Me and my big mouth! I had the exuberance and innocence of youth, but the fact of the matter was, I really had no idea what was in store for me. In retrospect, I imagine, however fancifully, that God was asking me to climb Mount Everest first so that every other mountain in my life after that would appear possible.

Johannesburg was about a thousand miles from Salisbury, and we arrived the next day, after stopping overnight in Louis Trichardt (a small town just over the South African border). Once we had arrived in Johannesburg, we went directly to the hospital, where measurements were taken by a technician. He took a plaster cast of my stump. He informed me that as my stump was too soft, I would have to wee in my hand and rub it over the stump to harden it for the socket. I was horrified. Dad told me not to worry, and when we visited a chemist, it was recommended, much to my relief, that methylated spirit be used as an alternative.

We stayed in a hotel not far from the hospital, and I swam in their pool nearly all day, and went for fittings every second day. When the artificial leg was ready, they brought out a 'contraption,' which looked heavier than me. It consisted of calliper braces on either side of a wooden leg, which connected to a large leather corset. The stump was inserted into a padded socket carved into the inside of the wooden leg. The corset was laced up, then a leather and elastic cover came over the knee, leading up to a leather belt, which strapped around the waist, and another strap looped over the shoulder. It was an awesome and daunting piece of equipment. I felt I would be lucky to walk ten steps with this THING, never mind keeping all the promises I had made to Mom.

Chapter two
Determined recovery

FOR the first time since the accident, my heart sank as I wondered how on earth I was going to cope with this monstrosity. It weighed a ton and was difficult to walk in. The strap and belt cut into my shoulder and waist until it rubbed me raw. I was desperate but, more than anything, I felt I could not let my mom down by failing to keep my promise to her. This was my 'Everest' and I did not have the maturity to cope.

Attempting to walk with what I had been given seemed at that point to be more than I was capable of. Through my tears I felt sure I detected a look of hopelessness in Dad's face, which added to my feelings of bitter disappointment. He needed Mom here to pacify me. I felt as if I were drowning in a dark place amidst the pain and effort of learning to walk in the monstrosity I had been handed. In truth, I was just too young and immature to accept the possibility that it would now become a big part of my life. The moment I realised my tears were adding to my father's anguish, I put my feelings aside, put on a brave face and proceeded with grim determination to try to learn to walk with the infernal contraption.

After endless hours of pain and walking between the bars, all that could be done had been done and we left for home. My shoulder and waist were raw, bleeding and bloody sore. I had not offered a word of protest throughout the pain and suffering and, to add to my misery, I had developed a raging temperature. Dad laid out a bed for me in the back of the station wagon and we headed for home. Both of us needed my mom very badly. Dad drove non-stop nearly a thousand miles, arriving home late at night, by which time I was burning up. Sometime after midnight, Dr Pockroy came out to the hotel to see me, and half an hour later I was back in hospital with pneumonia. The time spent in hospital gave the rawness around my waist and shoulder a chance to heal. I was determined, primarily for my mom's sake, to walk out of there. She had been horrified when she saw the walking apparatus that had been made for me.

A week later Dad brought my leg to the hospital; I strapped it on but when he handed me the belt and shoulder strap I shook my head, my injuries from that infernal strap and waist belt were still too sore and I was damned if I was going to rub them raw again. I had thought about those infernal straps throughout my recovery and decided I would find a way without all that paraphernalia; I had to! Leaving them off, and with the aid of crutches, I walked to my mom as I had promised her I would before I left for Johannesburg.

'I am still learning, Mom, and can't run yet but it won't take long,' I said, hoping she would not notice that every step was a massive struggle. I saw a tear run down her cheek, which was quickly wiped away as she cuddled me in her arms.

'A great king once lived in England called Richard the Lion Heart,' she said. 'You have all the key attributes he was blessed with as well as his name. So, my little Lion Heart,' she continued, 'with your determination and tenacious attitude, nothing will be impossible for you in this life. Your path is preordained by the Lord who gave you back to us'.

It all went over my head at the time, but I left my mother's arms with renewed faith and confidence. Inside me was instilled a will to succeed and to succeed better than anyone else. I owed this to my mother, who always had faith in my ability to do anything I wanted and to do it in style, no matter what obstacles were there to be overcome. Throughout my life she was my greatest mentor and confidante.

The leg still felt cumbersome but never again did I use the belt and shoulder strap. I walked with the aid of crutches until my stump had taken the shape of the socket and I had become accustomed to the apparatus strapped to my right leg. The crutches gave me a chance to get used to wearing the leg without the cumbersome straps. I felt embarrassed about the calliper braces, but I hid those feelings and got on with the job of learning to walk again. Thankfully, the Orthopaedic Centre at Salisbury Hospital made me an elastic strap about three inches wide, which fitted onto the corset just above the knee, over the knee cap and was attached to the limb below the knee. When it was tightened, it helped keep the stump in the socket, which had been the purpose of the original straps I had ditched in disgust. I was blessed with a mom and dad who always found ways of equipping me with the latest and best of everything, and fortunately they had the financial resources to do so.

After we got back from South Africa, Mom and Dad decided we should move into the hotel where it would be easier for me to be tutored and to attend doctors' appointments. Eight miles out of town built on the banks of the Hunyani River was the popular Skyline Motel which, though small, boasted an amusement park and the most delicious afternoon cream teas I had ever tasted in my young life.

Often on a Sunday, after lunch had been served and cleared away in our own hotel, Mom and Dad took my brother and me to the Skyline. This was a great treat for us, not only because of the wonderful gastronomical fare but because the hotel's paddle steamer, the *Hunyani Queen*, took people for rides up the river and back down again.

I can remember wondering as I looked overboard into the murky water what might happen if we were to strike a rock and sink. Would our fate be sealed in the mighty jaws of a hippo or crocodile, would we drown, our bodies never to be found? It never happened of course, otherwise I wouldn't be alive to tell this tale.

When the Christmas holidays came around, we moved back to

the farm. Dad taught me to drive a half-ton Commer 'bakkie' (small truck), which, in time, I drove all over the Umwinsedale Valley. It was a picturesque location through which the Umwinsedale River flowed, with the river supplying an abundance of water to all the farms in the area and beyond.

The valley was surrounded by hills peppered with broad msasa trees indigenous to Africa, which have a distinctive amber and wine-red colour when their young leaves sprout during spring (August-September). The hills and veld were home to wild animals ranging from leopards to buck, such as duiker and reed buck. We rarely saw leopards, those agile and stealthy predators, with their yellow-coloured fur patterned with darker rosettes, but were aware of their presence in the area. Not only are they able to take down large prey due to their massive skulls and powerful jaw muscles, they can also climb trees, thanks to exceptionally strong shoulder muscles.

Seldom, too, did we see wild boar or bush pigs, easily identified by their harsh grunt and pig-like appearance. They lived in the dense bush surrounding the farm and were a thorn in the sides of farmers because of their appetite for domestic crops, which they raided under cover of darkness. They were aggressive, courageous and positively dangerous to pursuing dogs or hunters, often turning on their pursuers and slashing them with their razor-sharp tusks. And it would not be Africa without the ubiquitous troops of monkeys and their larger cousins, the baboons. Baboons are destructive in their ways, but at the same time it's very funny to watch the antics of the comedians of the troop. They were a nightmare to most farmers for the same reason as the wild boars.

The granite outcrops and thickets were full of dassies (rock rabbits), meerkats and mongooses scurrying to and fro, foraging for food. These we saw on a daily basis. Meerkats are members of the mongoose family and are small burrowing animals, living in large underground networks with multiple entrances, which they leave only during the day. They are very social, living in colonies averaging twenty to thirty members, collectively known as a 'mob', 'gang' or 'clan'. According to African popular belief, mainly in Rhodesia, the meerkat is also known as the 'Sun Angel', as it is deemed to protect villages from the 'moon devil' or 'werewolf', which is believed to attack stray cattle or lone tribesmen. A meerkat's diet consists mostly of insects, and they are known to be immune to certain types of venom, especially that of a scorpion. Their behaviour towards each other is 'all for one, one for all'. They are assigned duties such as standing sentry or babysitting while others are engaged in play or foraging. When a predator is spotted, the meerkat performing as sentry gives a warning bark, and when safety is restored, he makes peeping sounds. The babysitter takes the young underground to safety and is prepared to defend them to the death if the danger follows. If retreating underground is not possible, she collects all the young together and lies on top of them.

The mongoose was a fairly common sight. They have long faces and bodies, small rounded ears, short legs, and long tapering tails with brindled or grizzled fur. Due to their agility and thick coats, and their immunity to snake venom, they are well known for their ability to fight and kill snakes, particularly cobras.

Mongooses are extremely territorial. My brother-in-law reared two of them, and as they grew, it was uncanny how they were able to correctly determine the hierarchy within the family. My brother-in-law, the elder of the family, was treated with caution and respect. His wife was the mother figure for the mongooses; they snuggled up and whispered sweet nothings in her ear, while the three sons were treated with rather less homage, more like inferior underdog siblings, especially the youngest of the three, who always seemed to get the short end of the stick.

My sister-in-law, when she visited, was extremely wary of them and kept her distance. She had seen their show of active, bare-toothed aggression to those they considered to be non-family members. She was convinced that as Striker and Rambo ran around the exterior walls of the house muttering to each other while she was sunbathing, they were formulating a devious assault plan on her defenceless person. She might not understand their mongoose chatter, but she could detect a conspiracy when she saw one, knowing they wanted to rid their territory of her unwelcome presence. They were much-loved pets within the family, and it was a sad day when the local vet was unable to save one from a jaw infection. The other one simply disappeared without a trace after having lived so many years as part of the family. It is likely he was grief-stricken over the loss and went away to die and was taken by a hawk or other predatory bird.

With the wild animals I have briefly described and the abundance of spectacular bird life, it sometimes felt as if we were living in our own private paradise.

My recovery was into its seventh month as Christmas came and went and with my twelfth birthday on the horizon, I went back to school for my final junior year. I had missed a lot of work, but my dedicated teacher came to my rescue by spending her lunch hours with me, helping me catch up.

After the lunch break, all students were expected to participate in either football or cricket, depending on the time of year, and I was absolutely convinced I could still participate as a goalkeeper or wicketkeeper. With a lot of encouragement from the masters and my team mates, I gave it my best shot, but it was a disaster. More time was being spent with stoppages while I strapped my leg back on, than with actually playing the game. I was keen and competitive, but was in a quandary since I knew I was spoiling the game for the rest of the team with my insistence on taking part. I wanted so much to prove to myself and others that my accident hadn't changed anything, and that I was still the same as before. It wasn't a question of not being able to participate. I knew I could! I was satisfied that I had achieved what I had set out to do: which was that nothing had changed. But of course it had. At the time, though, I was too young to realise that everything would now have to be done differently.

I have never believed in the word 'can't,' a word, as far as I was concerned, that is used as an excuse not to try. I spoke to Mom and told her I was not going to attend sports after school any more, as well as the reasons why. I needed to find something I could be good at, and could compete in, without the use of my legs. If I could just find that 'something', I would become the best I could at whatever it proved to be.

Mom agreed this was a mature approach and we would investigate other activities the school had to offer, which amounted to Chess, Debating, Public Speaking and Sewing, none of which rang any bells with me. I went to see the headmaster to explain to him why I would not be attending the afternoon sport sessions any more and handed him a letter Mom had helped me draft to the teams and coaches, thanking them for their encouragement, and apologising for spoiling the game for them.

At Monday morning assembly, Mr Lloyd, the Head, read out my letter, which embarrassed me no end. He called me up to the rostrum where he presented me with a Certificate for Sportsmanship, usually only given for an excellent performance in a given sport to a school athlete. The teachers and headmaster stood up and gave me a standing ovation as I left the stage, and the cricket, football and athletic teams all came forward to shake my hand. I felt confused, embarrassed and yet elated, all at the same time. I am sure the teams were secretly relieved at my decision to abandon ship as it now meant they could finish their matches with minimal interruptions, and I could not blame them.

Upon my arrival home, there was a brand new Phillips sports bike on the veranda waiting for me. Perhaps the wheels of the bike could take the place of my legs to some degree. I never do things by halves; a few days later I was laid up in bed with a raw and bleeding stump, resulting from over-exuberance with my new acquisition. Once healed, I took to riding it more rationally and spent many happy hours pedalling through the Umwinsedale Valley with my dog, Champ, running alongside.

Year-end exams went off well for me, considering I had missed so much school. As I was going on to high school in the new year, I took my teacher a huge bouquet of flowers and Mom and Dad bought her a brooch for all the lunchtimes she had given up to help me catch up. Without the effort she put in, I would not have passed the year-end exams. She seemed delighted with her gifts.

After Christmas, there was a flurry at all the school outfitters as pupils purchased their new uniforms. I was duly equipped and ready for my final five years of education. On the first day at high school, I located my classroom and some old friends from junior school. Two thirds of my class was made up of pupils from other schools, but new friends were soon made and I settled in with ease. I was at a loss once again on the sport/extra-curricular front; apart from the usual chess or the debating teams, there was nothing for me to participate in. I soon got fed up with watching my school friends play rugby as it got somewhat lonely sitting on those big stands all by myself. These afternoons were killers for me; everyone was participating in something, and my exclusion began to eat me up inside.

I had a very intelligent and understanding Mom who could see there was a problem. She soon found a remedy and asked me if, after lunch in the hotel kitchens, I would help her prepare the cold meats which Dad sold in the shop and on the trucks. A salary would be forthcoming for my efforts, and within a few months, I was proficient in the production of gammon hams and other delicacies. Not only did it fill my afternoons, but it instilled in me a love of cooking, which I still have to this day.

Chapter three
Mozambican holiday

CARLOS Brito was a Portuguese entrepreneur from Beira in Mozambique. He wanted to build beach chalets and a motel complex to attract Rhodesian holidaymakers. He had been given a lease on a portion of beach stretching from the Estoril Lighthouse to the Savane River, comprising twenty-five miles of pristine southern African coastline. Beira is a small port and fishing town about a third of the way up the east coast of Africa and fishing was about all it could offer – until Carlos had an idea to turn it into a holiday resort. The Hotel Association sent him along to talk to Mom as she had a reputation for getting things done, and done right. Their meeting didn't last long, and an invitation to visit the site in Beira and continue the discussion was put on the table. Mom, who loved a challenge, didn't need to be asked twice and as soon as the school holidays arrived, we were on our way. As it turned out, it was quite an adventure.

We crossed the border at Machapanda, a small railway border town with a goods yard to receive freight from the port of Beira en route to Rhodesia. We stopped at Villa Perry for lunch where Dad ordered a local favourite, 'Chicken Peri Peri'. At that time there were no fridges or freezers in the middle of the African bush so, as they say in the classics, 'The meat is on the hoof'. We sat outside and watched as a hapless chicken ran past our table twice, pursued by the chef wielding a wicked-looking knife. We were all aware of what its fate would be. There was a loud squawk and then Dad's lunch was gutted and plucked in preparation for the pot. An hour later the chicken was presented to

Dad in all its glory. The rest of us opted for ham and cheese sandwiches but that didn't stop Dad from eating his lunch with great relish.

After lunch, we continued our journey through swampy terrain on a dirt road, which came to a sudden and final halt on the banks of the Pungwe River. In the absence of a bridge, we were guided to the left of the road and watched as a wooden pontoon was pulled across the river by about twelve locals, who held a thick rope that disappeared into the water and was tied to a tree on the opposite bank. On its arrival, the pontoon was moored into the bank of the river below us. There was a two-foot drop to be negotiated before the car was safely on the pontoon, and to that end planks were placed between the bank and the ferry.

Mom took one look at the precarious set-up and climbed out of the car with my young brother firmly in tow. Her body language spoke volumes! She had no intention of landing up in crocodile-infested water and would ensure the survival of at least one member of her family. I remained in the vehicle with Dad behind the wheel negotiating the descent, which was not very stable, to say the least. Once the 'memsahib' and sibling were aboard, we set out for the opposite shore.

The frail craft took the current and headed downstream at a rate of knots, only to be reined in by our illustrious crew as they pulled into the opposite bank, all the while entertaining us with their melodious chanting. The whole trip took a matter of minutes but I could see by Mom's face that she was relieved it was over. Dad and I had found Mom's reaction to the event highly amusing, but decided against reminding her we would have to go through the same hazardous procedure again on the return trip. No point in spoiling her holiday.

We arrived in Beira about an hour later and stopped to ask directions to the Brito residence. Once we reached our destination, my brother and I went off to explore the beach where we found a forlorn old shipwreck that was acting as a breakwater next to the Macuti Lighthouse. Carlos is a very popular name in the Portuguese community, and we soon made good friends with another Carlos, who took us on a guided tour of his lighthouse, and arranged to take us surfing the next day. Once this outing had been arranged, we returned to our folks, who were having tea with the other Carlos (any more Carlos's around and we would have had to start numbering them).

We were made very welcome and after a quick shower and a change of clothes, we arrived downstairs for an early buffet: plates laden with lobster, prawns, crabs and small clams, all expertly prepared by Maria, Carlos's good lady. After gorging ourselves on the delicious fare, we left Mom to her meeting and went off with Dad to explore the beachfront and town.

Next morning, we were on the beach early where we met our lighthouse friend, Carlos. He had two surfboards with him made by the local boat builder at Club Nautico, a yacht club a little way down the beach. The surf at Beira Bay was not the best as it had a close shore break and the waves were more suitable to dumping than surfing, but great fun nevertheless. Sandbanks surrounded the bay, which kept the man-eating nasties in the deeper waters of the ocean.

As it would not have been prudent to get my good artificial leg wet, I used one of the old legs I always took with me to run in and out of the waves, which was a must if I intended to surf and frolic with my brother. The old leg was half-an-inch shorter than the one I used on a daily basis, which resulted in a pronounced limp, but what the hell, I had a limp anyway. Surfing in the sea on the boards or an air mattress was never a good option because sand got trapped between my stump sock and skin, rubbing the stump raw, but it was either take the consequences or sit on the shore. I elected to take the consequences.

Mom spent the day with Carlos, the planners and designers, and most of her suggestions were implemented. So started the Estoril Motel and campsite, which was enjoyed by thousands of Rhodesians over the years and became known as 'Rhodesia by the Sea'. It was a paradise. Mom and Dad bought a beautiful Turners caravan, and Carlos always made sure they were allocated the best spot at the campsite with magnificent views over the bay and close proximity to the pavilion to enjoy the food and drink on offer.

Chapter four
My passion for racing begins

I had my eye on a moped (a small motorcycle) that had taken my fancy. The answer I got from Mom when I broached the subject was an emphatic 'no', and nothing I said made the slightest difference to her decision. She was adamant: no motorbike for me, ever. I am sure to this day that a certain plan was hatched by Mom and Dad to take my mind off the motorbike.

As it turned out, this plan was to shape a big part of my future and see me back on level terms with my fellow man. There is a cost attached to everything in life, whether negative or positive, and this particular choice would prove to cost Mom dearly and give her more heartache than I would ever have wished.

As a family, we attended the Salisbury Agricultural Show in September and found the motorboat stand of particular interest. We seemed to be drawn there as if by an invisible magnet. A number of second-hand boats were on display, which, if one was interested, could be taken to nearby Lake McIlwaine, a reasonable stretch of water twenty-five miles from town, fed by the Hunyani River. The lake boasted a small game reserve supporting an array of wildlife: ostrich, rhino, wildebeest, buffalo and various forms of antelope, and on the opposite side of the dam was a lion and cheetah park.

Cottages were for hire and several boat clubs dotted the lake shore. The all-round facilities were excellent and consequently well supported by the Salisbury public. We were invited to go to the lake that weekend, and by Sunday night found ourselves the proud owners of our very own speedboat, which Mom, for reasons known only to herself, christened *Vicky*.

We were at the lake nearly every weekend after that, and it was at that time this one-legged, almost thirteen-year-old boy developed a love for speed, which grew and grew throughout his life. Even though our boat was more of a family runabout, with seating for six people and a top speed of twenty-five mph as opposed to a high-speed racing craft, it wasn't long before I entered some local regattas.

The first events I took part in saw *Vicky* at the back of the field, though I managed a second and a third place in two different handicap races. To be handicapped, meant that the slower boats started in front of the faster ones one at a time at various intervals. *Vicky* was painfully slow and started in front of the field, but somewhere deep inside me an ember had been ignited: I wanted to go faster and faster still. As the champions flashed past me, I knew in my heart I could compete with them given the right boat; the playing field would be level as I didn't need my legs, and then I could win. If only I had a faster boat!

As luck would have it, Dad got in conversation with Roy Geldard, a boat builder and the Rhodesian champion, who had won half the races that day. He told us he was building a new boat for the show and invited us to his house to have a look at her. Was that a mistake on his part?

Within five minutes of seeing this particular boat, she was ours: lock, stock and barrel. Her name was *Skeeter* and she was beautifully designed along the same lines as Roy's own racing boat. *Skeeter* was painted in black and yellow and alongside her written name was emblazoned the unique and eye-catching motif of a mosquito wearing red boxing gloves. Fixed to the transom was a brand new Scott Atwater 40 horsepower motor, which was one of the best and fastest racing motors America had produced. The whole package was impressive to say the least. We soon found a new home for *Vicky* and the long wait ensued until the end of the show when we could take possession of

Skeeter and put her on the water. I could hardly wait! We took delivery of her one Saturday morning, and it was immediately off to the lake for the family launch. Mom poured champagne on the bow and drank the rest; good job we only had a small bottle, I thought with amusement.

Dad accorded me the privilege of starting the engine for the first time and tossed me the keys. It was an exciting moment. I let the engine warm up, engaged the forward gear and accelerated past the jetties and out onto open water. It did not go unnoticed that the family generously elected to remain on shore, wanting me to enjoy the moment with no distraction.

Although the impulse was to push the throttle to the stops, to do so could have resulted in engine damage, and I resisted the urge. A brand new motor has to be run in, meaning it has to be run for a period of time at quarter or half throttle to give the moving parts time to settle in. We drove *Skeeter* sedately all day but on the last run I gave her a short burst of full speed; the hull seemed to quiver and she jumped forward, as if to say, 'This is what I was built for'. I didn't waste time in motivating a modification programme for *Skeeter*.

Dad ordered a racing prop from Michigan in the USA, and upon its arrival, we shot off to the lake for a test. The results improved speed by another five miles per hour, and if I moved to the left side of the boat, *Skeeter* travelled four miles per hour faster. The bottom of the boat was shaped like an aircraft wing and lifted the boat out of the water at speed, resulting in less drag, the consequence being a speed increase. The left side of the hull was obviously a lot more efficient than the right, resulting in this increase in speed.

I was now sure *Skeeter* was the fastest boat on the water, and we were soon bound for the next regatta to test my belief. The weekend finally arrived; my first practice was not to impress but to learn, and learn I did! I spotted Mom walking towards me in the paddock. She took my photo and then put her arms around me, squeezing me so tightly I was glad of my life jacket, which I was convinced had protected me from serious rib damage. 'You look after yourself, my precious son. Don't take any chances,' said she, releasing me from her vice-like grip, which would have put a python to shame.

'Don't worry, Mom,' I replied. 'I am going to do it for you and win all the races, so you'd better watch!' I followed Dad's advice for the race and tailed Roy during the practice, following him into corners, learning the fastest way to go round the buoys. It was the most fantastic sensation and I stuck to him like glue. *Skeeter* flew over the top of the wash from his boat, willing me to give her full throttle, but I resisted the temptation. My first-ever real race was about to begin and a five-minute siren signalled the start of the large clock at the end of the jetty. When the two hands reached the zero, the race was officially started.

Dad and I had watched the champions and observed how they always picked a spot well away from the line, clock and milling boats. With about twenty seconds to go, they would accelerate and hit the line at zero, going at full speed while the rest of the field was still in process of accelerating. In this way, they got a jump on the rest of the field and reached clear water before the first turn. Roy used this strategy. I could see him looking at me from where his boat was stationary. I knew exactly how many seconds it would take me to get to the line and I felt very calm, and even though I had expected butterflies, they didn't manifest. I remained cold and calculating and watched the seconds ticking away. I was a boy on a mission, filled with purpose, his sights set on that chequered flag for the first of many times in his life

I hit the line at full throttle as the clock hit zero, and Roy and I went into the first corner together. Down the straight I was catching him. I slipped behind where the passenger seat had been before it had been removed, and *Skeeter* flew past him.

The crowd on the shore could not believe their eyes - a quiet, one-legged boy running away not only from the rest of the field, but from the Rhodesian and international champion. The commentator remarked that Roy had let me pass as a goodwill gesture, but as the race progressed and the gap grew wider between us, he was forced to swallow his words. Mom was doing the catering for the regatta, but as it was her son's first real race against the Central African champions, she had taken time out to watch from the clubhouse.

Dad later told me that as I went into the first corner alongside Roy, she covered her eyes with her hands, saying a prayer for my safety, and at the same time peeping through her fingers to monitor my progress. According to reports related to me after the event, it appeared she almost fell over the clubhouse balcony when she saw me go past Roy. I am sure that if *Skeeter's* motor had not been making so much noise, I would have heard her shouts of, 'Come on, Dee' from the back straight, where I was leaving the rest of the field standing.

My lost leg was no longer part of the equation. I didn't need it to achieve my objective; three years in the wilderness, and I had just won the long jump again.

I have it on good authority that Mom's excitement, apart from making her hoarse from all her shouting, had forced her to sit down for a moment after I had taken the chequered flag.

With a shake of her head, she expressed her pride and excitement for all to hear, 'He said he would do it and he damn well did'.

With that, she was up and running down the clubhouse steps to greet me as I came ashore. I heard pride in her voice as she said, 'Congratulations, my champion-to-be. I watched every second. You take care of my property out there'.

'I will Mom,' I replied. 'Don't forget to watch my next race. I'll be the boat in front,' I said, bursting with pride. With an 'I will,' she turned and hurried back to her kitchen.

The race was an easy win for me, and I knew it had hinged to a large degree on all the preparation Dad had put in, and the advice he had given me. At last I felt on equal terms with my peers in a sport that did not require me to run, jump, or kick. I no longer felt inadequate because of a leg that hindered me every time I dived for a ball or attempted to protect a goal. Roy and a number of other pilots came over to congratulate me, all of them making a huge fuss of me. The South Africa champion commented wryly, 'I can see we are going to have plenty of trouble from you today, and in the future'.

Roy had his boat in and out of the water three times that day. No matter what he did, he couldn't come anywhere near me on the water. I won five races and came second in the two handicap races after overtaking the whole field.

At the prize-giving, my performance was praised by everyone, but for me, the most important and meaningful accolades came from Roy, who was quick to point out that Geld Craft boats had filled the first three places in every race, with champions being in all his boats with the exception of the boat that had won all the scratch races piloted by a thirteen-year-old schoolboy with one leg.

The applause rang out from the assembled crowd and the elation bubbled inside me; it was a feeling I have never forgotten. The despondency and frustration, the inadequacy – all those old feelings brought on through the loss of my leg were gone, swept away on a tide of euphoria. At that moment I felt immortal.

'This is you,' an inner voice seemed to say as I left the rostrum with eight trophies in my arms, seven for the races I had won, and one for having been named the most successful pilot of the day, which of course I was!

The clubhouse was abuzz, and people were trying to figure out how and why I had been so successful. I had taken on the champions of three countries, all experienced pilots, and had thrashed them. But what the crowd in the clubhouse did not have was insight to the burning drive inside me to succeed. The only ones to have that privy information were Mom and Dad who knew me inside out.

The gods had thrown their dice that day, and my numbers had spilled from their cup as they did forever after. Upon reflection, I wish I had been a little older in order to appreciate the enormity and significance of what I had achieved – several races won outright against international competition.

I had just celebrated my thirteenth birthday and was very much an amateur in my new-found sport, but I had found something I could excel in and no one could take that away. I had needed this boost so badly. According to the Commodore, I was a champion in the making. Because I had surpassed my own expectations, I imagined I should have felt a greater degree of excitement than I did, but this was not the case and instead, what I remember best, was more a feeling of satisfaction and accomplishment.

Our journey through life is not to create our destiny but to discover it. I have a sneaking suspicion that was the day I discovered mine. Mom, meanwhile, had taken centre stage among a group of ladies in the corner of the club singing my praises; I even spotted Dad among the crowd so I knew he considered my achievements important enough to leave the bar after four in the afternoon. Mom and Dad were footing the bills, and I went to show them my silverware as well as to thank them for everything.

My results made front-page news in the *Rhodesia Herald* the following morning, and at the school assembly the headmaster (Jeeves Hogard) called me up onto the stage to congratulate me in front of the whole school. Reading from the front page of the paper, he gave an account of what I had achieved over the weekend. Pride in my achievements grew as the headmaster went on with the accolades. I would never don a first team blazer for rugby or cricket, but by the same token they might never be able to beat national or international champions or get their photos and stories on the front page of the national newspaper.

Roy was in his early thirties and had been racing for at least ten years, but that did not stop us from becoming firm friends as we raced together in Northern and Southern Rhodesia, South Africa and the Belgian Congo, winning more times than not. He often said to me,

'I should never have sold you that bloody boat!' He meant what he said and, in fact, built a number of boats in an attempt to beat *Skeeter*. The last one he was to build he called *Copy Kat* so close did he try to follow the plans used to build *Skeeter*, but he never managed to meet his objective. Sadly, he was killed in a light plane crash a couple of years later, leaving behind his lovely wife and a young family.

Dad bought a plot at Wingate, a boating club, with the objective of building a boat shed to house *Skeeter*, which was a much more convenient option than towing her the round trip of fifty miles backwards and forwards from home to lake every weekend. It also provided us with accommodation at the lake. My younger brother, Clive, was by this time age ten and an expert water skier, a skill I intended to acquire as my next goal in life.

We wrote to the Cypress Garden Ski School in Florida for advice. They had no information or contact with one-legged skiers and pointed out that it was difficult enough for people with two legs. I used to tow Clive behind *Skeeter* and thought how easy he made it look, which made me more determined than ever to succeed. The problem was the difficulty I had in controlling my artificial leg in water. It kept veering off to the right and I could not pull it back. The ski rope would pull me right through the centre of the skis, and I would land face first in the water with the skis dragging behind me.

Roy made a clamp that held both skis straight, and once I was on my feet in the water, I was able to pull the clamp off and throw it towards the jetty as we sped past. It worked like a charm, and after about three months I didn't need the help of the clamp any more. I therefore considered myself to be one of the first, if not the first, one-legged water skiers in the world.

Salisbury had a roller-skating rink and I soon mastered the art, with surprisingly little effort, thanks to Mom, who used to teach the Friday night roller rink dancing classes in England as an instructor. My mom knew in her heart of hearts that I would come across things

I would not be able to do in life; she also knew that I would damn well try and more than likely succeed. Any time we visited Johannesburg or Durban, a trip to their ice rinks was a must.

Obviously, I had to adapt and do things slightly differently from people with two healthy legs, but since I was one of the first amputees to master these disciplines, I think my sense of pride was justified. Artificial legs in the fifties were hard enough just to walk on without attaching a set of wheels or blades to them. A lot of amputees were self-conscious about the apparatus, but being so young, I was completely oblivious to any stares or comments, my sole concentration being on anything I set out to do. Passers-by were welcome to remark or stare at whatever I was doing till the cows came home as far as I was concerned, as long as they did not impede me from enjoying my task at hand.

Chapter five
Another accident

BOAT racing events were held all year round in southern Africa. I was fourteen years old and the year was 1956 when I was chosen to represent my country racing boats for the first time. Club Nautico in Beira was holding their first regatta, and I was selected to go as part of the Rhodesian team. Dad, Clive and I went for the weekend and we stayed at Club Nautico on the beach and raced in the harbour, where people could come and stand on the sea wall to watch the boats. The water was rough and the swells were rolling in from the open sea, but *Skeeter* seemed impervious to these conditions as she flew from wave top to wave top. I made many new friends during the regatta and left Beira with three huge trophies, some medals and a couple of pendants to add to my growing collection.

The people in Beira had only seen water skiing in the movies and my little brother Clive, towed by *Skeeter* with yours truly behind the wheel, wowed the crowd with a spectacular performance. We returned from Beira in triumph, and Mom, as always, displayed our trophies on the hotel's reception desk for all to see. The topic of conversation for the next few days with our hotel residents was her two boys and their achievements.

That same year my father bought me an F1 hydroplane, a racing craft capable of travelling at eighty plus miles per hour. This small pocket rocket was like a thoroughbred Arabian stallion, as skittish as hell and bloody fast. With the slightest error of judgement, a pilot would be tossed across the water like a skimming stone. I never broke any bones but suffered dislocations and torn ligaments aplenty, which was an accepted part of a package that involved speeds on water.

My sixteenth birthday in 1958 dawned with me still in one piece. I took and passed my driving test, after which Dad and I looked at a number of cars, and I was fortunate enough to leave the dealership with a new Morris 1000. Dad commented that it would be good to have the use of his own car back. He never mentioned which one, as we had six in our household and most of the time I had driven our Commer truck.

With the hydroplane and *Skeeter,* I won many races and championships and was an automatic selection for the Rhodesian team with both boats. As final exams loomed, school work became the priority, so my boat racing was curtailed and Lake Mac and White Waters Dam in Gwelo were the only races I entered. In any event, the motor on the hydro was getting a little tired and needed attention.

We sold the hydroplane with motor, and replaced it with a new B-class hydroplane from America and Koenig motor from Germany. Dad and I worked on the boat together, and my knowledge increased significantly as he taught me all the lessons he had learnt from his motorcycle racing days. The many changes and modifications we made to the boat and motor brought amazing results, which was of supreme importance to me given my extreme competitive spirit. My first hydroplane had lacked the right equipment to blow any opposition into the weeds, but I had learnt a lot from it and with my new set up, the best that money could buy, I knew I had no excuse but to lead the way.

A skilled pilot could be the best in the world technically, but without the right equipment and set-up underneath him, he might as well sit in the clubhouse and enjoy the facilities. It is necessary for a good pilot to learn to read the water as it tells him which way the wind is blowing and its strength. He also needs an awareness of the wake from boats in front, as this can cause the boat to dig in and barrel roll.

It sounds like bragging and probably is, but this perception did not present a problem for me as I was usually leading the field.

Mom was dead against this advancement in my chosen sport. She understood quite clearly that only the brave were capable of piloting such a craft. As far as she was concerned, I was still her little boy and hers to look after. To have her son flying around a race course at ninety miles per hour with fifteen or so equally mad participants on his tail was not what she considered safe or sane. Pottery or weaving would have been more to her liking, but she was my greatest fan and admirer and without reservation gave me her one hundred and ten percent support. Though she trusted my ability as a pilot, I knew that just for good measure, she threw in a prayer or two along the way.

Mom and Dad had bought a flat at Katanga House, giving them a second home for the occasions they did not feel like taking the trip back to the farm for one reason or another. It was their home away from home and just around the corner from the hotel. When the hotel got to be too much, the sanctuary of the farm was still available for them to enjoy.

One day I gave my friend Chris, who lived close to our hotel, a lift home from school. My heart lurched in my chest when I dropped him off and he introduced me to his sister Linda. She was thirteen, very beautiful, and I was besotted with her at first sight, but I didn't dare ask her for a date, in case she said no. I felt I had no hope of attracting a girl like her. How could someone as lovely as her go out with someone with one leg and who walked with a limp? I was certain she could have anyone she wanted and would not be interested in me. It took an enormous amount of courage to eventually ask her out, and when I did, her reply was, 'I'd love to'.

She must have seen more to me than I saw in myself, and it was she who gave me the confidence I needed with the opposite sex. She made me feel completely at ease, she taught me to dance, and she never showed the slightest embarrassment at being seen out with me. I had the most beautiful girl in Rhodesia on my arm, who only had eyes for me; she was to set the precedent and fulfil the penchant I had for all the beautiful, usually blonde women I was to have in my life. In the years that followed, Linda moved back to Cape Town with her folks where she became involved in photographic modelling and later international films! Given her beauty, there were no surprises there. I never lost contact with the family, and although we all went our separate ways, we communicate regularly, even today, some fifty years later.

The year 1959 proved to be a time of great trouble and upheaval in what was then the Belgian Congo: the white population was forced to flee the country with just the clothes they stood up in. They arrived in Rhodesia in droves until our hotel was bursting at the seams. Most of them had no money to pay for their keep and spent most of their days at the Belgian Embassy trying to get a passage to Europe. We had refugees sleeping in every conceivable corner of the hotel.

Major Mike Hoare was staying with us at the time in search of mercenaries to join the fighting. To that end, with breakfast out of the way and with Mom's approval, he set up a recruiting station in our dining room. There would be queues of old experienced mercenaries and young wannabes outside the hotel waiting to be called in for interviews. Mike spent the evenings speaking to displaced Belgian nationals, who had fled the fighting, gleaning every ounce of information he could from them on the situation there. Whenever our visitors from the Congo had obtained a flight overseas, they left cars and possessions as payment for the accommodation and food supplied by Mom. Consequently, Mom eventually amassed the largest collection of left-hand drive cars south of the Equator.

That same year I was thrilled to be chosen to represent Rhodesia at the Gold Cup Regatta in Livingstone, Northern Rhodesia. I was to race against my old adversaries South Africa and Northern Rhodesia. With permission from my headmaster to take two days off school, I set off alone early one Wednesday morning on the nine-hundred-mile drive to Victoria Falls. The journey was quite boring to a young man such as me. There were very few towns to pass through along the way, and the scenery of trees and scrub, which is typical of any land above the Tropic of Capricorn, made my journey monotonous.

Seeing the odd baobab tree in its strange form, however, was always interesting. It is so different from any other tree, and only one of its species is found in Africa. One of its species is in Australia and six are in Madagascar. The baobab tree is known as the 'tree of life,' with good reason as the animal and human inhabitants of the African savannah regions depend on it for many things. It can and often does provide shelter, clothing, food, and water to all living creatures within an accessible distance. Its trunk can hold up to a hundred and twenty thousand litres of water, which can be tapped in dry periods, and its fire-resistant cork-like bark and huge stem are used for making cloth and rope. The leaves are used as condiments and medicines. The fruit, called 'monkey bread,' is edible, and has a high Vitamin C content. Mature trees are usually hollow, providing living space for many animals and humans.

For most of the year, the tree, which grows to a height of one hundred feet, is leafless and looks very much like it has its roots sticking up in the air. For that reason, it is sometimes known as the 'upside-down tree'. Trees are even used as bars, barns, wine and beer shops and more. Without a travelling companion to relieve the tediousness of the drive, contemplating such wonders of nature, that I had learnt about at school, helped.

The tarmac road was good but Africa is so vast that if I passed twenty cars on the thousand-mile trip it was a lot. The journey, thankfully, was trouble-free, and eventually I found myself driving across the bridge straddling the Zambezi River into Northern Rhodesia.

The Zambezi River, frequently interrupted by rapids, is the fourth longest river in Africa and the largest flowing into the Indian Ocean from Africa. Hippopotamuses are abundant along most of its calm stretches and crocodiles and monitor lizards are to be found in many places. Bird life is abundant with species including heron, pelican, egret and the African fish eagle. Riverside woodland also supports many large animals, such as buffalo, zebra, giraffe and elephants and the river itself is home to several hundred species of fish, including catfish, tiger fish and bream.

It was my first visit to Victoria Falls and Livingstone, which was little more than a large village. I located the riverside chalet allocated to me and made my way to the boat club situated two miles above the falls. Victoria Falls is known by the locals as 'Mosi-oa-Tunya,' which translated means 'smoke that thunders'. It is a very apt description as the mist from the falls can be seen in the sky from a distance of eighty miles. Awesome, to say the least. In the rainy season it is the largest waterfall in the world and regarded as one of the seven natural wonders of the world. It also serves as an ambassador to the seven natural wonders of Africa. At first sight, it is unbelievably impressive, being a mile wide and three hundred and sixty feet high.

Some local boat boys helped me float the hydroplane, then rowed it to my allocated pit site. It was facing upstream, and I noticed with fascination that the speedometer was reading twenty-two miles per hour. I gave the boat a quick run after satisfying myself that the crash boats were in position on the falls end of the circuit. I thought it might be fun to drift over the falls, but I wasn't taking any chances, not being absolutely certain I would survive the ride. With all that done, I put the boat away, had supper, phoned Mom and hit the sack.

After breakfast the next morning, the scrutineers could find no problem with either the boat or my gear, so I settled into a comfy chair to watch the opposition go out to practice.

It wasn't long before I knew which man I would have to beat, and I waited for him to go out again. As his boat left the jetty, I hopped into mine, started the motor and accelerated it onto the plane. I followed him onto the course and stayed slightly to his right, from where I could watch his throttle hand and see how much of it he was using down the straight. The boat bottom at the rear is concave and the air is channelled between the front sponsons, which lift the front of the boat out of the water, the air rushes back, hits the concave and lifts the rear of the boat out of the water, reducing drag. With the boat properly set up, it will prop ride – in other words, the whole of the boat is out of the water with only the propeller of the boat in it. The propeller has a special cupped lip to stop cavitation. As the boat is completely out of the water, if not balanced correctly, it will take off like an aircraft.

The throttle on a racing hydro is called a 'dead man's hand'. It is like an open V and the more it is squeezed together, the faster the boat goes. When the two parts of the V are touching together, the motor is at full throttle. The throttle has to be squeezed all the time because the moment it is released, a kill switch cuts the motor dead. This is a protection device and happens in the event of the boat flipping or the pilot being thrown from the craft.

My opponent was at full throttle while I was just over three-quarters, so it appeared to me that I had the faster boat. I stayed behind him as it suited me to let him think I couldn't catch him – devious Richard. When practice was over, it was time to get down to some serious racing.

The current of the river made the start difficult as the boats were drifting towards the start clock at twenty-three miles per hour. I found an island located in line with the starting point that had a fairly substantial branch sticking out into the current. The added bonus was the absence of any crocs on the island. I held the boat there against the current, and at the prescribed time hit the start button and accelerated towards the start line, which I hit at seventy-five miles per hour, about two seconds late, with the boat at full throttle. We were flying.

The South African had miscalculated the current and, arriving too early at the clock, had been forced to circle. Consequently, I was halfway down the front straight at full throttle, riding on the prop, by the time he crossed the start line. I won the race by nearly a lap, the land equivalent of two miles, even though I had slowed down as no one was catching me. I followed the same procedure in the second race with the same result and was thus chosen to represent Rhodesia for the Gold Cup Challenge between the competing nations.

I cannot describe the elation I felt deep in my heart competing against the best southern Africa had to offer, annihilating them, and being chosen to represent my country. I had grown a few inches since I got up that morning! Unfortunately, I had no one with whom to share my pleasure and joy with and that saddened me.

The last race of the day was the Gold Cup Challenge. I accelerated away from my island, getting an excellent start once again; this time I kept the throttle wide open and lapped everyone in my class, completely demoralising the opposition and winning the Gold Cup in my class.

On my slowing-down lap, I was flat out on the prop going down the front straight when I felt the front lift. I moved my weight forward and backed off the throttle, but it was jammed wide open and the boat kept rising into the wind. I knew I was in trouble when the water stopped hitting the sponsons, and I found myself airborne and being tossed around like a leaf in a storm. The boat was tail walking at over eighty-miles per hour, and then it caught a gust of wind on the flat bottom and took off, destination 'Venus'.

I was thrown out of the boat and flew thirty feet into the air, according to the 'crash boat' crew who witnessed the accident. The boat flipped back over and hit me full in the face. I hit the water, which was as hard as concrete, and could see the boat tossing and turning way above me. The whole incident must have taken no more than a couple of seconds, but it seemed to me that everything was happening in slow motion.

I skipped across the water like a stone until I slowed enough to sink in a shower of spray, and, knowing I was about a mile from the actual falls, remember thinking, 'I hope the crash boat gets to me before I go over the edge'. There was also the danger of crocs to be seriously considered. These reptiles bask on the islands in the sun waiting for fish. As the fish sense the danger of going over the falls, they swim back upstream against the fast flowing current. The crocs make short work of them for lunch. An attack was improbable with such a swift current, but I supposed there might be the odd, very hungry crocodile willing to brave it.

My Day-Glo orange racing life jacket pulled me to the surface like a cork out of a champagne bottle. It had a huge white collar, which fastened under my helmet, its main purpose was to keep an unconscious occupant from drowning and to pinpoint the pilot in the water. With both arms floating at my side, I could feel the current pulling me along. I wiggled my fingers, and could feel all of them beneath the water; everything seemed to be in place, except my left leg was hurting like hell.

I looked to one side and saw the crash boat heading towards me. By this time, I realised the collar of my life jacket was red with blood, and I froze as my imagination ran riot. I put my hands up to my face but could not feel my fingers touch it, and pulling my gloves away, found they were soaked in blood. My mouth felt full of grit and liquid. When I spat out the contents, I saw it was my teeth and blood.

I turned to face the crash boat and saw the girl in the front put her hands to her face, but not before I read her lips as she exclaimed, 'OH MY GOD,' which did nothing to improve my anxiety. The crew hauled me from the water and removed my life jacket. As the boat headed at full speed for the Red Cross tent on the riverbank, I remained in a sitting position as my mouth kept filling with blood. I was carried to the hospital tent where a doctor proceeded to patch me up. The extent of the damage became apparent as the blood was wiped away. My nose was broken, most of my teeth were missing, I had bitten through my tongue, and there was a huge hole under my chin through which the underside of my tongue was visible. As I regained feeling in my face, so came the pain. My left leg felt like someone had tried to tear it from my body. I had ice on my tongue, a splint on my nose, and a needle was being threaded to stitch all the loose bits back together again. Considering the speed and ferocity of the accident, I considered myself to have come off very lightly. Ten stitches were put under my chin and three in my face. My tongue was swollen, and it seemed the flow of blood was endless. I even had gum guards placed over my upper and lower very broken teeth to prevent the jagged bits from cutting into my mouth, damaging it further. It took an hour and a half for my tongue to stop bleeding before I was able to limp from the tent. I was in a great deal of pain, and I can only attribute the way I was able to handle it to the stamina of youth and my higher than average pain threshold.

In view of the injuries I had sustained, and the medication I was given, the doctor had forbidden me to involve myself in the rescue of my boat, but I nevertheless accompanied the crash team on the venture. When a boat is involved in an accident, it is usually kept afloat by air trapped in the nose, but the nose of my boat had been ripped open and it had sunk to the river bed three metres below. When this happens, a small flotation device is deployed; a bit like a fishing float except larger.

The team dived down to attach flotation packs, rather like large balloons, to the wreckage. Once inflated, the boat floated up to the surface, allowing it to be towed to shore, where several helping hands packed the trailer for me, tying the boat down and attaching the trailer to my car. I would have been hard pressed to do all this myself, as my leg was too sore to lift anything.

I took the team for a drink, although I could not have one myself because of all the medication I had been given. I had missed the prize giving. My trophies, along with the Gold Cup, had been accepted on my behalf by the Rhodesian captain, who at the same time brought the crowd up to date with my injuries. I might have felt groggy from the medication and my body may have felt like a steamroller had run over it, but that was no indication of what I felt inside, which was exuberant, sublime happiness and ecstasy to the degree I could have executed somersaults and cartwheels if only my poor body had allowed it. The enormity of my achievement began to sink in; I had won every trophy it was possible to win that day and beaten the best Africa had to offer and, most important of all, I had done it for Rhodesia as part of her team.

Back in my chalet, a feeling of drowsiness began to take over together with a feeling of utter loneliness; I had no one special to share my happiness with. I just wanted to go home and had an early night in preparation for the long trip ahead of me the next day.

I phoned Mom before retiring to tell her of my wins and the time she could expect me home. I mentioned the damage to the boat but not wanting to worry her unnecessarily, refrained from mentioning any personal injuries. I knew I would be in enough 'kak' from her once I returned home, so it might as well wait. I had been prescribed painkillers but elected not to take them, wanting to be alert for the journey home. I tried to sleep but the pain made it impossible. When I left Livingstone at two-thirty in the morning I felt like death warmed up and think I must have driven all the way home on autopilot.

I was attempting to climb out of the car when my mother first laid eyes on me. She put her hand to her face and exclaimed, 'Oh, Dee,' followed by a huge lecture as she checked out my injuries. I winced in pain when she prodded my hip and the blood-soaked bandages on my face. I tried in vain to distract her by piling my trophies on the roof of the car, but to no avail. There was definitely no chance of her sharing my joy at that point in time: her son was badly injured. When I eventually got a chance to look in the mirror and saw how badly my face was swollen, I was horrified. I didn't recognise the person who looked back at me.

Chapter six
Speedboat champion

BY four that afternoon, Mom had me in Dr Pockroy's surgery; I was checked out and all my dressings were changed. The ligaments were torn in my left leg, and although they were strapped up, they were very painful. The next day my dentist could do very little for me because of the swelling and stitches, and I looked far worse than I had just after the accident. I was not a sight for sore eyes, with my swollen, lopsided face and gruesome-looking blood-encased stitches, which were too sore to clean. It was only by the matter of my supreme will that I was able to open my mouth at all so the dentist could take imprints of my jaw, from which new soft shields could be made to protect my mouth from the jagged remains of what were once my Colgate-smile teeth.

My whole body ached from the impact of hitting the water, and my painful leg was another story, which forced me to use crutches to get around. Meals became interesting, a culinary experience, consisting mainly of steak and chips blended to a smooth consistency. I thought perhaps Mom should put 'steak and chips milkshakes' on the hotel menu, but she didn't find the idea one bit amusing.

Mom was adamant that the 'damn thing', meaning, of course, the boat, had to go, to which I protested vehemently. I might as well have addressed my protests to a brick wall because Mom was just not listening. The moment the crash happened I knew I would be in big trouble, so her response to it all came as no surprise. I had no alternative but to eventually keep my mouth shut and take everything she threw at me.

The next ten days were taken up with doctors' appointments.

Everything was improving except my good leg, which seemed to be getting worse, so much so that I could hardly get in and out of the car. I had used crutches since arriving home, which, I think in retrospect, might have saved me from permanent, if not crippling, damage. A lot of bruising remained but the swelling eventually subsided, the stitches came out, and I was beginning to look a bit like my former self, except for the smile. Although a dentist is not my favourite person in the whole world, and I would rather avoid one like the plague, the broken teeth had to be cut out of the gums so I had no option in the matter. The whole procedure was extremely painful but, once done, was worth every minute. My jaw had been fractured in a number of places; what had been left of my teeth after the accident had had to be surgically removed. It was false teeth for me. On the bright side, at long last I had my smile back.

The rest of the injuries were healing well apart from my left leg, which seemed to get worse by the day. Never one to mollycoddle myself, lounging in bed was not an option; I was happier spending time with Dad helping him repair the boat. The engine had been underwater for a number of hours, which required it to be stripped and all the parts checked out for damage. In spite of my battered body, I was fortunately still able to drive myself around without having to depend on anybody else. I decided, very wisely probably for the sake of my ego, to give the fairer sex a break until I had healed properly and was back to my former gorgeous self.

Joss Nangle, the top orthopaedic surgeon, who had dealt with the loss of my leg as a boy, was getting out of his car one day as I was walking past on my crutches. He invited me to sit in his car as I explained the accident and brought him up to date with the current situation. After listening to me, he expressed concern that the pain in my leg was worsening and advised me to make an appointment to see him at the practice. Lying on his couch that afternoon, he asked me to lift my leg, which I was unable to do. I consider myself to have a very high pain threshold, but when Joss Nangle tried to rotate my leg, I went through the roof. I had never experienced pain like that before.

He looked at me quite calmly, but there was a serious tone to his voice when he said, 'Hospital for you, young man'.

'What's wrong,' I asked, remembering the pain when he rotated my leg. 'This leg needs to be X-rayed. I suspect a hip dislocation with complications. If you do any more walking on it, you will end up a cripple'. I sensed he was making a statement of fact.

'That's impossible! I have been on crutches since the accident,' I said, hoping he would not detect the fear in my voice. 'We'll see!' he went on and dialled for an ambulance to come to his surgery.

I phoned Mom to tell her what Joss had said and was met with a deathly silence that said it all – big dog box for me once more!

The X-rays confirmed Mr Nangle's suspicions that at some time during the accident, the ball and socket of the thigh joint had parted company. The torn ligaments had masked the real problem in the early stages, which had now become a massive one. All the subsequent walking had badly damaged the ball joint, and after much deliberation, it was decided I should undergo an operation, which held a fifty/fifty chance of success, the operation never having been performed in Africa before. My hip's ball joint would have to be pinned into the pelvis to allow forward and backward movement of the leg only, no side rotation. Mr Nangle seemed reasonably sure of success, and as it seemed the only option open to me I voiced my complete trust in this very clever man.

'I wish I had your confidence, young man, but we will only know once we are into the operation'.

As I was wheeled into the operating theatre, my sense of humour was intact and I couldn't resist saying to him, 'Make sure you get my wheel alignment right'. I didn't fancy landing up pigeon-toed. He burst out laughing and retorted, 'Just you go to sleep this time and let me worry about your wheel alignment'.

I always considered myself extremely lucky to have had a specialist of his enormous calibre piece me together for the second time in my life. I guess my guardian angel was still looking after me, for the time being anyway. I am sure if he had known what he was in for, he would have opted out and asked the Lord for a new and easier assignment.

I awoke to no real pain, just an unpleasant ache. Mr Nangle was pleased with the operation but warned me to expect to be in a wheelchair for eight weeks.

I tentatively suggested crutches as an alternative and was informed in no uncertain terms, 'You can't walk on crutches with a prosthesis'.

He should have thought twice about using that word 'can't'. During my second week in hospital when no one else was around, I strapped on my leg and surprised even myself by walking with the aid of crutches. I continued with this practice in secret and became quite proficient at it. If my mother knew what I was doing, she would have killed me.

She had been to see my headmaster to make arrangements for my school work to be brought to the hospital and for my exams to be written at home. Once she had all these arrangements in place, she gave me her full attention, thereby curtailing my walkabouts. She was obviously very worried that I would end up in a wheelchair for the rest of my life and spoke to me about selling the hydro.

I had undoubtedly been born with a love for speed, which my parents had inadvertently honed when they bought the speedboat. Being reasonable and sensible was the obvious choice to go with, and I realised that meant selling my boat or that 'damn thing' as Mom insisted on calling it. I certainly could not afford to damage my left hip any more than it had been already, but I had tasted victory and the feeling of elation that goes with it.

I thought about my life before the boats, when I was a bystander watching all my friends playing their chosen sports. What would I do without boat racing? There had to be something I could compete in to quench the need I had in me to succeed at something. Mom had some time ago suggested tiddlywinks which had become a standing joke between the two of us; maybe once I got into it I would enjoy this exciting game.

Mr Nangle had no idea how much this young man wanted to go

home, but he did know of the tenacious will of the person he was dealing with. I managed to persuade him that I could walk on my prostheses with crutches and proved my point by showing him.

Shaking his head, he looked across at me. 'I should have known better than to use the word *can't* when speaking to you. You are a remarkable young man,' he said. High praise, coming from him. Five days later after spending time recuperating, I arrived home on crutches.

One of my schoolmasters, who would be the invigilator when it came to writing my final exams, spent time with me in the afternoon to go over school work. We struck up quite a friendship and when I opened my workshop years later, he was one of my first customers.

As I began to put more and more weight on my damaged hip, like any injury, it hurt like hell. Sometimes I felt I might even have overdone it when the aching kept me awake at night. However, in my short life I had learnt that persistence gets almost anything working again, so I carried on regardless. There was the final regatta of the year coming up in a couple of weeks and to retain the championship, I needed a fourth place. Most of all I needed Mom's blessing to be able to do it. Mission Impossible.

Mom was confident I could not expect to race as it entailed kneeling in the boat, which would be impossible for me to do. The impact of the boat hitting the wash from boats in front would have damaged my hip permanently. She had not, however, thought of the option that I could lie on my stomach in the craft. This would alleviate any jarring on the hip, but if I came out of the boat at speed it could tear the pin out of my pelvis and that would leave me crippled for life.

I broached the subject on a couple of occasions, but Mom was adamant that if I went anywhere near that 'damned thing,' she would smash it to pieces before leaving home, never to return. Strong words from my mother and I knew she meant every last one. The obstacle I would have to overcome to get Mom's blessing to race seemed insurmountable. Every time I mentioned competing, she would throw me a look that would have scared a full-grown lion accompanied by a definite and emphatic 'NO!'

I tried everything to get her to change her mind and at times felt she would not be swayed from her path, but ultimately I wore her down by dogged persistence, constant nagging, pleading and cajoling. I was a sixteen-year-old and had the advantage over my mother of youth and unflagging stamina when it came to getting my own way. I knew and understood how hard it had been for my mother – going through the loss of my leg with me, the worries she had endured over my boat racing, and the damage my good leg had sustained.

Mom gave me the go ahead completely out of the blue one day when I had almost given up the fight. She gave no reason for her change of heart, just her permission and her blessing for me to enter the race but not before extracting from me the promise to take care of 'her property'. My mother was a very special person throughout my life, and right up until her death there was a special bond between us, which could never be broken or taken away by anyone. It may be assumed that a mother tends to bond with her most difficult child, but in my case that wasn't true. I was a perfect little angel and I know that because my mother told me so.

To please my mom I had promised her that I would sell the boat after racing it in this one last regatta. I had thought of every conceivable argument and reason to continue racing, while knowing at the same time deep inside that any further damage to my leg would probably see me in a wheelchair for the rest of my life. The risk was too great.

The boat had been repaired and was now well padded and surprisingly easy to pilot lying on my stomach. I drove a very careful race and took second place in the scratch race, which was all I needed to clinch the championship. I was well aware for the ten laps of the race what could happen to me if I tried any heroics.

Bowing to Mom's wishes, I had already advertised the boat for sale prior to the event and had a string of pilots clamouring to buy her. As I cut the motor and drifted towards the jetty, the pilot who had been first to phone with a more than adequate offer was waiting for me, waving a cheque. I took it and walked away, not daring to look back because I knew if I did I would have changed my mind. I had to force myself to step away from a part of my life which many a young man could only dream of and I resolved to console myself with the fact that for a special period of time I had had the blessing of living that dream to the full.

I felt extremely emotional having to part with one of my beloved boats, but I had made a promise. It was one of the most difficult things I have done in my life. I had kept my promise to Mom and that brought me some consolation but with the boat gone, I had no idea what I would do with myself. I knew one thing for sure: I could not risk any more injury to myself any time soon and my body needed time to repair itself. Life's complications do require answers. Upon the realisation that we have found an answer, life often changes the question – and once more we pursue the answers.

I went up to the clubhouse balcony to watch the rest of the day's racing and was glad to sit down as my leg was a bit achy. After changing out of my racing overalls, I settled into an easy chair, quite unnoticed by anyone, when I heard Mom, who had been assigned to do the catering, announce, 'I am just going to watch Dee race'.

'Dee' was a nickname assigned to me by my Mom, which only she ever used. I'm not sure why and can only guess it was short for 'Dick' or that she preferred it to 'Dick'. I never thought to ask her, but in any event, it was special.

The boats were already on the water in readiness for the race as she arrived at the balcony. 'Lady, you are spoiling my view,' I said. Recognising my voice, she spun around but before she could say anything, I waved the cheque in the air. 'Gone!' I declared.

'Oh, Dee! Thank you!' she said, bursting into tears as she came to hug me. 'You are a very special and different young man, who doesn't know the meaning of *can't* and I respect you for that. You have made me very happy in keeping your promise to me, and I am well aware of the sacrifice you have made to please me. I know that somewhere around the corner a different and exciting life is waiting for you and, as always, you will excel in it as you do in all things. I am glad that bloody thing has gone'. My mother was always coming up with these intuitive, inspiring speeches when she felt I needed a lift. She was always able to read me like a book, but her words of wisdom often required me to ponder what she had said and to seek and decipher the kernel of truth her words always carried. I knew in that moment what it was like to look into the eyes of the happiest person in the world, my beautiful mom.

The week before this particular regatta, Pat Green, Northern Rhodesia's top pilot, had died while testing his boat on the Zambezi River in exactly the same place I'd had my accident. His outfit had also tail-walked but when the crash team got to him, he was dead.

We had kept this news from Mom, as Pat was one of her favourite people. I found out later that she knew of his accident all along but had kept it to herself. It proved to be Pat's death that had prompted her to give me the go-ahead to race.

When I asked her why, she replied, 'My son, you are a champion and racing is in your blood. You have tasted death twice in your sixteen years, and by God's grace, you remain with us. Your life is in His hands, not mine, so who am I to deny you the pleasure you derive from your racing and to interfere with the destiny God has ordained for you'?

These words were very deep and at the age I was, perhaps a little over my head once again, but in all my years, I have never forgotten them. They say things happen in threes. A few months down the line, my friend Gordon Lanham Love, the South Africa open champion, broke his back while attempting to break the South Africa water speed record.

Chapter seven
The racing motor mechanic

IT was December 1958; I was approaching my seventeenth birthday early the following year and had passed my end of the year exams. I had applied and been accepted for an apprenticeship with the Central Mechanical Equipment Department, a Rhodesian government workshop servicing and repairing anything from a D8 Cat Bulldozer, used for building the mighty Kariba Dam, to a Vespa scooter belonging to a meter maid. I had always been interested in anything mechanical so I knew the apprenticeship I had decided on was the way forward for me.

The wage – sixteen pounds a month – was not generous by any stretch of the imagination, which made me a little reluctant to take up the apprenticeship. Dad insisted I go through with it and agreed to see me right as far as money was concerned, with the understanding that once I had made my first million, I would pay him back!

The car I had now was a Riley one point five and although I had sold my F1 hydroplane, I still had *Skeeter,* my racing boat that had changed my life in so many, many ways. We had set out as newbies, *Skeeter* and I, years ago: she as an unseasoned race boat and me a young boy following a dream. Together, we had achieved that dream; it had taken me on a journey which would last a lifetime. I have enjoyed every millisecond of that ride.

My weekdays now became occupied with work but the lake remained a popular choice on weekends, with three random months of the year dedicated to the City & Guild's Course at the Polytechnic.

I took to the mechanical profession like a duck to water and enjoyed every minute of it, but I missed the thrill of a competition and, most of all, the glory of winning.

One day a visitor from England staying in the hotel came across to chat with me while I was working on my car. He introduced himself as Bob Flight and was interested to learn I was a Rhodesian Champion on water. He remarked on my young age as he must have been around thirty-five. A lot older than me, he was employed by the motor manufacturer Standard Triumph and was on a short visit to the Rhodesian agent. As he was a race driver in England, he had talked Swift Motors into lending him a second hand TR2 to race in the Rhodesian Junior Grand Prix.

He did not know many people in Rhodesia so he asked me if I would I like to be a member of his pit crew for the event, which was to be held in a few weeks' time. I didn't need to be asked twice!

Practice was scheduled to commence at two o' clock on the Friday afternoon before the Saturday race day, and we arrived with plenty of time to spare. I was to help Bob with lap times and other incidentals. Watching the cars flash by, I felt a flutter in my stomach as I hung out the pit board for Bob to see his lap times. A part of me wondered what it would be like in one of these cars compared to my F1 hydroplane.

Once practice was over, the track was left open for a further hour for fine-tuning and problem sorting. Bob was happy with the performance of his car and asked if I would like to experience the reality of a race car. He really shouldn't have done that! I was overjoyed and very attentive as he explained to me the finer points of driving a racing car, such as the error of driving into a bend at too high a speed and losing control of the car, and coming out of the corner too slowly.

'A corner must be entered at a controlled speed,' he explained. 'Straighten the corner, hit the apex and accelerate out of it at as great a speed as possible, and this speed will then be carried all the way down the straight. It is this approach and smoothness that gives a quick lap time. Enter the corner too fast and you will lose all your speed trying to control the car as you negotiate the corner'.

I could see sense in what I was being told. I took the first two corners far too fast, and by the time I slowed down, I had missed the apex completely. I had stern words with myself during the next five laps and thought hard about what I had been told. This experience gave me a full understanding of how to get the car around the track quickly.

Driving into the pits afterwards, Bob's praises rang in my ears: 'You're a natural. As soon as I saw you relax and drive the car into the corner, I knew you had it'. I felt that familiar buzz of elation in my head but knew I had so much to learn. Bob won his race the next day, and I observed, from vantage points around the inside of the circuit, how he attacked various corners.

I would like to give my readers a little background on the technicalities of racing. The racing line is the route a driver follows in order to take corners in the fastest possible way. Determining the best line is an essential skill to learn, though there is rarely a perfect line through any corner for all circumstances.

To get the line right, it is vital to turn in at the correct point. The apex is the point closest to the inside of the corner, also referred to as the clipping point. Once the apex has been hit, it should be possible to reduce the steering lock and increase the throttle.

I bought a brand new TR3A the following Monday, and Bob very kindly gave me the race cam and carburetor needles he had brought with him from the UK. He also organised a substantial discount on the TR, and as a gesture of appreciation, I took him out for dinner before he left that week. If and when the club had a practice, I made sure I was there and drove my car around the circuit as hard as I could. My times were very respectable to the extent I was eventually lapping the track just two seconds slower than Bob had done.

I stripped the motor, carried out modifications to the cylinder head, and fitted the cam and needles Bob had given me. What a difference! I could feel the motor revving easier, and the increase in torque coming out of a corner was very evident, so much so that at the next practice, my times were as quick as Bob's had been at the GP meeting.

On the notice board at the motor club I spotted an invitation to Beira for their first-ever motor race, and I decided I would like to have a go, providing I could get the idea past a sergeant major called Mom. All I needed was to put a full harness safety belt and fire extinguisher into the car, and I was ready to go.

I broached the idea with Mom on the phone and began by telling her of my timed laps on the circuit and how much I enjoyed driving my car there. For good measure, before I asked her if she minded my entering a race just to see what it was like, I told her how much safer it was than boat racing as the elements, 'wind and rough water,' would be absent. Talk about a deafening silence. I hung up, feeling somewhat defeated, my mind working overtime to find plausible reasons to gain Mom's approval. To my surprise, she called me back out of the blue. 'Just take care of my property,' she said.

What a fantastic mom I had! The Lord in His wisdom had selected someone very special to raise me to adulthood with the foreknowledge that as the Creator of this boy, I was going to be more trouble than Lucifer. Only my mother could have filled the role of being my mother. She could not only read me like a book but had the patience, tolerance and understanding of what was going on inside my head and heart. I know that my brother Clive will corroborate what I am telling here.

I set off on Thursday afternoon, stopping at the border post to cross into Mozambique. After checking in at the motor club and with formalities finalised, I attended a rather good cocktail party. The following day I went out for the practice and duly qualified for the race. I realised straight off how crucial it was to keep the car in the centre of the track and on the racing line; anywhere off this line and one could expect to hit one of the large potholes that were dotted around the track. While the organisers spent a great deal of time filling in the ever-increasing breakup of the track, some of the would-be Mozambican Fangios (Fangio at that time was considered to be the best race driver of all time, having won numerous world championships) spent more time off the circuit than on, and a hell of a lot of time in the pits repairing the resulting damage to their cars.

I qualified the TR second behind a Honda factory race car of a thousand CCs. The exhaust note from the engine sounded like a swarm of bees, and the engine itself was capable of eighteen thousand revolutions per minute. It was a real pocket rocket, which left me for dead on the straights. The race got under way and the Honda shot off into the distance with me following in second place; I found it very boring and not nearly as exciting as boat racing. Up ahead, the Honda slowed down and as I went past, I noticed its wheel sticking out at a peculiar angle. The driver had apparently hit a pothole off-line on a corner, damaging the suspension. As a consequence, I won the race by miles and collected a large trophy and a medal or two.

Prize giving was a low-key event, with no special mention given of my young age, and I left for home soon after. I had plenty of time to contemplate everything I had experienced, and when I got home voiced my feeling to Mom that motor racing was not for me. My statement was met with a 'Go on, tell me another' look. Mom knew I would eventually find something, somewhere, involving speed and danger, although to me at that time with the sale of my hydro, it felt as if I had taken more than a few steps backwards in my sporting life.

It may be argued that the age I was then and the impatience of youth that went with it had a lot to do with my feelings, but I don't believe that was the case at all. I knew first-hand what it was like to have an artificial leg, which left me with no hope of achieving a good result in any sport requiring the use of two legs, and I knew, too, how important it was for my inner man to achieve something of value in the sporting world.

I tried to be philosophical about the whole situation, convincing myself it was only a matter of time before I found something I could both excel in and be passionate about. I continued dabbling in motor sport after being talked into buying an Alfa Giulietta, which I refrain from enlarging upon, it being in my estimation a heap of rubbish. Suffice to say, its acquisition was a disaster from beginning to end with more time being spent working on the car than on the track. After running out of brakes on one particular occasion, I stripped out the racing components and sold it.

Racing components consist of a lot of things: from wide wheels for a better mechanical grip, bigger brakes for better stopping, and special brake pads to prevent brake fade, to better shock absorbers for increased road holding, and bigger roll bars for greater weight transference. I have mentioned only a few components for handling and braking, but engines can be fitted with different pistons, hi-lift cams and bigger valves, and those are just for starters. A separate book could virtually be written to include all components available for better performance.

When I found myself with nothing to do, and remembering that my friend Chris from school days was playing there with his band, I drifted into the Sarum Youth Club at the old Belvedere Aerodrome, which was to become a regular feature in my life every Wednesday and Friday night. I can't for the life of me remember how it happened, but somehow I found myself elected Chairman of the Sarum Youth Club Committee that ran and administered the club. In six months, with the aid of a really good team, top rock and roll bands in Rhodesia queued to play there and though I was not the best dancer on the block, I enjoyed dancing with the good looking blondes that frequented the club along with all the other teenagers of the day, without feeling self-conscious. A thriving table tennis section was formed, which began topping the Junior League in Salisbury and for the three years under my chairmanship, from the age of seventeen to twenty, the youth club became the biggest and best in Rhodesia. Friends who I had co-opted onto the committee tackled their tasks with tireless energy, dedication and unflagging enthusiasm. Without them the Club could never have reached the heights it did.

Sarum Youth Club took up a small amount of my time but a large vacant hollow existed inside me since selling my boat and nothing I did seemed to fulfil its cravings. I grew to firmly believe that happiness is like a butterfly. The more you chase it, the more it eludes you. I tried to interest myself in archery, table tennis and horseback riding: they all left me stone cold. I was an excellent shot and had been shooting since the age of eight, but there are only so many rounds that can be discharged at a target and then it gets too repetitious. With my fierce love of animals, hunting was not an option. I was looking for something that kept eluding me, and after the Alfa debacle, motor racing was low on the list. I cast around, not knowing which way to turn.

I had gone to a timed practice at the Marlborough Circuit and was about to leave when Mossie Clements, a friend from the motor club, and one of the top rally drivers in southern Africa, offered me a drive in his Volvo 122S. My times were good but most important, I was enjoying the car, and Mossie asked me if I would be interested in joining him to race together as a team in certain international rallies and race meetings for Volvo. He mentioned he would get me a special deal on a new Volvo if I were interested. I had never rallied a car before, and at only eighteen knew I could learn a lot about the rudiments of rallying from not only Mossie, but the other older drivers I would be competing against.

After acquiring my new Volvo later that week, I set about acquainting myself with the characteristics of the car by making my first port of call the 'skid pan' on which cars can be made to skid so that drivers can practice controlling them. When I was finally satisfied with my performance, I felt ready for my first race for Volvo in the Rhodesian Grand Prix at the Khumalo circuit in Bulawayo.

Many of the towns in Rhodesia were given names originating from the African language such as Que Que or Shabane, but many were also named after white pioneers or important British dignitaries. Salisbury was originally known as Fort Salisbury after the Third Marquess of Salisbury, the British Prime Minister at the time and subsequently became known simply as Salisbury.

Bulawayo had grown from a few trading posts to become the second largest city in Rhodesia. It was set up originally as a kingdom in the northwest of Rhodesia by Mzilikazi, a Zulu chief who fled from Zululand during the Mfacane, the name given to the extended regional instability caused during the second decade of the 19th century by Shaka's expansionist ambitions. Mzilikazi, with five hundred warriors, set up his main homestead at the place which became known as Bulawayo. 'Bulawayo' is the Matabele name for 'the place of killing,' as it was there that the turbulence of the establishment of the new Matebele state, the witch hunts and executions, took place.

The Khumalo racing circuit in Bulawayo was a converted Second World War airfield and had a very fast sweep, or gradual corner, that could be taken at full throttle, depending on the way the car handled. On the first practice, I was losing a lot of ground to Mossie at the sweep, and his advice to me was to simply take the sweep at full throttle. 'I do,' was his comment. Problem solved, I thought. Never believe your opposition!

Out we went for second practice. I have never been short on courage, and if Mossie was driving at full throttle through the sweep, then I would be too. On the first lap into the sweep at a hundred and ten miles per hour, foot flat, using the whole track, the car lost all grip and swapped ends. Off the track I went in clouds of dust, and through the fence alongside the main road, which was close to the race track. The car launched itself into the air and across the main Salisbury to Bulawayo road, and disappeared into the bush on the other side. It was a miracle no cars were driving along the road at the time. I spun the

Volvo to a stop in a cloud of dust, selected first gear, and drove back to the main road and onto the circuit via the entrance gate.

The car seemed fine under examination in the pits, and I was preoccupied in trying to fathom what had gone wrong. Mossie, who had seen me disappear in a cloud of dust, walked towards the car as I was donning my crash helmet to go and post a time before getting back on the circuit. He asked what had happened.

'Going through the sweep with my foot flat is what happened. My car won't do it,' I declared. 'Oh no! You must lift off for a second to load the front end before you turn in. Didn't I tell you?'

Oh, how sweet was revenge. Once I had sorted out the sweep, I was half a second quicker than Mossie.

It was just as well I phoned Mom to tell her about my excursion into the scenery. The next morning on the front page of the Sunday papers, there was a photo of yours truly in his Volvo flying across the main road three feet in the air. We eventually came in third and fourth in the production car race. Volvo was pleased with the results, which was the important thing as they were picking up the tab. After prize giving, we drove the three hundred miles back home to Salisbury.

For the first time since selling the hydro, I felt committed to something purposeful and soon settled into the rhythm of racing and rallying. For me, it was a big learning curve on the rally front, but my teacher was one of the best in Africa. I befriended most of the South African champions as well as the British and Europeans, who came over in November for the Springbok Series, and was treated as a driver with equal capabilities by all concerned.

The 1960s and 1970s were exciting motoring times in South Africa and Rhodesia. A booming economy, the development of a motor manufacturing industry, and the arrival of performance cars with ever-increasing horsepower resulted in what is now generally referred to as the 'golden age' of motor racing on the subcontinent. South Africa drew the great names in motor sport to its shores, hosting an international Grand Prix at the Kyalami circuit near Johannesburg that formed part of the world championship, as well as international Grands Prix at the provincial circuits which were not part of an international championship. This, combined with the Springbok series at the end of the year, meant the calendar of international events in southern Africa was a full one. The Springbok Series started off with a nine-hour race at Kyalami in November, moving on to three-hour races in Rhodesia, then Lourenço Marques in Mozambique, and on to the regional circuits in Natal and Cape Province of South Africa.

Many drivers taking a break from the European winter brought their state-of–the-art machinery to sunny South Africa. Lola, Porsche, Ford GT40, Ferrari and the like competed for overall honours, mixing it with local production cars chasing the index of performance award.

Volvo ran their cars for an index of performance win and the team prize. An index time is calculated by race organisers and is worked out on the modifications done to the smaller cars or even road cars with minimal mods, which do not stand a chance against a car that has been purposely built for racing. The car closest to a hundred percent or above wins the index prize, which is just as coveted as a race win. A team consists of three cars: there was Mossie and I with the Volvos and our third members were Hamish Smith and Brian Evans in a Taunus 20M.

We had many podium finishes as well as winning most of the team prizes in the two years we ran the 122s; we competed in all the national and international events and the Springbok Series at the end of the year. I did less work on the Volvo in two years than I did on the Alfa in six months, and she never failed to finish a race. I had learnt from my car and various drivers the art of fast endurance driving.

Chapter eight
Unilateral Declaration of Independence

I had resigned in 1962 at the ripe old age of twenty from the youth club committee as my interest now lay firmly with the motor club, to which Mom's hotel had been awarded the catering rights for all events. Mom and Dad had by then also bought another hotel, the Victoria Court, to procure a railways contract. When catering was required by any venue, I was actively involved in the production of food for the buffet and carvery tables.

Having also completed my apprenticeship, written and passed my City and Guild Craft and Technicians exams, I spent a lot of time at the lake partying, water skiing and generally having a good time. Women, wine, fast cars and song were the order of the day, but I knew by then that I wanted cars and racing in my life.

Ankle movement is crucial for braking and accelerating in a Formula 1 car. My artificial leg had no ankle movement but I was keen to see if I could drive one and what it would be like. In England in the late sixties, I drove a Wilment BRM F1 around Brands Hatch with the greatest of difficulty, so much so that I was thankful to be the only car on the track at the time. With a fixed ankle on the right and the left hip pinned in one position, Formula 1 was always going to be a non-starter for me. I had never been under any illusions that it wouldn't be difficult. I had tried and was not able to properly control the car; while in a saloon or sports car, I was able to compete with the best. But my F1 experience did not stop me from climbing my chosen mountain and reaching its summit. My mountain was to be the best I could be in saloon and sports car racing along with rallying, and I reckon I did a good job of that.

My time at Volvo drew to a close in 1963 when, sadly, I decided to say goodbye to them in favour of a switch to Ford, where I could see far more opportunity. The new Ford Cortina was notching up a string of victories in Europe, and Colin Chapman had been commissioned to build a Lotus version for the race and rally circuits. Ford had intimated to me that a Lotus Cortina would be on the cards if I performed and produced the results they were looking for. I raced the GT for the first year with Ford in all events open to it. The car was extremely competitive and trouble free to run, and true to their word, Ford put the Lotus Cortina on the table for the following season.

Unfortunately, political events were brewing that would make this impossible and would ultimately change the course of my life. After countless negotiations with world leaders, Ian Smith and our government declared Rhodesia independent on the 11th of November 1965, and as a consequence, the world imposed strict sanctions.

Our Prime Minister, Ian Douglas Smith, was a great leader of men and the mere mention of his name evoked strong emotions. Either you believed in him or you despised him; I would have gone to hell and back for him, as would most Rhodesians. These are just my views on an extraordinary man, a Second World War hero, a man who was called upon to defend Western culture and all that it stood for.

As Prime Minister of Rhodesia he rebelled against the Crown with these immortal words:

To us has been given the privilege of being the first western nation in the last two decades to have the determination and fortitude to say: 'So far and no further.' We may be a small country, but we are a determined people who have been called upon to play a role of worldwide significance. We Rhodesians have rejected the doctrinaire philosophy of appeasement and surrender. The decision, which we have taken today, is a refusal by Rhodesians to sell their birthright. We have struck a blow for the preservation of justice, civilisation, and Christianity, and in the spirit of this belief we have assumed our sovereign independence. God bless you all.

In the 1960s, the power structure of the world was changing. The British Empire was dissolving and being taken over by the Americans with their free enterprise system, and the Russians with their belief in the communist system. Not only that, but within free nations, people were questioning long-held beliefs as well as the ethics of it all. For a man like Ian Smith, these changes were against everything he held dear as he had a largely Victorian belief in moral values and British primacy.

It must have taken an enormous amount of courage for Smith, when he became Prime Minister, to rebel against the British Crown. The nationalist movements within Africa were guided by communist ideologies. The British government, prompted by MacMillan's 'winds of change' speech, was rushing to placate these movements and give them independence and power in their own countries.

Smith refused to buckle to these policies for Rhodesia, shocking the world with his own Unilateral Declaration of Independence. It was mutiny of the highest order, and the British imposed sanctions. They famously declared that Smith's Rhodesia wouldn't last six weeks, and that Ian Smith was a racist, when nothing could have been further from the truth. As it happened, Smith's Rhodesia lasted nearly 15 years.

America joined the international sanctions against the Smith regime; since Ford was an American company, they withdrew from Rhodesia. My sponsorship went out of the window. It began to dawn on me that to realise my dreams would mean leaving this paradise I was living in and to follow the road Destiny seemed so intent on leading me down.

Chapter nine
A European adventure

IT was early autumn in 1965 when I attended the South African Grand Prix and met the Australian driver, Paul Hawkins. We became friends and he told me he would be returning at the end of that year to race in the international Springbok Series racing event. Paul would be driving for the Willment Race Team and would be driving mouth-watering cars – an AC Cobra, a full race Lotus Cortina and a seven-litre Galaxy. The Willment cars had competed internationally, which gave the local 'Fangios' a chance to compare their development with that of their overseas counterparts.

I wanted so badly to become part of this exciting circus, and got goose bumps just listening to the cars thunder past the pits. At the conclusion of the series, Paul gave me his address along with the addresses of a few other prominent drivers and team managers, and I assured him I would be on my way overseas as soon as I could tie up loose ends in Rhodesia.

After the Springbok Series was over, the overseas drivers and cars had returned to Europe where their cars would soon be prepared for the upcoming season in the UK and Europe.

I became a little sidetracked, well hugely sidetracked, actually. I had met and become involved with a gorgeous, simply irresistible girl on my return to Rhodesia from South Africa. Before I could look around, the months had flown by and it was Easter. My young lady gave me an ultimatum: me, she said, or Europe. After a millisecond contemplating the pros and cons, I chose Europe. Kicking myself for wasting so much time, I made all the necessary arrangements, and three days later, on a Friday, I found myself checking in on a South African Airways flight to London. My folks and brother, who had also caught the racing bug, were there with a few of my friends to see me off.

The flight was called an hour later, and I collected my possessions and walked out of the building onto the apron. There was a huge roar from behind me, and as I turned to see what the commotion was about, I was confronted with an airport balcony crowded with the motor racing fraternity. With raucous calls and wolf whistles, they bombarded me with streamers and toilet rolls. I felt a bit overcome, I have to say, and humbled too, that so many people had taken the time and trouble to bid me 'au revoir' or just maybe 'thank the Lord he's leaving'. I stood there covered in streamers and toilet tissue, deeply touched by their display of support and recognition.

These colleagues and dear friends who championed and supported me, had given up their time to wish me well, and now I felt it was up to me to fulfil one of the purposes I believed I was born to accomplish. I knew and understood the depth of my tenacity and determination, and to the best of my ability, I would strive not to let myself or them down either, and upon reflection, I don't think I did.

I arrived in England one Saturday in early May and headed for Earls Court, where I booked in at the Overseas Visitors Club (OVC) on the corner of Nevern Place and Earls Court Road. On the Monday, I approached Lotus with the hope of employment, but they, like all the other teams I approached, already had their full complement of employees. After a couple more rejections with private entrants, it was evident that I had left it too late for that season to find gainful employment combined with the fact that I had no track record in Europe to make me attractive as an employee. I decided my next objective would be to get myself noticed just so I could get a toe in the door. In the meantime I had enough money saved to see me through the lean times.

As the Monaco Grand Prix was the coming weekend I would go and make a nuisance of myself in the pits, help out where needed, watch the races and learn all I could. Undaunted, I bought a Thames panel van, fitted it out with a bunk bed, a two-plate stove, a hot blonde – I wish! – and after making it self-contained, I caught the midnight ferry from Dover. Hello, Europe – here I come!

I felt great excitement as I viewed the real Europe for the first time, scenically so vastly different from what I had known all my life in Africa. It was just after five in the morning when I drove my van onto French soil, and though I had no idea whatsoever of what lay ahead, I didn't really care because my whole being was centred solely on the Monte Carlo Grand Prix at Monaco. A voice inside me said, 'Go' and so I went – destination Monte Carlo.

I had never seen Europe and felt exuberantly footloose and fancy free. When I grew tired of driving, I would slip into the back of the van and sleep, and when I was hungry, I pulled over to eat. Crossing the Swiss Alps, I saw snow for the first time in my life and was immediately transformed into a five-year-old boy again, such was my awe and delight at its fairy tale quality. I spent a couple of hours throwing snowballs at anything that dared move. I found the scenery very different from Africa but no more beautiful or awe inspiring. I was just a young man focused, not so much on the trip but on the exciting destination.

I drove over the St Bernard's pass into Italy through Mentone to my final destination Monte Carlo, where I found parking and settled down for the night. I knew very little about Monaco, only that the Grimaldi family had ruled the principality, situated along the French Riviera coast, for generations. Prince Rainier had married the beautiful Hollywood screen legend Grace Kelly, and they had an equally beautiful eldest daughter, Princess Caroline, who was the fantasy of many a young man's dream, though not mine since she was dark-haired and my preference was definitely blonde.

I had heard of the world-famous Place du Casino, which had made

Monte Carlo 'an international byword for the extravagant display and reckless dispersal of wealth'. As time went on, I was to learn that it hosted world championship boxing bouts, the European Poker Tour Grand Final, and the World Backgammon Championship, as well as fashion shows and other events. Monte Carlo had been visited by royalty as well as the general public and movie stars for decades. Of most interest to me was the Monte Carlo Rally, which takes place outside the Monte Carlo quarter and runs mostly on French roads. This rally was one of the longest running and most respected in the world of rallying and marked the start of the World Rally Championship back then. Monte Carlo is also host to the Circuit de Monaco racetrack, on which the Formula 1 Monaco Grand Prix is raced.

The race is held on a narrow course laid out in the streets of Monte Carlo with many elevation changes and tight corners, as well as a tunnel, making it one of the most demanding tracks in Formula 1. In spite of the relatively low average speeds, it is a dangerous place to race and is the only Grand Prix that does not adhere to the FIA's mandated one hundred and ninety miles minimum race distance.

I had in my possession a letter of introduction from the Rhodesian Motor Sport Association (RMSA), introducing me as a Rhodesian Champion assigned by them to compile articles and reports on European motor sport for publication in the *Motor Sport Magazine* in Rhodesia. I also had a personal letter of introduction from the President of the RMSA and hoped these documents would get me a pass, any pass, to the various races. The next morning I went to the race offices and with the help of my letters of introduction, managed to get a journalist pass for all sports and Formula 1 races for the entire year.

I felt as if I had been given a sack full of Christmas presents. I was only just out of Rhodesia and all the famous names I had read about and seen in films were coming alive now in my actual physical presence. I could hardly believe the feelings of awe that overtook me; my eyes must have appeared the size of soup plates. Not only was I in the company of world motor sport champions but princes, and more importantly, princesses. Walking through the crowd on pit lane, I saw Brett Maverick (the actor James Garner) from the popular TV show back home. I wandered around in a 'dwaal' (confused state).

Talk about 'star struck'. I found out later that the movie 'Grand Prix' was being filmed in Europe and James Garner was one of the stars. I became acquainted with him over the next few months, but to me he remained and would always remain 'Brett Maverick'. I could hardly wait to send a postcard home, but I knew I would never find one in existence big enough to pen all my experiences, and who would believe them anyway?

The press enclosure laid on a fantastic cold buffet to which my press pass allowed me access. I helped myself to the fare, which was excellent, but finding a table in the sunshine proved difficult. One of the diners saw my predicament: tray in hand and nowhere to sit. He waved me across and cleared some papers from the chair so I could sit down. He introduced himself as Tim, a reporter for one of the English motor magazines. He identified my accent as being 'South African,' a country he told me he had visited as a reporter on the South African Grand Prix.

I tried to explain where Rhodesia was, and after a couple of roughly drawn maps on paper serviettes, we got the location sorted. We had developed an immediate bond, and I made a mental note to thank RMSA for their help in obtaining the press and pit passes, for without these I would have been be stuck in a stand somewhere on the outside of the track instead of where I found myself: at the very heart of things. I felt a sense of great elation. As the expression goes, I had really 'landed with my bum in the butter'.

Tim guided me around the pits after practice and introduced me to a number of team managers. I made it my business to jot down their names and the locations of their workshops, keeping conversation brief as most of them were on their way to team debriefs. When I returned to the UK, I planned to follow up on them. Race day dawned bright and sunny. Crowds began lining the streets and commandeering the various pavement cafés and restaurants. The cars lined up to begin the first Grand Prix I had seen out of Africa, and what a venue I had chosen for the occasion! I didn't think then and I don't think now, that there is any finer street circuit anywhere in the world. It supremely defines the excitement and atmosphere of a F1 Grand Prix.

I watched the Grand Prix from the pits and partook of the amenities and food at the press enclosure. You are not able to see much of the race track at Monte Carlo, but the atmosphere and excitement of the event is electric. There were many retirements and the race finished with only four cars still running. I had arranged to meet Tim at the press enclosure at the end of the race and after watching the antics at the royal box at the finish line, made my way there.

Tim and a couple of the other journalists had hired a yacht, and I was invited to spend the night on board and partake in all the merriment. It was anchored about half a mile from the pits, which was logistically convenient. That evening we partied with an amazing array of cocktails and enjoyed the company of what seemed like an abundance of young women who needed very little invitation to join us. We attended the prize-giving at the Club Sportive and with only four finishers in the race that day, it was soon over, which left plenty of time for more hard partying. In the early hours, we went back to the boat, and with no race scheduled for the following day, a sleep-in was definitely on the cards.

When I finally awoke at eleven the next morning, I found Gabby, a very pretty girl I had met at the prize-giving ceremony, sleeping next to me. I think I can say with certainty we had not whiled away the time playing tiddlywinks. Everyone else on the boat was still sleeping, and since Gabby needed to get back to Paris, I very gallantly walked her to the station.

On shore, it was anything but quiet as large numbers of newsmen and photographers crowded together on the main beach. A passing couple informed us that the focus of attention was Brigitte Bardot and her then boyfriend. I was speechless and wondered if anyone back home would believe me when I told them I had seen the delectable Brigitte Bardot in the flesh, so to speak, and had 'been in her company,' even if only at a rather large distance. Before Gabby departed, she gave me her address and phone number in Paris so I could look her up if the occasion ever arose.

When the rest of the layabouts on the yacht surfaced, Tim and I went for a late lunch and bumped into one of the scene setters he knew from the Grand Prix film company. He was looking for someone who had some knowledge about the preparation of race cars and asked us if we knew of anyone. I am not sure what his actual designation was but only that he set up all the props for scenes before the actors arrived on set. Specifically, he wanted someone to look after the Formulae Junior mock-ups, which were camouflaged to look like actual Formula 1 cars. The cars had to look as close to the real thing as possible and required someone who would be able to carry out repairs if need be.

Tim pointed to me as the man for the job, and rattled off a little of what I had told him about myself. This suited me as I was conversant with every aspect of the running gear and was skilled with glass fibre. I told the scene setter of my capabilities and following Tim's recommendation, he offered me the job immediately.

The film crew's biggest problem was that when the cast was ready for filming, the cars were not and vice versa. It would be incumbent on me to ensure the cars were ready performance-wise to do what was expected of them during filming, and that they were in the right place at the right time – with the actors. A huge bonus for me was that I could fit in a whole load of sightseeing when my services were not required, and at the same time get paid for the privilege. The deal was sealed back at their caravan. I was given a schedule of times and locations when and where the cars would be required on set, and what specifically would be required of them for any given sequence of film. When would this fairy tale end? I was now employed on the set of a Hollywood blockbuster movie and in the company of world famous people. The serendipitous course of events that had brought me to this point made me more determined than ever to succeed. I had felt disappointed with myself for my late arrival in Europe, but I was now beginning to see a reason in my late start as I was surely now in the right place at the right time. Who knows what changes are in store for us in this life and my life was changing daily.

During the afternoon, James Garner, Eve Maria Saint and Yves Montand wandered in and out of the caravans to ascertain location details of their next shoot and to leave contact numbers where they could be reached, if necessary. While Tim photographed the actors for his magazine, I was given introductions to them all. If I had pinched myself and found that I had been dreaming, I would not have been surprised, so surreal was the experience.

Tim and I returned to the yacht, which was leaving the next morning to sail down the Italian coast to Naples, and he asked if I would like to accompany them. I had a week to spare before meeting the film company at the Spa-Francorchamps Circuit for the Belgium Grand Prix, so I accepted. It had been my intention to write a very long letter home once everyone had left, but at the rate things had been going, and by the time I finally got to penning it, I would need a ream of paper. So much had happened to me since I had left Rhodesia, my feet had not touched the ground. Tim had a friend who agreed to garage the van for me while I was away and that done, we hoisted sail and turned the bow towards the open waters of the Mediterranean.

The next few days were like a dream. I managed to get a letter off to Mom when we stopped to pick up some fresh provisions, and a few days later we arrived in Naples. My new found friends were flying back to England; I thanked them all for having me and made arrangements to see Tim at Spa-Francorchamps the following weekend.

The next few days were mine to explore. The highlight for me was a visit to Pompeii; I climbed Mt Vesuvius because, 'I was there'. Having done and seen most of what interested me, I hailed a taxi to take me to the airport for a flight to Nice. Back in Monte Carlo with all the Grand Prix crowd gone, things were quiet, so I had an early supper and decided to check out the famous Place du Casino, not to gamble, but for the experience. It was an eye-opener: more money crossed those gambling tables than I had ever seen in my life. The next morning I enjoyed a leisurely breakfast before hitting the road, which involved a short drive to the Italian border and then inland over the Alps. Taking a slow tour through Switzerland, I arrived at Spa-Francorchamps around lunchtime the day after.

The Circuit de Spa-Francorchamps is one of the most challenging racetracks in the world, mainly due to its fast, hilly and twisty nature. It is a favourite circuit of many racing drivers and fans. It became notorious not only for fatal accidents on its ultra-fast, track but also its inclement weather. It could be raining in one area and the track would be wet, and in another, the sun would be shining and the track completely dry.

Eau Rouge is probably the most famous corner on any Grand Prix circuit anywhere. Having negotiated the La Source hairpin, drivers race down a short straight past the pits to a point where the track crosses the Eau Rouge stream, before being launched steeply uphill into a sweeping left-right-left collection of corners with a blind summit. Strictly speaking, the Eau Rouge corner is only the left-hander at the bottom.

At Spa I found my way to the offices of the movie company to let them know I was reporting for duty. I had been on the payroll for a week and so far not had to lift a finger; I had a feeling I was going to enjoy this job.

When I met up with Tim, he asked if I would be interested in driving him around the circuit in a BMW2002 for an article he was writing on European tracks for his magazine. I would have preferred being behind the wheel of a Carrera Six, but for the opportunity to drive Eau Rouge, I wasn't going to complain. Though Tim had no first-hand knowledge of the calibre of driver I was, he seemed happy to let me drive based on news cuttings he had seen in my scrapbook. Roads are used as part of the nine-mile long Spa circuit, which is the fastest open road circuit in the world. In the final years of the old circuit, drivers could average speeds of one hundred and fifty miles per hour.

Although I had never driven the circuit before, by the second lap, I could feel Tim settle in. He obviously had faith in my driving. I was rather erratic to begin with, trying to piece the circuit together in my mind and attempting to remember what was where and which way it went. By the tenth lap, I was hopelessly in love with this circuit and to this day it remains one of my favourites. The track, its location, the beer and the hospitality of the locals are all part of what makes Spa so special.

Once unofficial practice was over, scenes were scheduled to be filmed in the pits, and I ensured from my side that everything was in place and the cars parked, ready for use. A number of drivers were used in conjunction with the actors and several scenes were shot in various parts of the paddock. During the official one-hour practice for the actual race, filming was switched to the pits themselves, and Tim and I wandered off to the corners to watch.

Afterwards, I was needed in the pits for more filming in the paddock with the actors dressed in racing overalls, enacting their various scenes. I just hoped the director knew what he was doing as the whole thing looked very disjointed to me.

The first lap of the Grand Prix was filmed by a cameraman strapped into a Ford GT40 with the passenger door removed. The camera had been mounted on a protractor, and the car was driven by the ex-world champion, Phil Hill. In these particular scenes the cameraman took various shots of the F1 cars at the back of the field.

At the end of the race the stars would move in and interact with the F1 drivers so various agreed-on scenes for the film could be shot. It was all very interesting to watch, and I was fascinated. There did not seem to be any sequence to anything, which of course there wasn't; such is the way movies are made.

Chapter ten
Love at first sight

O N race day we had lunch at the press enclosure and then wandered down to Eau Rouge to watch the F1 cars going through the corner and up the hill. The race had barely started when there was a cloudburst and spectators, drivers, pit crew as well as Tim and I were drenched in the deluge. Cars were spinning off in all directions, and there were a number of crashes and injuries, but fortunately no deaths. With wreckage from the crashed cars strewn all over the local countryside, there were only five cars left to complete the race.

Filming finished up the next day and though my services would not be needed for the next two weeks, I still got handsomely paid. I was given a destination address and the date when the cars would be needed again by a member of the film crew, who seemed pleased that at last it had been possible to marry the cars and actors when they were required on set.

Paul Hawkins, the Australian driver I had met at the SA Grand Prix, had asked me to meet him at Le Mans where he was driving one of the seven-litre GT40s for Holman & Moody. This plan fitted in beautifully with my time off as the famous 24-hour race was the coming weekend and after fuelling my van and checking oil and water, I set off to meet him. Tim had suggested that rather than eating at restaurants, I should stop off at monasteries en route where monks would supply me with wine, bread, cheese and slices of various meats. If I took along a carafe, they would fill it with wine and, according to Tim, I would eat and drink like a king. He was quite right; the fare supplied by the monasteries was top class, and the abbots were always pleased to receive the donation I gave for the hospitality afforded me.

I arrived at the racetrack in the northwest of France. It is the world's oldest active endurance sports car race, held annually since 1923 near the town of Le Mans, France. Commonly known as the Grand Prix of Endurance and Efficiency, race teams have to balance speed against the cars' ability to run for twenty-four hours without sustaining mechanical damage. At the same time, the cars' consumables – primarily fuel, tyres and braking materials – were monitored and affected the final race results.

The endurance of the drivers is likewise tested as drivers frequently spend stints of over two hours behind the wheel before stopping in the pits and allowing a relief driver to take over. Drivers then grab what food and rest they can before returning to the car for another stint. Today it is mandated that three drivers share each competing vehicle.

I eventually found my way in, which was no mean feat, I might add, given the number of ticketing check gates I had to get through. If there was any discrepancy in the ticket, entrance was disallowed and back you were sent from whence you had come. I parked the van and headed for the race office to pick up race tickets and passes before heading off in search of Paul.

On the way I bumped into Peter de Klerk, a friend from South Africa, who was in Europe for the season, working on a project for Aston Martin with John Surtees. Peter had been offered a drive in a Porsche for the race; the car had been specially built with a long-tail to give it stability down the long and very fast Mulsanne straight. Arriving at the Holman & Moody pit, I opened the door to find a veritable hive of activity going on inside, but with Paul still out on the circuit, I decided to come back later and went off to look around.

After a half hour of exploration, I had the layout of the pits imprinted in my mind, and I decided to watch practice from the corner situated after the pits down at the Dunlop Bridge. Decisions we make affect the course of a life. If I had not decided to go across the Dunlop Bridge that day, my life would have missed one of its momentous experiences, and one that my old friend Destiny had reserved for me since my conception.

The circuit on which the twenty-four hours of Le Mans is run is named the circuit of the Sarthe and consists of both permanent track and public roads that are temporarily closed for the race. Since 1973, the track has been extensively modified, mostly for safety reasons, and currently is around nine miles in length. Although it initially entered the town of Le Mans, the track was cut short in order to better protect spectators. This change led to the creation of the Dunlop Curve and Tertre Rouge corners before rejoining the old circuit on the Mulsanne. Another major change was on the Mulsanne itself, when the FIA decreed that it would no longer sanction any circuit that had a straight longer than one and a quarter miles. This led to the addition of two chicanes, reducing the time that the cars spent travelling at very high speeds on the old four-mile long straight.

Walking across the Dunlop Bridge to the funfair, a group of Swedish visitors befriended me, probably because they noticed the pit and press passes hanging from my neck. When they asked if I was a driver, I replied in the negative, but they pushed me to help them gain access to the pits so they could have a closer look at the cars.

There were two couples and a very pretty girl with long blonde hair, dark blue eyes and looks to die for, who appeared to be by herself. Le Mans took a back seat when she smiled at me. My whole reason for being there changed from cars to this vision of loveliness. I arranged to meet them at the pit entrance in an hour, which would give me time to hustle a couple of tickets. This objective achieved, I hurried back to find them. My heart missed a beat when I saw her again, and it struck me that she looked even prettier than I remembered.

As I had only procured two tickets, one each from Paul and Peter, the five of them would have to take turns visiting the pits. The first couple grabbed the prized tickets and headed for the cars, which by then had completed their practice. While we waited for their return, I chatted to my three new friends and became better acquainted with the vision of loveliness called Britt, who was there with her brother and cousin. There was no sign of a boyfriend and I simply could not take my eyes off her. I casually lifted her hand in mine and was rewarded with a light squeeze. I couldn't believe my luck and my heart was pounding in my chest as I asked her, 'Would you like to watch the race with me?' I awaited her reply anxiously.

'I would like that,' she replied simply. Then I recklessly took it further, throwing all caution to the wind by asking, 'Would you like to have some lunch with me and watch practice when your family has returned?' An affirmative reply made my heart do its own twenty-four-hour race. I couldn't believe my luck.

When Britt's brother returned and handed the tickets to his cousin, he came across to thank me. Britt spoke to him in Swedish, and I saw him nod his head in agreement and say something to her.

Britt turned to me and said, 'My brother said I can go, but I must be back at the campsite this evening'. I assured him I would have her back before nine. At last I was alone with the gorgeous Miss Askogh. As we walked into the pits, I held her hand and once again she squeezed my hand tightly in return and looped it under hers. From the pit lane, we crossed the track to the press facility where we had some lunch, watched most of the afternoon practice at the top of the grandstand, and told each other our life stories.

Britt had asked about my limp and consequently I had to show her my amputation when she did not believe me. When it came to removing my trousers so she could see the scar on my good leg from the boat accident, I flatly refused but promised I would show it to her in more private surroundings. At eight pm, I took her back to her campsite, where she related everything about the afternoon's events to her relatives in Swedish.

Her campsite was built at track level, which meant you had to look up to see the pits and control tower as well as the stands and press facilities. From their campsite, she pointed out the press box where we had sat and told them about the buffet table laden with food. Thoughtfully, she translated everything she said back to me in English.

I looked at the unopened tins of frankfurters and baked beans on the camp table and felt a little guilty. Nonetheless, I made arrangements to collect her the next day to watch the race with me. I sadly left her for the night and returned to the pits where I had arranged to meet Paul, who wanted to have a look at a car from America, the 'Chaparral'.

I found Paul at the back of his pit and we went off to meet with Hal Sharp, the designer and engineer of this most unusual car. Soon the three of us were deep in conversation on the technicalities of the car. The Chaparral was a car quite unlike any other; for a start, its radiators had been moved from the traditional front of the car to the side of it and were fed by two ducted air channels on either side.

Chaparral were leaders in the effective designing of air dams and spoilers at this time, so they had added an interconnected air dam at the front of the car, which closed off the nose ducting for streamlining at high speed. When opened, the ducted nose channelled air from the front of the car up over the bodywork, thereby creating extra down-force while cornering.

A large wing was mounted several feet above the rear of the car on struts, the design of which was the opposite of an aircraft wing in that it generated down-force instead of lift and was attached directly to the rear suspension uprights, loading the tires for extra adhesion around corners. The unique use of a semi-automatic transmission allowed a floor pedal that was in the position of a clutch pedal in other cars, thus allowing the driver to feather, or straighten the negative angle of the wing, when down-force was not needed, to reduce drag and increase top speed. The chassis was fitted with articulated plastic skirts that sealed against the ground, creating a vacuum: the effect sucked the car onto the road surface. (A lot of these technologies would later appear in Formula 1.)

According to Jim, it was like driving a giant vacuum cleaner capable of two hundred miles per hour. He was very interesting to talk to, and if I had had a bit more knowledge about what he was talking about, I would have asked him for a job. He was certainly a radical designer and an all-round nice guy.

Chapter eleven
Le Mans 1966

A S I was on my way to fetch Britt the next morning, I saw this vision of loveliness coming over the Dunlop Bridge in hot pants looking like a million dollars with a duffel bag over her shoulder. She gave me a lovely smile and waved. I hit meltdown when she came up and kissed me on the cheek and said, 'I hope you were a good boy last night,' and burst into very infectious laughter.

She slipped her hand in mine. 'Come on, I am very hungry. I want more of that delicious food at that press place,' said she, dragging me after her.

She was a natural, easy-going, stunningly beautiful girl with striking features who was neither opinionated nor artificial. What a find! Suddenly, I wasn't interested in the race or even the cars, and if I had been offered a drive in the GT40 pole sitter, you could have kept it. We put Britt's duffel bag in my truck and went off for breakfast, which was more like brunch by that time.

At the press box every eye in the place was on her and even the telex machines went quiet. I told Britt my agenda for the day and asked if she would like to come, but she shook her head and intimated that she was quite happy to stay where she was in the press box. She shooed me away and as I looked back, she blew me a kiss.

The start was everything I had expected it to be and more. At the end of the first lap, Paul in the Holman & Moody GT40 had the wheel for the first stint and was in the lead. He did not reappear on lap twelve, and I presumed something must have happened out on the circuit somewhere. Unless he could get back, he would be out of the race. I left to go across to the press enclosure to find my Britt eating again – not a care in the world, with the self-assurance and confidence of knowing she was the most beautiful girl in the room. She lit up my world with a smile and gave me a huge kiss on the lips, which woke everything up! I bumped into Tim on the stairs and introduced Britt to him. She reduced him to jelly in about thirty seconds flat.

He turned to ask me where I had found the delectable Miss Askogh. 'Behind the pits,' I replied truthfully. Tim handed me a cheque, which I was not expecting: his magazine was paying me for the pleasure of driving their ace reporter around Spa-Francorchamps in his hired car.

Tim told me about Paul's accident; apparently, on his way down the Mulsanne straight at two hundred and twenty miles per hour his rear bodywork had detached itself from the car, which went flying through the air for a quarter of a mile, resulting in a monumental shunt. According to Paul, 'the f---ing Yankee mechanic' had not fastened the Dzus fasteners properly, nearly killing him in the process. Paul's command of the English language was colourful, to say the least. The sister car to Paul's had been called into the pits and the Dzus fasteners checked and duct taped.

Tim went off to write up the race so far and then to telex it to some paper or other in order to make the midnight deadline. Britt and I waited for him to return and then we went downstairs to the buffet table. We had a lovely dinner and polished off a couple of bottles of wine. I asked Britt if she wanted to come with me to the pits but when she declined, I presumed she wanted to go back to her camp. No – she wanted to go to my van as she was feeling a little tired, and she said she would wait for me there.

I wanted to poke my nose in to see how Peter was doing as well as see if I could find Paul anywhere, so I took Britt back to the van and tucked her in. She gave me a lovely cuddle and kiss – what a girl! I hurried away; the sooner I had seen my mates, the sooner I would be back in her company. Peter had just gone out in the car and was not due in till after midnight, and Paul was busy talking to one of the technical boffins. Anticipating what awaited me in the van, I headed back there post-haste.

The best laid plans of mice and men can and sometimes do end up in 'bin thirteen'. When I got to the van, I found Britt sound asleep so I climbed into the other bunk and had to be satisfied with dreams. I awoke at seven as Britt was stirring, and I told her I would be back later with breakfast for her.

On my way to the pits, I joined Paul, who was on his way to a sauna and massage at the drivers' facility. He had some business to attend to so I grabbed some coffee, croissants and fruit for Miss Askogh and returned to the van.

She was up, looking gorgeous as usual, and asked, 'Why did you not wake me when you came in?'

'You were snoring so loudly that I had to sleep outside in the cold,' I said, trying to keep a straight face. 'What is this snoring?' she wanted to know. I told her and had to duck in a hurry as she hurled her knapsack at me.

You don't know what you missed,' said she, followed by her lovely laugh. If only she knew my thoughts had kept me awake half the night. Britt jumped from the van, threw her arms around me and whispered in my ear, 'Early to bed for you tonight; no more running off to the pits for you'.

'As you wish, madam,' I replied, hoping she couldn't hear the excitement in my voice. The night seemed so far away. Britt made short work of the food and complimented me on my choice. This girl was always hungry.

We went to the changing rooms where Britt had a shower and emerged in a black wet-look cat suit. If she had anything on underneath, I defied the gods to show me where. I would find out eventually if I could just contain myself till then. I went weak in the knees in anticipation of what was to come for me that very night. I took her hand in mine as we meandered towards our lunch.

By the time we made it to the press facility, there were only fifteen or so cars left out of the fifty-five that had started. We found Tim, who was telexing a report back to his office, had a late lunch and then settled down to watch the finish. In the final hour, Le Mans winds down and most drivers hold station, or in laymen's terms, hold their positions until the end of the race.

Ford finished first, second and third; Peter, in the Porsche, finished sixth, a creditable performance on his first attempt. We were invited to join the festivities being held in the Ford pit where we met Henry Ford, who seemed more interested in Britt than anything else, but who can blame him? She looked stunning. I just felt so privileged to be part of the Ford celebration and to be part of Le Mans racing history, as well as to have a girl such as Britt to share it with. What a lucky sod I was!

After finding Britt's relations and making arrangements for all of us to meet in the morning, we walked slowly back to the van where she dragged me in kicking and screaming to have her way with me as she had promised that morning. The details pertaining to the rest of the night, I'm afraid, are censored and mine to cherish!

The next morning the pits were like a morgue, but walking into the changing rooms, I thought I passed Steve McQueen in Gulf racing overalls. I shook my head and looked back. He had stopped at the entrance and was talking to somebody so I got a real good look.

Yep, it was him alright. My folks at home would never believe this. When I came out, there were movie crews all over the place, filming in half a dozen locations in the pits; it turned out they were in the process of making a film entitled 'Le Mans,' starring Mr McQueen.

When I told Britt, she appeared more interested in a shower and food – she was hungry again. I escorted her to the ladies' shower and hung around, being very aware of Steve McQueen's reputation with the ladies. I did not fancy her bumping into him.

She emerged from the shower looking devastating, as usual. She was wearing another sensational body hugging cat suit, which was pink with silver challenge stripes running down both sides. Without glancing at anyone except me, she threw her arms around me and planted a huge kiss on my lips.

'You can make love to me like that forever and ever, you gorgeous man. Come on, I am so hungry for food,' said she with a wry smile. I felt a warm glow start inside and spread through me as realisation dawned that my prowess as a lover now had international recognition from this most beautiful girl.

I knew in that moment that my old friend Destiny had instigated my path to Le Mans. I had met the girl I wanted to spend my life with. Somehow I had known this for the two days since we first met. My heart rate and blood pressure must have been running around 200 plus as we climbed into the van to drive into the town of Le Mans for breakfast.

Over breakfast I told her I had feelings for her and wanted to see her again; lo and behold she felt the same way. I had a two-week break before the next race in France and wanted her to accompany me around Europe to share the sights, but she had other commitments involving her mother. I wondered if this was her attempt at saying goodbye.

After breakfast, it was back to her campsite where we found her relations packed up and ready to leave. She spoke to her brother in Swedish and then asked if I would like to come to Sweden with them. I was elated that she wanted me to accompany her. So much for my worried forebodings that she might be saying goodbye.

Britt and I followed the other three back to Sweden where I was made welcome by her parents, Eric and Anna. They lived on an island just outside Stockholm called Lidingo, and both spoke good English, so we had no trouble conversing.

After a short time, I felt a bond had developed between us as I was asked all the usual questions parents would ask a young would-be beau for their daughter. I guess with Britt's help I passed with flying colours. Of course, the main topic of conversation and mutual interest, after Britt, was racing. In his younger days, Eric had been a speedway rider on the ice circuits and had the scars to prove it.

Anna listened to the stories her daughter regaled her with about this young man who had stolen her heart in the space of a week. My scrapbook was thrust under Anna's nose on more than one occasion, so she could read for herself articles written about me in various newspapers.

Mother and daughter looked and acted like sisters, while the boys, Eric and I, opened some bottled chicken (beer) over which we shared racing experiences.

Once she had fulfilled her obligation to her mother, Britt took me all round her beautiful country and into the neighbouring ones as well, not that I was terribly interested in the countryside or any other countryside for that matter.

As far as I was concerned, it was the same as any country in Europe with its small villages, lots of islands, and people who did not speak English.

My sole focus was Britt. During the trip, infatuation turned to something much deeper, and by the time I was to leave for France, I was very much in love with this beautiful girl.

I had never had feelings like these for any other girl, and as luck would have it, Britt felt the same about me. To top it all, her parents approved of me and already treated me as one of the family.

I decided to fly instead of driving to France for the race at Rheims, which would give me more time with my girl. Britt had lectures scheduled for her coming year at university, so Eric dropped me at the airport, and I asked him if he would collect me on the Monday.

'No,' he said firmly, 'I think you will find Britt here to pick you up, and I want to tell you that Anna and I give you two our blessings. We want you to know that we consider you part of our family. I know that you and Britt will have a long and happy life together, be it here or in your beloved Africa'. He gave me a hug and motioned me towards the aircraft sitting on the apron. I felt elated at this show of emotion and approval after such a short time. I had thought myself to be in love many times in Africa but any feelings I might have had for anyone else paled in the light of what I felt for Britt. I believe we were true soul mates and I felt blessed to have found her.

When I arrived in France, I found Tim waiting for me and we drove to the track. The circuit at Rheims was nowhere near as good as the Spa and was an easy one to drive; it was a classic road circuit – fast, narrow and dangerous. It would have been greater fun in a faster car. Tim's hired BMW was not the greatest turn-on. Nevertheless, I considered myself extremely lucky to be given the opportunity to drive.

After the race, I sent a long letter home to Mom, not about racing or film stars, but about the beautiful Britt. Tim gave me a lift to the airport and we made arrangements to meet up in London before the British Grand Prix, which was two weeks away.

I saw Britt immediately I stepped off the plane in Stockholm. She looked as gorgeous as ever and I realised I had missed her for every second of the four days I had been away. As soon as she saw me, she ran out onto the tarmac and threw her arms around me, smothering me in kisses. I nearly dropped the bottles of champagne I had bought.

'I missed you so much, my beautiful man,' she said. Holding her away from me, I looked into those dark blue eyes and kissed her passionately, 'I just want to run away with you and hide, I am so afraid I will lose you,' I replied.

Britt looked at me with a very serious look on her face, 'You and I are meant to be. I will be what you want me to be for as long as you want, and if at any time you want me to go, you only have to be truthful and tell me'.

The feelings for this girl culminated in tears, which ran down my cheeks without shame as we walked together arm-in-arm into the terminal. She hugged me close and I felt a warm safe glow within me. I was so glad to be with Britt again; at that moment she was the most important person in my world. When I told her that Tim had said I was like a 'puppy who had lost its bone without her,' she replied, 'Yes, but you are my puppy and I am yours'.

I had only been in Europe three months and already I was in big trouble. This girl meant so much to me.

Britt was coming to the British Grand Prix with me, but as there was no direct ferry to the UK from Sweden, we had to drive to Denmark where we caught the ferry to the UK on the Sunday.

On arrival we drove down to London, spending the night at the Overseas Visitors Club (OVC). Every eye in the OVC was on Britt because, as always, she looked fantastic.

This was my year, and I felt that if I could just get my ass into racing and development, there was nothing else this world could offer that I would want. Although the thought crossed my mind, no question of marriage to Britt had arisen as she still had two years of university to complete and I hadn't even started learning how to develop a fast car.

We left early the next morning before the London traffic and stopped at a transport café for breakfast. Madam was hungry again! Plans had been scheduled to film a number of scenes at the circuit, so we arrived early at Brands Hatch. The crew took one look at Britt, and we were both signed on as extras for some of the scenes.

For the next two days we enjoyed the hospitality afforded in the tent provided for the extras. Britt was harassed by one of the producers, to avail herself for a screen test. She turned him down with the excuse that she had varsity to finish and a footloose, fancy-free foreign race car driver to take care of.

I was highly delighted by her answer. Her words showed me the depth of the feelings she had for me. I don't know of any other girl who would have turned down a screen test for university and a one-legged race driver from Africa.

Britt and I watched practice and the race and once all the necessary film sequences had been shot I loaded the cars to be shipped to Holland. Then we drove back to London where we spent a glorious week together: shopping in Kensington and spending the money we had earned as extras, among other activities.

Wherever we went, people would pause to look at her, and I thanked the Lord in every prayer that he had guided my footsteps to the Dunlop Bridge at Le Mans on the day I met my Britt.

Tim took us to dinner and remarked that he and I were sitting with the most beautiful girl in London. Upon my suggestion that Tim should change the wording from 'girl' to 'couple,' I was bombarded with bread rolls from two different quarters.

Later in the week we caught the ferry to Germany, once there I put Britt on one for home. She took my heart with her when she left, but I had a Grand Prix to attend, after which, I consoled myself, we could spend time together again. I turned the van south to Holland while subduing the longing inside me to swim after Britt's ferry.

I arrived at Zandvoort and settled in a quiet spot I had found for the van. Tim found me on his arrival from London, presented me with a cheque for work done, and asked if I would do the honours and drive for him again. Of course, I obliged.

We headed out in the BMW 2002 after practice and I was amazed at just how slippery the corners were. Tim confirmed that the car was fine and the slipperiness was due to fine sand that blew from the beach onto the circuit. I was quite pleased I wasn't driving anything more powerful.

The race completed a hat trick for Jack Brabham, as he had won Rheims, Brands Hatch and now Zandvoort. The necessary filming had been completed and I now had two weeks off before I was scheduled to arrive for filming at the German Grand Prix.

Britt and I arranged to meet in Cortina, as her summer vacation from university was drawing to a close and the family was going to their ski lodge. I left Holland and motored through to Cortina. I arrived at the lodge before the family and had a bit of time to explore. Another tourist party, which had just come back from a day trip to Venice, advised me of all the do's and don'ts of such an excursion and made it sound so appealing I decided to go the next day.

Chapter twelve
The dogged skier

I phoned Britt to tell her my plans and the following day I left on my excursion to Venice. I wandered around the cathedral, went up the clock tower on the square and then on to watch glass being blown at the glass factory. It was fascinating to see how all sorts of little trinkets were made from blown glass, and I had one of the workers make me a swan for Britt. I walked along the canals, had a late lunch at a café on St Mark's Square and, as tourists do, hired a gondola to show me the sights.

On my return to the lodge, longing to see my Britt again and hear her voice, I gave her a call, 'Hurry up and get here,' I pleaded. 'I have this gorgeous blonde following me around who fancies my body, and she won't leave me alone'.

She was very explicit in her retort about what she would do when she caught up with said blonde. She finished the conversation with, 'And as for you…' and her beautiful infectious laugh rang in my ears. She was always in a good mood as well as hungry – maybe the two go together.

She arrived the next day and as she hugged and kissed me, she whispered, 'Where is she?' and burst into laughter once again. I whispered in her ear, nibbling it at the same time, 'She is the girl in my arms'. 'That's good,' she said.

I had prepared a fondue of fresh bread, prawns, cheese and fillet steak for lunch. I had cubed the meat, cleaned the prawns and melted three cheeses together with some white wine, herbs and fresh coarse ground black pepper. The meal was washed down with some good champagne I had picked up in Rheims. It was a meal fit for a king. I had been well trained in the hotel at home by my mother and was quite capable of presenting a meal to my guests.

The compliments flowed as we ate and drank into the early evening, surrounded by the snow-draped Alps and in air as fresh and exhilarating as the champagne we were drinking. I felt completely relaxed and privileged. Not many people would be lucky enough to be in that part of God's world with a very beautiful girl, great company and good food and drink.

Britt snuggled up next to me. 'Is there no end to your talent?'

'You have only just scratched the surface,' I replied with a smile.

She cuddled into my shoulder as we headed for our room. I let out a long contented sigh. At that moment life was perfect!

After a light breakfast next morning, we were off to the ski slopes and, although I had never skied on snow before, I consoled myself with the thought that I was a dab hand at water skiing so how difficult could snow skiing be? At the least you could stand on it without sinking. I watched the children and learners on the slope, intently trying to convince myself it couldn't be that difficult.

We caught the ski lift, which took us up the mountain; the higher the ski lift took us, the greater the feeling of uncertainty became in the pit of my stomach. Things were looking a whole lot more difficult than I had imagined the higher we went. I began to wish we'd stayed in bed. There was no turning back now; I was well and truly committed with a gorgeous girl to impress.

We reached the top of the ski lift and peeled off. As I approached the edge, I realized that an almost vertical drop lay at my feet. Britt's brother was over the edge in a flash and skiing down the near-vertical slope from side to side until he disappeared from view. It looked so damned easy, but at the same time it was so damned steep!

I turned to Britt and said sheepishly, 'This is too professional for me. You go and I will come down the easy route'.

'This is the only route,' was her reply.

'I'll take the ski lift down then,' said I with a sinking feeling in my stomach.

'You can't. This is the only way off this mountain unless you are injured and a helicopter is sent,' she said with trepidation creeping into her voice.

No one had bothered to tell me that the only way down from the top of the mountain was by ski or helicopter, but there again, after listening to me, everyone thought I was a dab hand at it. If they had told me, I doubt I would have been quite so stupid. Knowing myself like I did, though, I soon concluded it would not actually have made a scrap of difference – even if I had known.

I was standing on top of this mountain and with my tenacious attitude, I would somehow have to get down or face the humility of being stretchered off the mountain, something I would never allow to happen as long as there was breath in my body.

'You go on ahead and organise me a headstone, and I will get down to you somehow. I need to sort this out by myself but it may take some time,' I said with resolution.

'What is this headstone?' she asked. When I told her, she hit me. 'I will carry you down,' she said, with a look of panic in her eyes.

'I will get there on my own,' I replied, with what I hoped was conviction. 'I love you, my darling, as well as that laugh of yours, but right now I don't need you laughing at me. I need to concentrate, and you, at any time, are a distraction. Give me some space and I will work it out as only I can. I will see you at the bottom,' said I, trying hopefully to exude an air of confidence.

'I will go but as soon as I reach the bottom I will be back. I do not like this talk of a headstone,' she replied with a worried expression on her beautiful face.

I gave her a kiss and a whack on her lovely rump, while at the same time rather fervently hoping that I would see it again.

'See you at the bottom, then,' she said. Placing her goggles over those beautiful eyes, she slipped over the edge and worked her way down the slope from side to side, disappearing into the mist and leaving me alone on the edge.

I emulated what I had seen Britt do, or tried to. 'See you at the bottom,' I said to myself, and over I went. I was a lot slower and a whole lot less confident than my Britt, but if I had learnt anything in life it was never, ever give up on anything. What seemed impossible today would become old hat tomorrow.

To avoid picking up speed, I pushed the snow ahead of me like a snowplough. It was a nightmare, but with a lot of sitting, I managed to stop myself from falling or going too fast. The slope began to ease and I was gaining confidence with every yard.

Fifty minutes later a skier flashed to a stop beside me with the flourish of a professional. Her face was flushed with the excitement of the slope, and mine was flushed with the exertions of the slope. I wished they were both flushed from another type of exertion!

I addressed the lady with a smile and an air of nonchalance, 'Where have you been? I have been up and down twice looking for you'.

Flipping her goggles onto her cap, Britt burst into laughter and said, 'You have done very well. I was watching you from back there, and I can tell you have never skied before. Why did you not tell me?' Her voice sounded so good and I was so happy to see her I wanted to grab hold of her and kiss her. I loved this girl so much.

'Stupid pride and an inner urge to impress you,' I said.

'This is a very difficult run and not one for a beginner, and you don't need to impress me any more than you have already,' she added.

I mentioned water skiing in a muffled voice.

She burst out laughing again. 'Come,' she said. She held my hands and skied backwards coaxing me down the slope – how easy she made it look. It took me four and a half hours to get down that mountain but I did it and was proud of myself. I had learnt a hell of a lot on the way down. Britt had stayed with me and pointed out what I was doing wrong. She was a good teacher and we arrived at the bottom to a rousing reception from the rest of our party.

It takes an accomplished skier twenty minutes to negotiate the slope, but my Britt was nevertheless proud of my accomplishment, and over dinner had everyone in fits of laughter telling them of my trials and tribulations.

The next day I took to the nursery slopes as a duck to water, and with the help of my girl mastered the art of skiing. By the end of the day Britt was sore from laughing so much, and I was sore and stiff from the exertion on the slopes. On the way back to the chalet, I began to loosen up, and after a nice hot shower, I felt like a million dollars. We had a lovely dinner and a few drinks before retiring to bed for an early night. The remainder of that evening is mine to remember, as was the day.

The rest of the party was leaving for home, and Britt was accompanying me to the German Grand Prix at the Nürburgring. We spent a day by ourselves at the chalet and then packed up and drove into Switzerland where we found accommodation in a lovely little village.

During that week we fell more deeply in love. We were on the slopes almost every day, ate our meals in front of a roaring fire, had lazy breakfasts in bed and lots of you know what.

With great reluctance, we left for Germany and arrived at the Nürburgring, which is a motor sports complex in the Eiffel Mountains located forty miles south of Cologne, and seventy miles northwest of Frankfurt.

The Nürburgring was built in the 1920s around the village of Nürburg with its medieval castle, and is widely considered to be the most demanding and difficult purpose-built racing circuit in the world. The north loop is thirteen miles long with an elevation change of a thousand feet from its lowest to highest points. With one-hundred-and-seventy odd corners, the track is notorious. Only heaps of lap practice would give any sort of continuity, and a quick lap time would only come once the layout of the circuit was etched indelibly in the mind.

My few laps with Tim would prove to be an experience, nothing more. Tim gave me a running commentary, from a map he held, on where the track went next, every twist and turn. As I had had experience in Africa rallying on navigator's notes, it worked very well.

Two film companies were in attendance at the time, ours and the crew who were filming 'The Day of the Champion', so there was unavoidable friction between them about who should film where and what, but it didn't affect me because, apart from a bit of filming around the track and the first lap of the Grand Prix, that was it.

Britt and I enjoyed the facilities laid on for the press over the weekend, and Tim lent us the BMW so we could motor to all the viewing points around the track. Having the press tickets meant we were allowed in anywhere.

My work was finished with the film company as this was the last Grand Prix they would be filming in Europe. Early the next morning I went in to pick up my very generous pay with gratuity bonus and to bid the company farewell. It really saddened me to leave them as it had been such a fantastic experience and given me such insight into two worlds.

My Britt had to go back to university in the next few days, and I knew I would miss her as I had become accustomed to having her around. I had to find something to do.

It had been an amazing journey, and as I looked back over the last few months – it was now October – I couldn't quite believe how the time had flown and all the things that had happened in that relatively short space of time.

Britt and I bade each other an emotional goodbye. Before she boarded the ferry at Kiel, destination Gothenburg, she held me close and whispered, 'Stay safe, my Love,' turned and was gone. I waved until I could see her no more and then watched from the cold windy dock until the ferry had disappeared from view. I felt deep sadness driving to the British terminal where I would catch my ferry to Hull.

Chapter thirteen
A catastrophic loss

EARLS Court was so inhabited by Rhodesians, South Africans, Australians and New Zealanders that it felt like being at home. I slept in the van on the street for a few nights until I made up my mind what to do next. I phoned Britt regularly to let her know what was happening and promised to get a number she could phone me on. It just wasn't the same without her around.

One evening I went to the Steering Wheel in Curzon Street, a pub frequented by motor racing types, and ended up talking to a mechanic from Bath in Wiltshire. In the course of our conversation, he mentioned that one of his club members in Bath was battling to sort out a Carrera six he had bought. Apparently, the car would complete a couple of laps and then either fell off the track or expired out on the circuit somewhere.

After a phone call to Gordon, the gentleman who owned the car, I went down to Bath to have lunch with him and discuss the problems he was facing. We ended up taking the car out to Castle Combe, a local track, for a test drive. I realised immediately how atrocious its condition was and how badly it needed major surgery. I told Gordon I could look at it but would need a workshop. It so happened he had a friend in London, who prepared saloon cars, and arrangements were made to ship the Porsche there.

When the car arrived, I had it up on trestles and began stripping it. It was in such a sorry state I found it hard to believe that no one had been killed in it. I spoke to Gordon on the phone and gave him a list of the spares that would be required, and an estimate of my labour costs, which he thought too expensive. He elected to find a less expensive avenue, which was fine with me.

I left the car at the workshop; he posted me a cheque to cover the cost of the strip and inspection. Gordon phoned me a week later and asked me to apportion the job. I refused, explaining that if I did part of the work, it would make the car faster but if it crashed and he was injured, I would feel responsible.

I was not willing to half prepare any car. Gordon saw my point and agreed to meet me at the workshop where I went through the car with him. He was horrified at what he saw, and even more horrified to think he had been trying to race it in that condition. It was agreed that he would supply all the spares, pay me weekly and towards the weekend, he would check on the work in progress.

It eventually took three weeks for me to finish the job, and when we took the car back to Castle Combe, there was a huge difference in performance and handling. Before it had even been properly set up, it was circuiting eighteen seconds quicker than it had ever done before. Gordon was over the moon, finding it hard to believe he was driving the same car. Before, he had never completed more than two laps without something falling off. By the fifth lap, he was twelve seconds a lap quicker than he had ever been in the car. He ran it for a full hour without a hitch, a new experience for him because it had never survived a long stretch without expiring.

Colin, who owned the London workshop where I had prepared the Porsche, had bought a crashed Lotus Cortina. It was obvious the car needed a lot of attention as it had been rolled, and had motor, body and suspension damage. All the basics were there, and it was full race spec, but he didn't have the time to rebuild it and asked if I was prepared to do it for him. We struck a deal that I would carry out the rebuild, and foot the bills for parts on the understanding I would race it the next season.

Being as determined as I was to get into racing, I didn't think things through carefully enough, and saw the deal only as my introduction to racing. I went ahead with the work and by the end of the week the car had been stripped, and I had acquired a used body shell from Ford, all on the understanding that the car would be raced. I repaired or replaced whatever components were needed, and by mid-autumn we were ready to run her on the track. We borrowed a trailer, hitched it to the van, and off we went to Castle Combe.

It is standard practice for me to keep a book to record all the settings, such as day temperature, shock settings, diff ratio, etc. I also keep a note of timing and jet settings, so there is always a full record of everything pertaining to the vehicle on that particular test day as well as lap times before and after every change.

I ran her in for about twenty laps and after altering a few settings, started building some lap times, which were recorded in my log. We ended the day with some very respectable times. Colin drove the car and was most impressed. I had a few more tricks up my sleeve to make the car even quicker. But this would require the use of the workshop again.

A week later, I decided to finish the car. Not seeing it in the workshop, I presumed it had been moved to free up needed space. When I asked Colin where the car was, he told me that he had needed some money urgently and had been forced to sell it. When I inquired about the money and labour I had put into the car, he told me to give him a detailed invoice, and he would see what he could do. I was devastated. I had really looked forward to racing that car. I recalled words my dear old dad used to say, 'Never put your faith in people. You will always be disappointed'. How right he was.

At the end of the day, I received a cheque for a mere three hundred pounds for all the hard work I had put in. I felt very let down, but had learnt a valuable lesson.

I found a notice on the board at the OVC posted by three South

Africans who were looking for a ride around the UK. They had their own camping equipment, and I arranged to meet them to discuss their proposed venture. At lunchtime the following day, after a call to Britt, we set off for Land's End. We zigzagged all the way up the west coast into Wales and on to Liverpool where we stopped off to see my grandfather, aunts and cousins.

I was met with news that my Grandfather Mawson had died two weeks before. Having left England at the tender age of four, I knew so little about him or even how old he was. After a visit to his grave, we continued our journey all the way to John O'Groats. The boys had relations to visit so we hauled out the maps and planned the trip that allowed us to stop off with them. We zigged up the west coast and zagged down the east coast of Scotland with glorious late autumn sunshine all the way.

We visited Hadrian's Wall where we were highly amused by the conflicting stories we were told about it, depending on who was telling the story. On the English side of the wall, the English said they had built it to keep the Scots out, and a mile down the road in Scotland, the Scots informed us they had built it to keep the English out. Personally, I'd put my money on the Scots.

We had been to Gretna Green and no one had come away married, I had swum in Loch Ness, and had not seen the monster, let alone been eaten by it. My three companions had not ventured into the water with me because they were either too scared or too cold, probably the former.

We met nationalists in Wales who made us very welcome when they discovered we were not English, and that my mother's maiden name was Edgerton Jones. Many of the innkeepers along the way offered us warm hospitality, and their wives provided lovely breakfasts before we left to continue our travels. It was a great way to see the land of my birth and to meet its people.

We arrived back in London fifteen days after leaving. Several messages awaited me in the OVC post box, and a couple of letters from Mom, which were most welcome.

I returned a call from Gordon, who asked me how the Lotus project was going. When I told him what had happened with Colin, he promised to look into it for me. Gordon needed some updates done on the Porsche, and said there were another two race cars needing attention close by. I agreed to come down and Gordon found a workshop just outside Bath where I could attend to the cars.

One of the car owners was a farmer who provided accommodation for me in the shape of a very nice loft room with bathroom en suite. The three of them looked after me well and took me everywhere. It took me a couple of weeks to get the cars sorted; they were happy and very complimentary about the work done and were generous with their payments. Gordon handed me a cheque for five hundred and sixty pounds from Colin for the balance outstanding on the Lotus Cortina. This was a nice surprise, and I left the following morning, feeling that I had made three firm friends in the West Country.

Back at Earls Court, I had a call from Jeff Uren at Willment Racing Team, he was interested in my services and had heard about me from Paul Hawkins. I caught the tube to his offices and we went to look at the workshop, which consisted of a shed and a yard, not what I had expected at all from a front-line racing team. It was very dirty, with racing parts lying all over the floor from half-completed jobs, but I was there to learn and when he offered me a job working on a variety of cars, I decided it would do me for the winter. There didn't seem to be much going on anywhere else, the season was over and most of the racing cars had been shipped either to America for the Can Am or to South Africa for the Springbok Series. And at least the shed was heated.

Brian Muir from New Zealand (Yogi Bear) seemed to be the only resident driver around: he was the driver of the Ford Galaxy. The Cobra Daytona Coupé, BRM F1, Lotus 40 and the open Cobra were cars, I believe, that were for hire to all and sundry would-be race drivers. Most of the work was checking the cars and small rebuilds, but I was learning and had come to England to work on cars like these. I remembered the feelings that I felt in South Africa just looking at them. One Friday night we took the Lotus 40 to Wembley Stadium and drove the singing star Tom Jones around the stadium. As we drove, his hit song 'What's New, Pussy Cat?' was blaring out over the loudspeakers. The screams from the female fans were so loud they drowned out the roar from the exhaust on the Lotus.

Tom Jones stood on the passenger side of the car holding on tight to the roll bar. After the ride around he said, 'Thanks,' jumped from the car and disappeared down a tunnel, much to the disappointment of his female fans.

I worked another month or so and then left Willment as I wanted to spend time with Mom, who was coming for a holiday. Britt had finished university for the year and was flying across to be with me and to meet Mom.

A message was waiting for me in the box at OVC to phone Eric, Britt's father. As soon as he answered, I had a sense of foreboding, which grew when he burst into tears. A voice I hardly recognised came over the phone, 'Dick, Britt is dead'.

My heart stopped and my insides froze as I tried to comprehend what I had just heard. I could make no sense out of it.

'Anna died with her,' he went on, between sobs.

'Eric, what the hell happened?' was all I could think of to say.

'Accident; car crash,' I caught in between sobs.

My whole being turned numb as I contemplated never seeing my always laughing, always smiling, always hungry Britt again. I was struck dumb with nothing to say as the pain grew inside me like a raging tornado. I wanted to refute as some stupid mistake the claim this man was making over the phone, to tell him I had spoken with my Britt only the night before.

The last words she ever spoke to me rang in my ears: 'I love you and will be with you soon for always, my Love'. Yet I had this man on the phone stabbing at my heart as I listened to his sobs.

Eric had become so incoherent from crying that Britt's brother took over the phone from his father. Orla's normally brash voice sounded subdued by the events that had befallen the family. Arrangements had been made for me to fly to Sweden the next day, he said, and he just wanted confirmation that I could make it.

I managed to get a few words out, confirming that I would be there. Nothing would prevent me going to my beloved Britt, not even if Satan and all his followers were to stand in my path.

When the plane landed and I stepped out onto the stairs, I remembered that beautiful girl running into my arms the last time I was here. The tears ran down my cheeks unashamedly as I walked towards where my Britt should have been, an awareness of loss building inside me like a volcano before eruption.

I was able to get a clearer explanation of the accident once sombre greetings had been exchanged. Britt's Mom had gone to fetch her to bring her home, but they had both been killed in the crash. They say it takes a minute to find a special person, an hour to appreciate what you have found, and a day to fall in love, but it takes a lifetime to forget.

Britt still lives in my heart today. She had been the jewel in my crown, and I felt overwhelmed by the enormity of my loss. I had attended some of the greatest races in the world, had been involved to a small degree in the world of film, and had met and loved the most beautiful and loving girl in the whole world, who was now being laid in the ground next to her mother. I placed a red rose on each coffin, and as I turned to go, I heard Britt's voice as clear as a bell, 'Stay safe, my Love'.

I don't remember much more of the funeral because of the turmoil that was churning inside me. The grief and anger I felt was contained within, building with every second and threatening to burst forth. I felt a strong impulse to scream my frustration and anger at the altar. But I hesitated as my thoughts turned to Eric and his feelings. I had lost the love of my life, but he had lost not only his daughter but also his beautiful wife.

A couple of years down the road, possibly because some part of me knew I would not be back in the future, I went to Britt's grave and put flowers on before coming back to South Africa. I phoned the house, but Eric was not prepared to see me. He had gone to pieces after the loss of his wife and daughter: too many memories; he just couldn't bear to have any more reminders of his loss. I heard shortly afterwards that Eric was dead. I believe it was a suicide, which I can understand given the close-knit family they had been.

My gorgeous Britt had come in and out of my life like a moth drawn to a flame. She had been my friend and lover and had given me insight into what it would be like to love someone forever. I wanted to cry out in grief, but my eyes remained dry; I wanted to demand an explanation from God, but no words were forthcoming. The hurt began to settle heavily on my heart, and still no tears came.

I flew into Heathrow, collected my van and drove down the road to Virginia Waters where I found a quiet spot to park for the night. Mom was arriving early the next morning, and if I stayed there I would not have to drive through the London traffic to fetch her.

I lay on the bunk that Britt and I had shared many times, closed my eyes and heard her voice crystal clear once again as her presence washed over me, 'Stay safe, my Love'.

I was calm, quiet and unemotional and was unaware that I was crying. I reached up to touch my face which was soaked from the tears that were streaming down my cheeks. A flood of emotion overwhelmed me, and the tears came! And came! And came!

I must have cried myself to sleep and I awoke with a start just after five. Mom was arriving on SAA at six-thirty. I drove the few miles to the airport and, after parking the van, took a clean shirt and trousers along with my wash-bag to the ablutions in the terminal. Half an hour later I was spruced up and ready to meet Mom, who was expecting my Britt to be with me.

'God,' I thought, 'What am I going to do without her?'

The flight from Africa had already landed by the time I arrived at the International arrivals hall. When Mom came out of Customs, she located me and I could see her looking for Britt. I realised then how full of her my letters must have been, and consequently Mom had been keen to meet the young lady who had stolen her son's heart.

When she eventually stopped hugging me, I was faced with the obvious, dreaded question, 'Where is this girl of yours?'

I could feel emotion rising within and wasn't ready to answer truthfully so I played for time by answering, 'Her flight was delayed. We'll pick her up later'.

On the way into town I filled her in on events to date, which I had been unable to do by mail. We parked outside her hotel and I turned to her, tears streaming down my face. Before I got too choked up, I blurted out, 'Mom, Britt died three days ago'.

There was a deafening silence as she turned to me and said, 'I knew something was wrong. I can read you like a book'. She put her arm around me and hugged me. Out of the corner of my eye I saw tears on her cheeks and felt their dampness on my shoulder. 'I won't mention your young lady again, but if you need to, please talk to me about her!' She left it there!

We sat together hugging in silence, finding comfort in being together once again. The days sped by, filled with visits to galleries, pubs and shows. We spent the last few days of Mom's visit in Liverpool with her sisters and a brother.

Back in London for the last day, I took her to Britt's favourite restaurant in Virginia Waters and told her the whole story. I had never seen my mom quite so touched by emotion as I told the tale of my girl and the love we had shared, leaving nothing out.

I took her to Heathrow the next morning, and soliciting a promise from me to 'take care of her property', she left for Africa, leaving me with my memories and with the loss of my beautiful Britt once again descending heavily on my heart.

Chapter fourteen
Fighting through

I had an inexplicable desire for my physical body to feel the searing pain my heart and soul so deeply felt, and knew a labour-intensive job might be the answer.

I saw a notice on the board at OVC, advertising for people to dig holes for the planting of trees near a motorway. 'Just what I need,' I thought. I rang up and the job was mine. On my arrival at the yard, I was issued with a small tent, a sleeping bag, and the digging and measuring equipment necessary to dig the holes to a specified size and depth. Armed with digging tools and my very warm, quilted Paddy Hopkirk rally jacket to ward off the freezing cold of the winter of 1966, it was 'Hi ho, hi ho, it's off to dig we go'.

I was feeling neither hi nor ho, more like numb and on autopilot, but after a stern talk with myself, I was ready for the big dig. I arrived on site to find a crew setting up their tents. After introducing myself, I got out my digging equipment, and picking up a tab, went straight to work. The tab indicated who had dug that particular hole so that the labourer could be paid for it. By half past four, night had begun to draw in, and I had dug four holes. I moved half a mile further on and pitched my tent, noting that the others had not as yet started any digging. They were playing cards and making tea, ready for an early morning start, or so I presumed.

I took some clean clothes up to the local village and arranged with the landlady of the pub to have a bath every night for the duration of my stint. After my bath, I had a drink and some supper and decided to retire early to my tent. I was up and dressed as the day dawned. It would have been too easy to lie in a warm sleeping bag and pretend that all was well, but I walked resolutely back to where I had finished the night before and continued digging. The rest of the crew was still asleep, and I hoped they didn't expect me to dig all the holes by myself.

By the end of the day, having worked like a Trojan, I achieved the goal I had set myself, sixteen holes. That night, after a bath and dinner, I was asleep before my head touched the pillow.

I had no idea what the others were doing. I had seen them dig for a couple of hours that morning and then retire to their tents the moment it had started to drizzle. I worked on, thankful to have my mind and body occupied with the work at hand and not on Britt. Whenever I thought of her, tears would tumble down my cheeks uninvited, which had the effect of increasing the ferocity of digging until I was on the verge of collapse. This would to some extent alleviate the pain I felt over my loss.

At the end of the week, I had over sixty tabs to hand in, whereas the other three diggers had a paltry twenty-five between them. I had leaned down a considerable amount and my clothes were beginning to hang on my frame, but the time was flying by. At night when my head hit the pillow, I was too tired for thoughts or memories.

Life continued for three weeks in the same vein, and then it was Christmas, which I spent at Earls Court alone. After the festivities, it was back to the big dig, only to find I was the lone digger, my three amigos having abandoned ship. They must have decided the backbreaking work was not for them.

I finished up work on New Year's Eve and, handing back the equipment to the firm who had employed me, I was well rewarded for my labour and banked a sizeable sum of money. For me, the most important thing of all was that I had kept myself from moping around and wallowing in self-pity over my loss.

I got a call from Jeff Uren at Willment who asked me to take some race cars to Kendal for a show. I was at a loose end; the money was good and certainly beat digging holes, so I accepted the assignment. When I got to Kendal, I was told by one of the organisers that Donald Campbell was scheduled to run his boat *Bluebird* in an attempt to break the existing world speed record on Coniston Water in the early hours of the following morning. *Bluebird* had been specially designed and built for this purpose, and I found myself with this amazing opportunity to watch her in action.

Coniston Water, sheltered by hills on both sides, is the third largest lake in the Lake District of Cumbria in England. It is five miles long, half-a-mile wide, has a maximum depth of one hundred and eighty-four feet, and covers an area of 1.9 square miles. An early morning start the next day saw me at a good vantage point to watch the record-breaking attempt. I was excited at the prospect of seeing this man and his beautiful boat smash the record, little realising what the outcome would be on that fateful day.

After Campbell had made a very fast first run, he turned and lined up for the run back down the course. As he was approaching the end of the mile, the boat lifted out of the water and started to fly just as mine had done on the Zambezi, except that Campbell was travelling three times as fast. *Bluebird* back flipped, hit the water and broke up. The incident was over in a flash, followed by the deathly silence that always follows while everyone tries to digest what has happened.

The silence was soon broken by a woman's scream, and the sound of boats starting up and heading for the crash site. I had just witnessed a man die chasing a dream, destroying his beautiful boat in the process. There were a few pieces of wreckage floating on the water but *Bluebird* and her pilot, or what was left of them, were on their way to the bottom of Coniston Water.

The accident I had just witnessed left me unmoved and unemotional. Racing drivers know the risks and accept them as part of the deal. We are willing to lose life and limb in exchange for the thrill of the race; it seems to be in our blood. Donald Campbell knew the huge risk he was taking but he thought it worthwhile. He died doing something he loved. How many people will be able to say the same thing?

If there is an accident in a race I am competing in and someone is killed or badly hurt, it does not affect me or alter the speed at which I am travelling. I have to have enough faith in my own ability and in my car to single-mindedly ignore what has happened and continue the race. There would be someone along in the near future who would break the record that Donald Campbell had been trying to break.

I left the beautiful Lake District and, once settled back in London, picked up 'rats and mice' jobs for a couple of days. I was looking forward to Friday when the monthly Rhodesia House party would be on the go. These parties were always great fun but, on this occasion, I and three of my friends had cut the time very fine to catch the last tube home from Charing Cross.

I ran as fast as I could to keep up with the others but obviously got left behind in the end, and the next thing I knew I was flat on my face, sliding down the tunnel leaving flesh and blood as I slid along. I looked up as I came to a halt and saw a man trying to catch a lady, who I presumed to be his wife, as she also fell to the ground. I looked back when I heard a scream from behind, and found the same scene re-enacting itself with another woman sliding to the ground through the arms of her partner.

There was a lot of blood from the grazes on my legs and elbows which hurt like hell but I was at a loss to figure out what had happened until I tried to stand and realised my foot and shoe were missing.

Looking back, I spotted the missing pieces lying in the tunnel. My ankle, minus the foot, was sticking out of my torn trouser leg and it began to dawn on me what all the hysteria was about. The two ladies had obviously fainted at the sight of what they thought was a man shearing his foot off at the ankle. What had actually happened was that the bolt holding the foot onto the limb had snapped. I got to my foot (I can't grammatically say 'feet' as I had left one up the tunnel!), but it was difficult to walk with my good leg, which was now three inches longer than the other. I managed to limp my way back to the foot and removed the sock to ascertain exactly what had happened. While assessing the damage, the lady who had fainted came around briefly and on seeing me standing looking down at what must have appeared to her to be my severed foot, let out a scream and slithered to the floor once again.

The guards at the station had heard the commotion and came running to investigate, only to stop dead in their tracks when they saw me, blood all over the place, standing on one leg and holding what appeared to them to be my severed foot, with two ladies lying prostrate on the floor. What a sight it must have been! One of the guards stopped to assist the distressed lady and the other ran on towards me. When he reached me and I explained the situation, the look of relief on his face was priceless.

To cut a long story short, a taxi was summoned and I eventually arrived back in Earls Court in the wee hours. The next morning I was very sore and stiff with grazes where no self-respecting person should have them. I took out my toolbox and with a centre punch and a hammer, managed to get the broken bolt out of the leg. My landlord was good enough to go down to the local hardware store to purchase the appropriate cap screw I needed for repairs.

Once I had reassembled my leg, I shot off to the OVC to meet Tim for a drink. He had just returned to England from America where he had covered the Can Am Series, which is a series of races run in Canada and America on similar lines to the Springbok Series in SA. It begins in Canada, takes in most of the American circuits and ends in Long Beach, California.

Tim was horrified and saddened to learn of Britt's death and shocked to see the state I was in with all my grazes, cuts and bruises, which were drawing a lot of onlooker attention. He was reduced to fits of laughter, once I had finished relating to him the cause of all my bodily injuries.

At lunch, and on Tim's insistence, I told him Britt's story once again from start to finish. By relating the story to Tim, in one afternoon, I felt I had undone all the good I had tried to achieve in putting painful memories of Britt on the back burner of my mind. I had tried so hard to smother the deep aching loss by working all the hours God had given me to dig those holes. To a degree, I had achieved what I had set out to do, but after leaving Tim and returning home, memories of Britt came vividly alive once more, reviving the torment and an aching heart.

That night I felt compelled to face my loss head-on instead of trying to smother the memories, joyful and painful, so indelibly etched in my mind. For the first time since Britt's death and in the darkness of my room, I found relief in exploring and coming to terms with the memories I carried. Finally, sleep overtook me and set me free from the torment that had been my constant companion since her death.

Chapter fifteen
Building racing cars

THE next morning I received a telephone call from Gordon, who had bought a later model Porsche that had been well raced and was now in need of some TLC and 'lots of bloody work,' as he put it. My prayers had been answered. I was fed up with the 'rats and mice' jobs I had picked up around Earls Court, even though they had kept me busy and I had put my heart and soul into every one of them. Rebuilding the Porsche would be a welcome assignment. I was longing for the racing season to begin so I could start what I had come here to do, become an integral part of the racing world.

I wasted no time in Bath and soon had the car in pieces. I made a list, ordered the parts and went about getting everything cleaned and ready for assembly. It was a dusk-to-dawn rebuild for me and my mind was so engrossed in my work that, once again, I was too tired at night for any memories to haunt me. In just three weeks the work was finished and we ran the car at Castle Combe. I made a few adjustments and drove a half a dozen quick laps, which uncovered a few more problems, such as locking brakes, roll bars adjustments, etc., which only took a few hours to resolve back at the workshop. We returned to the circuit the next day. I ran the car for an hour and then handed it over to Gordon, who proceeded to almost wear it out in one afternoon.

Gordon settled the bill, adding a generous bonus and with money in my pocket, I headed back to London. I bumped into a friend of mine from Rhodesia, George Thornton, who had just returned from the Can Am series in America. We rented a top floor flat together in Earls Court and he and I continued with the various jobs on offer at the OVC. George had met a South African on the Can Am series, Pierre du Plessis, who wanted to open a race preparation workshop and was looking for South Africans to join him. Pierre had found premises in Brentford and we drove out there to talk to him.

George decided to take up a position preparing a GT40 for national and international events and afterwards the three of us went for a drink.

Pierre asked me what I did. After a brief explanation of my experience to date, he asked if I would be interested in the design and development of a Chev Camaro to be run in the 1967 British saloon car championships. This kind of work was exactly what I had come to the UK to do, and I accepted there and then. The only stipulation I made was that I alone would be responsible for the design and any development on the project, which Pierre agreed to on the proviso that we would have a weekly meeting to discuss work in progress, and the proposed direction the development was heading.

The first thing I needed to do was speak to someone running a similar car to familiarise myself with the do's and don'ts to ensure compliance with certain rules pertaining to the British championship. Pierre had plenty of contacts in the UK, so we went to various team workshops asking all sorts of questions about the V8 cars running in the championship. I eventually ended up with a blueprint from which to work and all I needed now was the car, which was on its way from the USA. It was an object of engineering beauty, a 1967 Z28, (Camaro Black Panther) and it seemed criminal to have to gut her in order to fulfil our objectives.

It took a couple of days to strip out all the electrical and heating equipment as well as all the glass, with the exception of the front and rear screens. I removed every last thing from the car until she was just a body shell. The months of planning and preparation were on the verge of achieving reality; the dream was about to begin. The progress made on this Camaro project was slow, steady and methodical. I started at the front, working my way steadily to the back, and a few months later the car was ready for its engine.

The actual motor was being built in Derby and was nowhere near ready by the time I was, but as this arrangement had been undertaken by the owner of the Camaro, it was out of my hands.

Testing had to be done on the modified components of the car, so I built a motor from scrounged bits and pieces and completed it myself. The motor sounded fantastic and the car looked every inch a winner. The wheels had not yet arrived from America, so I widened the steel rims the car had arrived with, fitted some race tyres and we were ready to test her. I had worked my butt off and had spent many a night sleeping at the workshop so I could continue my labour of love early every morning, often working around the clock.

A week of testing at Castle Combe revealed that the car was almost perfect, requiring only slight alteration of suspension settings and spring rates. Brake fade was the only problem I had expected and anticipated because when I unpacked the brake discs and callipers, I had remarked that they were too small to stop the Camaro. My comments had been disregarded.

'GP Speed Shop' was the name of Pierre's new venture and as my role was one of development, I had a lot of time on my hands. I got involved with the other mechanics and cars when my services were required, and I accompanied the team to all the races in which they took part. We contested the RAC British Sports Car Championship, and our cars raced from Croft in the north to Goodwood in the south, and from Villa Real in Portugal to Karlskoga in Sweden.

When the European season was over, on the cards were the Can Am series in America and the Springbok Series in the Southern Hemisphere. We raced the twelve-hour endurance races at Rheims, Spa-Francorchamps, Hockenheim, and the BOAC 500 at Brands

Hatch, which was closer to home. On average, our drivers placed about eighth against the works cars, and we were among the top privateers competing. We brought across South African drivers to compete in some of the events and had a good reputation around the pits and paddock.

The memories of my Britt were melting into the recesses of my mind, but now and then, when faced with the realisation I would never see her again, the tears would still freely flow, and I would withdraw within myself to relive the moments we had shared.

Gordon asked me to come to Snetterton, where he was racing the Porsche, so I took the Camaro back to London and drove up to join him. Two works Lotus Cortinas, driven by Jim Clark and Graham Hill, were also competing. I had been longing for a look at them and would have given almost anything to drive one, so when I found Gordon, I told him I was going to the Lotus transporter to see them. The mechanics looking after the two cars lifted the rope for me to duck under for a closer look – after I had explained that I was a Ford works driver from southern Africa.

They were discussing a differential problem they were having with one of the cars, and it transpired they needed someone who could build one for them. I intimated that I was able to do that and have never been hustled into a transporter so fast in all my life. All the spare parts I needed were on hand, and I chatted to them while I was working, telling them a little about myself. Half an hour later I was finished and the diff was being fitted to Graham Hill's car. The mechanics ran it on jacks and seemed surprised to find it perfect. But when they offered to pay me for my efforts I declined, figuring that they might be handy contacts to have one day.

As the race meeting was drawing to a close, the Lotus mechanics made it their business to seek me out to express their appreciation. Graham had competed in two events and the diff was still perfect. They gave me their business cards and invited me to contact them if I ever needed their help. I didn't know it then, but I would be calling on them sooner rather than later.

We had three cars entered in the BOAC 500-mile race at Brands Hatch and I was helping out where needed. Walking through the tunnel, which goes under the track, I suddenly felt my right foot break (again!) and managed, by holding it together, to get to the side of the tunnel. The new bolt had not broken, but the block that it screwed into had broken out of the bottom of the leg. Obviously it had been damaged when the bolt snapped at Charing Cross Station. I stood there on the side of the tunnel with my shoe, sock and foot in my hand and a feeling of despair beginning to rise.

I saw Graham Hill walking down the ramp and was just about to call out to him for help when I heard a voice from behind him say, 'There's the lad who built your diff, Graham'.

There is a God after all! I was so happy to hear the voices of the two mechanics I had helped with the diff. They came across to me and I explained my predicament. As they burst out laughing, I could see Graham thought it funny as well to find a forlorn figure standing in the Brands tunnel with a lower extremity of his person in his hands. My two friends supported me back to their pit while Graham carried my severed appendage with a degree of dignity, pausing along the way to show interested parties what could be found in the Brands tunnel these days. We soon got everything back into place with good old Araldite (an epoxy resin glue) and duct tape. I thanked my helpers for their assistance and made my way back to the pits, albeit on a wobbly foot. I would have been of little help in packing up the pit or loading, so I left them to it and got a lift back to Earls Court.

The following morning in the workshop I mixed some fibreglass resin and poured it into the leg, making sure the foot was pointing in the right direction. The fibreglass would seep down and anchor the block in place.

At long last the motor I had been waiting for arrived from Derby. I was keen to get the car to the track with this special engine, so in it went and I was off to test it out. I found the engine to be running erratically with a loss of power pulling out of corners and plenty of misfiring under load, which sounded to me like a camshaft timing problem. Out the engine had to come. It wasn't a problem of my making and if I had started playing around with it, it would then have become my problem, so straight back to Derby it went.

I was waiting for rims from American Racing Equipment because the brakes were still fading on the car, and the more open magnesium rim might have helped with the cooling. The motor arrived back from Derby for the second time, and, once fitted, sounded a lot better. I had increased the cooling to the front discs and there was nothing more I could do to stop the fade.

The Camaro was entered for the last event of the season at Oulton Park and qualified second on the grid to the championship leader Roy Pierpoint in his all-conquering Falcon. The car was the talk of the paddock, having qualified in second place first time out, with its owner Hugh Dibley at the wheel. In the race, when challenging for the lead, the brakes started to fade and later in the lap the car ran out of brakes completely. I had voiced an opinion that the brakes supplied were not up to the job of stopping the car, and had been proved right, whereas everything I had built or designed myself had performed well above expectation.

My two friends from Lotus approached as we were loading the car, had a good look around and were so favourably impressed they asked me to come and see them when I got back from the Springbok Series. Two years before, I was a nobody from Rhodesia and now I had Team Lotus wanting to talk to me. I had achieved what I had set out to do, which was to interest people who mattered in my development designs and workmanship – and I now had a track record to be proud of in Europe.

I went across to Europe to a race with one of the GT40s and upon my arrival back at Dover, the customs officer emitted a rather forceful 'Ah ha!' and proceeded to inform me I was 'persona non grata' as I held the passport of an illegal regime and was trying to enter the UK. I had a Rhodesian passport and was living and working in England. To be truthful, I hadn't given it a second thought until that day because I had been in and out of the UK so many times without incident.

One of the more awake of the bunch, after perusing my travel document, exclaimed, 'Mr Mawson was born here and is thereby entitled to enter the UK'. Perusing all entry and exit stamps in my passport, he added, 'Besides, he has lived here for a while!'

A phone call from the 'Ah ha' gentleman, presumably to the home office, allowed me passage to my abode.

With the British season over, we began preparing cars for the Springbok Series. Pierre and I rebuilt Mike d'Udy's Lola T70 coupé, took her out to a circuit for a shakedown run, and once we had bedded in some new brake pads, she was loaded onto the trailer ready for the trip to South Africa. Ed Nelson wanted to fit a new motor to the GT40 but was racing in Europe from where he would also be shipping the car to South Africa. George asked me to build a sub-assembly for the car. A new block arrived, and after I had fitted new competition parts into the motor, it was boxed up ready for George to fit into the car in South Africa.

We had rebuilt and made ready a GT40 belonging to Colin Crabb for the same series, and the car was ready for the trip as well. A GT40 came from Europe for a suspension rebuild and Pierre said, before shooting off to Bournemouth for a short break with his wife, that if I wanted to rebuild the car for the customer, it was mine to do. Once again, I was glad to be kept busy and I finished the rebuild a day before the cars were being shipped to South Africa. The owner was so pleased when he saw the results of my labour that he included a generous bonus in my pay packet. I took the cars to the docks the next day, along with their spares, and came back to close the workshop for winter. The flat was packed up and vacated, and it was off to sunny South Africa for me. The Springbok Series consisted of a nine-hour race in Johannesburg for openers, followed by four three-hour races. One in Lourenço Marques, Mozambique; one in Bulawayo, Rhodesia; and two in South Africa, in Pietermaritzburg and Cape Town.

The races were designed for sports and saloon cars running concurrently and together constituted this popular series. All the overseas drivers got to avoid the winter in their own countries in exchange for the sunny climate of Africa. This series ground to a halt in the late eighties and was sadly missed by all concerned.

Chapter sixteen
Return to Africa

IT was a pleasant flight, but because the Kenyan President was flying in around the same time, our landing was delayed at Nairobi. The captain announced the delay and, to kill some time, flew the aircraft to Mt Kilimanjaro. He banked the aircraft first right and then left so all the passengers could get a good look at the majestic mountain. When we finally landed, I was not allowed off the plane as I held the dreaded Rhodesian passport and one of the hostesses had to stay on board with me. Some people have all the luck, don't they?

She produced some drinks and snacks from First Class and, while the cleaners went about their tasks, we had a party in the rear kitchen. We were on the ground for just over an hour without the luxury of air conditioning and as the heat became more intense, we moved the party to the aircraft door to get some fresh air. Eventually, the passengers boarded and we resumed our flight to Johannesburg.

Walking out of the arrivals gate at Jan Smuts Airport in Johannesburg, I spotted my folks and headed towards them. I could see shock in my Dad's eyes when he saw me. Mom had not thought to mention I was a good forty pounds lighter since last he had seen me. He told me afterwards that he had hardly recognised me.

We drove to Durban where I was to supervise the offloading of the cars. The ship docked that afternoon and I supervised their transfer to a rail car. After spending a couple of days in Durban with my folks, I caught a flight back to Johannesburg to meet Roger Taylor, the mechanic in charge of the Lola for the Springbok Series. I was also reunited with the cars that had made the journey down by rail. The usual checks ensued, which included altering the timing and jets to compensate for Kyalami's altitude of six thousand feet above sea level, followed by testing at the racetrack and unofficial practice. I was sure there was a vibration from the motor at certain revs and voiced my opinion, but it was going quickly enough and Roger and Mike were happy with it.

We qualified our Lola fourth for the race and all seemed well, but without any sign of George or the car at practice, the situation certainly didn't look good. I was told that the car had arrived late and George was frantically changing the engine. They arrived very late but managed to run the new motor in and qualify for the race. Ed Nelson had Mike Hailwood, the ex-world motorcycle champion as co-driver with him in the GT40. Partnering Mike de'Udy in the Lola was Hugh Dibley, the owner of the Camaro I had built back in the UK.

The nine-hour was always a Le Mans start with the fastest car lining up at the front. We were down in fourth and got a good start. We sat in fourth position for three hours or so until the oil pressure started to fall and the car had to be slowed. Sadly, the car was forced to retire after about four hours as the motor was beginning to knock. To continue would have destroyed it although major damage inside the engine had probably already been done. Ed and Mike went on to win their class in the GT40 and came a creditable third overall. In effect, they were co-leaders of the Springbok Series.

Roger and I returned to Krugersdorp to pull the motor and repair the damage, and after stripping it, we found very little inside that was of use. We had a week to repair the car, run it in and get it to Cape Town for the next race, over a thousand miles away. As we could not run the high-revving Traco motor, a compromise was obtained by running a larger engine. We managed to finish the build and after an all-night drive to Cape Town, we used allotted practice time to run the engine in. Mike was trying to bed the motor in and set up the car at the same time, which, in my experience, never worked, but we qualified third and were happy with that.

The first hour of the race saw the two Lolas of Paul Hawkins and Mike dicing for first place, until Paul was forced to pit with a puncture, handing us a two-lap advantage over the rest of the field. Just after the second hour, Mike collided with Doug Serrurier's Lola and we lost a lap attending to the car. Mike rejoined, believing we were a lap ahead, but the control tower insisted that the three Lolas were on the same lap. Roger put the pit board out, and Mike started to push it, but he must have forgotten that he had the larger motor and over-revved it. With twelve minutes to go, his motor threw a con rod and, consequently, the hot oil caught fire.

Our race was run but we were classified fourth. Ed won his class, which put him in the lead of the Springbok Series, ahead of Paul by three points. Mike denied over-revving the car, saying he was sure it had suffered oil surge in the corners, which had resulted in the blown motor. My rejoinder was that if the motor had been suffering from oil surge, it would have blown long before the two hours and forty eight minutes it had run.

We drove back to Johannesburg overnight to repair the damage. There was much to be done. Apart from repairs to the motor, there was fire damage to the glass fibre body and all the electrics had been destroyed. The motor was out and washed by Monday morning, and I shot into town to the engineers while Roger attended to the rest of our problems. The next race was the Rhodesian Grand Prix at the Falls Road circuit. I would have loved our Lola to win my home race but it was not to be. There simply wasn't enough time to repair all the damage.

We now had two weeks to get the car ready for the Lourenço Marques race in Mozambique. The car was race ready, run in and pre-race checked by the time we hit LM where the emphasis of our lives revolved around practice and prawns, for which LM was famous.

Once again, the Lolas were in control and we were hoping for a few more points in the series. Mike was quickest in practice, followed by Paul and Doug Serrurier.

Because of the heat, the race began at five in the evening with Paul and Mike dicing for an hour and a half for the lead, until Mike arrived in the pits with a mother of a misfire. We checked plugs and leads, which were all fine, but discovered a broken rocker and a bent push rod under some very hot rocker covers. With the parts replaced in a flash, the Lola rejoined the race only to return a few laps later with a similar problem. This time the rocker stud had pulled out of the head, resulting in another early retirement.

This problem left us with just over a week until the last race of the series, which was to be held on Boxing Day.

The practice run in Pietermaritzburg went well and we were second on the grid alongside Paul. Once again the three Lolas were in the front of the field with Mike and Paul dicing for the lead, with Doug Serrurier (a local F1 driver) sitting in third place. Mike over revved the engine again, this time admitting he had missed a gear and as a consequence was out of the race with a bent valve. What a disastrous Series for Mike, Roger and me.

Doug Serrurier, driving with Jackie Pretorius, won the race with Paul coming in second. Ed Nelson had won his class and therefore the series by three points and in the process had beaten one of the most successful drivers in sports cars – my mate, Paul Hawkins. The calibre of this man was such that Enzo Ferrari himself had signed Paul to head the Ferrari sports and prototype challenge in Europe the following year. I was very pleased for George, who had put a lot of work into his winning car and deserved the series win.

Our car had not finished a single race, and I believe it was all down to the way the car had been driven, and nothing to do with bad preparation. In fact, I had built the sub assembly for George's GT40 that had won the Series, and I knew my motors were good. Furthermore,

Roger and I were considered two of the best mechanics on the series, as well as in the business. Mike then asked us if we would build another motor for him to have a crack at the South African land speed record.

David Piper had raised the record to one hundred and eighty-nine miles per hour in his Ferrari just outside Bloemfontein in early December. All well and good, but the highest gear we had for the Lola would only give her a top speed of one hundred and ninety miles per hour, and we needed at least a two hundred and ten miles per hour gear to take the record. Back in Krugersdorp, I built another engine while Roger headed to a gear manufacturer with a sample. The gear was ready for us two days later; we assembled the gearbox and headed for Cape Town where the attempt was to be made.

The attempt to break the land speed record consisted of two runs over a measured mile – one up and the other back, both in the time limit of one hour. The South African Police were the official timekeepers and had closed a section of road near Malmesbury for us. Our first run was two hundred and four miles per hour; the second run was aborted as the fifth gear stripped when selected. Our only option was to put the fourth gear into fifth and space the rest of the gears accordingly at the run site. This done, we started the run back with eight minutes to spare and both runs gave us an average speed of one hundred and ninety-four miles per hour, a new record. So at least we had achieved something in the last three months – apart from building engines for Mike to blow up.

After shipping the car back to Europe, we left Cape Town for Johannesburg from where I caught a flight home to Rhodesia. Salisbury had grown a lot since I left, or maybe it just seemed that way to me, having been away for four years. Rhodesia had been independent all those years and was prospering. I was quite amazed at how this little country had become virtually self-sufficient, with only the need to import fuel. Exports of tobacco, beef, gold and flowers were made to Ireland, Belgium and Holland. Our DC8s were flying out twice a day to Europe and returning loaded with commodities needed by the country to survive world sanctions, and then reloading again to fly back to Europe. Sanctions were actually a joke and had accomplished the opposite effect of what they were supposed to achieve.

Living in Rhodesia during those exciting times was, unquestionably, the highlight of my life. There was a shortage of luxury items because of international sanctions, but that was all, and an ever-increasing insurgency war was being contained. More importantly, we revelled in the challenge of proving British Prime Minister Harold Wilson wrong. 'They won't last six weeks' was his comment on our declaration of independence.

I'm so thankful that Ian Smith, our Prime Minister, was there to guide us through. Despite most world governments' derision of Smith, among ordinary people he was universally admired. His service during the war, and his subsequent stand after it, increased his popularity, which in turn stood us in good stead for breaking sanctions.

Wilson sent warships to the Mozambique coast in an attempt to prevent tankers dropping off oil destined for Rhodesia. This action backfired and gave the Rhodesians even more support. Sanctions were backfiring as well. Instead of importing products from Britain, we started making them ourselves. Previously, we had largely been an agricultural nation, now an industry of necessity was starting to take off. Initially, the products were terrible. People used to joke about their quality. But gradually they got better and even surpassed their prototypes.

There is an expression about politics making strange bedfellows. The Russians were intent on arming the insurgents, but were desperate for our chrome; while the rest of the world needed our highly sought-after gold, beef and tobacco. The Rhodesian dollar was at an all-time high and we were giving the finger to the rest of the world.

The first thing I did when I walked into the motor club was to seek out and thank the chairman and secretary of RMSA for those very important letters of recommendation they had given me for my trip to Europe. I saw my good friend Taffy Swire Griffiths and passed on salutations from the land of his birth (Wales), and greetings from the Cornish pixies to his lovely wife Betty. I told him about the huge advantage the letters had given me, and he said I should have phoned him, and he would have joined me.

The first week back home I just chilled out and became reacquainted with old friends. I was sad to find that some of them had died, happy to find others married, and pleased to learn I had become somewhat of a celebrity around Salisbury.

Mom had told me in London that Dad was drinking heavily, a problem which had escalated over time. Most nights he would sleep in the hotel as he was too drunk to come home. As the eldest son, I tried talking to him, but he just agreed with me and went his own way. Mom was worried. She found it difficult to run the hotel and look after Dad, who gave her little help with anything. I spoke to Mom about my returning to the UK, but she explained that she and Dad would rather have me in Africa to help out.

If I was going back to Europe, I would need to move now as it was the beginning of February, and the teams would be hiring from the middle of the month. I had a number of options open to me in Europe, most notably with Lotus, who had posted me an offer so good they were convinced I would not refuse.

My immediate family, however, was the most important thing in my life right then. I if I could pull Dad straight by staying, then stay I would. My family had stood by me in the past and now it was my turn to repay that debt. I knew in my heart that I would miss the excitement and glamour of the European tracks. I had made some good contacts there. If and when I decided to go back, it would simply be a matter of picking up the pieces in a few days.

When I phoned my friend at Lotus to give him the news of my non-return, he was really upset but accepted my decision. He told me to call them if I was to come back at any time and give them the option of first refusal. I thanked him for the compliments and wished the Lotus team well for the new season. My staying seemed to have a good effect on Dad. Things appeared to be stabilizing, and I felt that my decision had been the right one. Life moved on.

I bumped into an old girlfriend who was in the throes of a divorce. The last time I had seen her was in London, where she worked as a Playboy bunny at the Park Lane Club. We decided to go to Beira to visit my old friend Carlos Brito and Johnny the Greek from Bar Arcadia, another old friend, who owned the best seafood restaurant in Beira. They made a big fuss of us and we spent a lovely couple of days together. On the way home, we stopped off at Inyanga, located on the eastern border of Rhodesia, for a week of relaxation. The beautiful mountains, trout streams and the bonus of my gorgeous companion did me a world of good and had the effect of enabling me to put my life back into perspective. On our return home, we went to our chalet at Lake McIllwaine, which the family had bought while I was away. Although I had not water-skied for a number of years, it was not long before I was skimming over the water again behind our powerful boat.

I bought a Renault Gordini in South Africa with the view to racing it. If I had to miss out on the European season, then I was going to race my own car at home. The Renault Gordini was a fast little car and its endurance was fantastic. I raced it for half the year with a variety of successes. Ron Lupson, a good friend, had the same car and won the saloon car championship that year.

Around the same time we sold the farm, Dad and Clive, my younger brother, who was now twenty-four, had bought a company, Continental Upholsterers. From the premises, Clive was building his own auto electrical business. Dad was supposed to run the office and upholstery side of things, but the problem was that he would get in at nine-thirty in the morning only to disappear half an hour later to the Chalet Bar, where he would sit and drink until three in the afternoon, stagger back to the workshop, and drive himself home. This state of affairs left Clive trying to run the entire operation, leaving him little chance to build up his own business.

I was asked to join them to build a motor repair and servicing department and this was the start of M&M Motors. Dad gradually faded out of the picture, and Clive and I were left to run the upholstery section of the business as well as our own.

More than anything, I enjoyed the longevity of endurance racing and I entered a six-hour and two three-hour races, but the year to me was a mish-mash. Losing Britt had left a huge void in my life that I couldn't seem to fill, and on top of it all I missed the glamour, excitement and competition of the tracks in Europe. I was happy to be home with my old friends again, but inside I was pining for my quiet ghost.

Later that same year I went to the factory to talk to Alfa and came away with a sponsorship to race for them the following year. After selling the Gordini, I found a GTV, which I bought with the view to racing it. Alfa Africa in Johannesburg supplied me with competition parts for the car, which I fitted when I returned to Salisbury.

Rhodesian drivers took great delight in ragging me about my racing equipment, which was all the latest fireproof Nomex gear, including fireproof underwear, a fireproof balaclava and a Bell Star helmet, all standard requirements for anyone racing overseas.

There were many comments made, the best of which came from my good friend Ron Lupson. 'Dickey Mawson, International Grand Prix Driver' was his usual comment when I was all suited up in the change room, but I knew there was no malice intended so I let it go. He was aware of what I had achieved overseas and was proud of my accomplishments. Later that year, during a three-hour endurance race, one of the GSM Darts caught fire and the driver got badly burnt. As a result, the Rhodesia Motor Sports Association made it compulsory to conform to international regulations, and fireproof suits had to be worn by all drivers. My mate Ron was silenced quickly by the price of these items. When he was decked out in all his gear, I commented that it was a big improvement as his full face helmet hid his ugly face. Then I had to hurriedly duck as he threw his tog bag at me.

Ronny and I were the best of friends throughout life and never a cross word came between us. He was a person who added greatly to my life and I loved him to pieces. He was a good and true friend and left huge footprints on my heart when he died in New Zealand in 2008.

Clive and I opened a panel beating division at the rear of our M&M workshop so to all intents and purposes, we could now strip a car down to the last washer and rebuild and refurbish it in-house.

Clive had bought an E-Type Jag. Rhodesian car factories were building Alfa, Nissan, Citroen and BMW and apart from fuel, Rhodesia wasn't short of anything. Mossie, my Volvo partner, was making a fortune manufacturing and marketing RHP Sauce, a copy of the internationally known brand of British HP sauce, which tasted just like the original. We made our own corn flakes, produced the finest beef and tobacco in the world and even made our own whisky, a Scottish malt concentrate blended with Inyanga water. Sanction busting was the national sport and everyone was into it. Our business was growing in leaps and bounds. We had our own accountant, who was also a director, and employed a staff of ten but, like many small businesses, cash flow was to become a problem.

In 1970 Clive decided to get married and chose the same wedding day as a friend of ours, Brian Evans, who was marrying one Alannah Veloza. The receptions for both weddings were to be held at the motor club where Mom was doing the catering. Clive's marriage to Paddy was held on the farm owned by her parents, Don and Zoë Baker, some eighty miles from the reception venue. The rest of the family and I attended the wedding that morning, but Mom and I had to leave almost as soon as formalities were over to set up the buffets for the receptions at the motor club. We were organised and ready to go by the time the guests started drifting in at around seven that evening. The motor club was packed to bursting, and I don't know of anyone who didn't enjoy themselves.

Brian and Lana were spending their honeymoon camping at Troutbeck in Inyanga, a mountain retreat on the eastern border of Rhodesia, and Brian had invited a load of mates down for a game of golf the next morning. Lana didn't mind the arrangement even though it was her honeymoon. She and Brian had been together for some time and us Rhodies were a close-knit social bunch anyway and always up for a party and a laugh.

We arrived at the hotel a few minutes after six the next morning, congregated around cups of coffee and then set off to the first hole. We had played six holes and had to play across the lake for the seventh. The hole was on top of a thirty-foot hill accessed by steep steps cut out of the earth. I managed to land my ball on the green of said seventh hole while most of the budding 'Gary Players' (he was South Africa's world golfing champion) were knocking the little white ball from one side of the hill to the other. Those of us who had landed on the green, more by luck than judgement, I might add, played out the hole while golf balls whistled overhead from all directions.

I was on the opposite side of the green to the steps and decided to go down the side of the hill as a short cut to the next tee but slid on the dewy wet grass, causing my right leg to buckle under me and down I went, all the way to the bottom of the hill, leaving my leg at the top. My caddy, who was about to follow me down, stared in wide-eyed horror at what he was seeing – me at the bottom of the hill, and my leg complete with sock and shoe lying at the top. He dropped my clubs and took off, probably for the Mozambique border thirty miles away. I am led to believe, by those who tell the story, that to this day he has not been seen. After everyone had finished laughing, I was reunited with my leg and clubs, courtesy of the groom. Naturally, the whole wedding party soon got to hear about the disappearing caddy.

The Lions Club of Rusape had posters advertising a boat race, up not down, the Rusape River. Only mad Rhodesians would have considered such a race in a river known to be crocodile inhabited and bilharzia infested. Bilharzia is the second most devastating parasitic disease after malaria in Africa. It is found in parasitic worms carried by fresh water snails, and it's prevalent in many Asian and African countries. The chronic disease affects internal human organs, among a lot of other horrible things, and although it has a low mortality rate, you don't want to contract it.

Naturally, a few friends and I began work on a craft to get us up the river. The race was scheduled for a day in November, which was our rainy season when the river would be fast flowing and the crocs scarce. The most important feature of the raft, as far as we were concerned, was the positioning of three cases of Castle Lager to a place where everyone could reach them with ease as we negotiated the river. To that end, we lashed the cases together and placed them in the centre of the raft. Running up rapids with your inner tube raft was, after all, thirsty business.

Imagine a bunch of intoxicated motor sport enthusiasts trying to carry a raft up fast-flowing rapids at half past eight in the morning, a task made almost impossible by the slimy rocks. I, for one, could hardly get up the rapids for laughing. Eventually, we managed the feat, leaving behind an assortment of walking wounded in the pool at the bottom of the rapids.

As we approached the road bridge packed with spectators, I slipped off my leg and laced the stump liberally with tomato sauce. The idea was to give the spectators the impression that a crocodile had had my leg for breakfast. The whole team were shouting 'croc, croc'. Honestly, I reckoned that the nearest croc was at least five hundred miles away from the bunch of drunks which had invaded their river. Then I heard a voice from above shout, 'Give the poor croc his other leg, he's still hungry'. It was my good friend Ron.

As we came out on the other side of the bridge, we were pelted with half-eaten rolls, bacon sandwiches and empty beer cans. People drinking at eight o'clock on a Sunday morning – disgusting! We went on to win the race, but everyone was feeling a little worse for wear as all the beer crates on board were now empty.

Britt and I had done some canoeing in Sweden, and the raft race had flooded my mind with memories of my quiet ghost. The event and probably the alcohol-induced emotions served to bring on feelings of extreme melancholy. As everyone was congregating at the motor sports clubhouse, I felt I couldn't face the braai and went home to be with my Britt.

My penthouse in Warwick House was on the ninth floor and looked out over the whole of Salisbury. It was without doubt the best penthouse in town and was furnished by Mom, who had impeccable taste when it came to interior design.

I lay down on my bed and was transported back in time to Europe to relive my days with the gorgeous Miss Askogh. I awoke the next morning with feelings of nostalgia and a wish that I could return to Europe. At the same time I felt truly in favour with my maker. He was definitely smiling on me.

I had everything a young man could wish for and was enjoying my life. If I returned to Europe, Britt would not be there. Women, wine and song, in that order, came and went. Most weekends were spent away with a variety of women. I had no particular favourite and can only say I was a little in love with all of them. But I had found no one yet to match my Britt, and I felt that finding someone to fill her shoes would be impossible.

The year was now drawing to a close. I had had a successful year with Alfa; the competitive racing had been great between Ron and I, and the Springbok Series was with us again. Ronny's Renault had been very fast all year as had my Alfa. We had tested our cars the week before the three-hour race at Bulawayo; and with everything in order, we embraced the challenge of facing the might of the European and South African entries.

We arrived in Bulawayo a day early. After a sauna and massage to relieve the stress of the three-hundred-mile drive, we went to the track for unofficial practice. I knew an outright win by my little Alfa would be impossible, but an index of performance win was a distinct possibility.

I qualified for the race on a full tank of fuel and worn tyres, and Ron qualified on the smell of an oil rag and new tyres. He planned to stop halfway through the race, while I was driving without a stop, apart from the one compulsory pit stop. It would be a matter of 'a splash and dash' to take on fuel during the race, as the rules required. It worked like this: I would pull in at some time during the race, the pit crew would remove the fuel cap, dump a teaspoon of petrol into the tank, and I could be back out on the track in less than twenty seconds. With this plan, I knew I could finish in the top three. I fitted new race tyres and brake pads to the car and went out for two laps to bed them in and check the wheel balance before practice finished. Once satisfied, I topped up with fuel and I was ready to race.

Ron had qualified one and a half seconds faster than I had, but had not run his car with a full tank, so it would be slower in the actual race than it had been in practice as he would be carrying a lot more fuel. Ron informed me that he would flash his lights as a signal for me to move over when he came up to lap me. I mentioned a few unprintable words about what he could do with his flashing lights, but I don't think he took me literally. As the flag dropped, we were away and I shot past Ron, leading him for a couple of laps as he was obviously battling with the extra weight of the fuel while settling in.

I let Ron overtake me and sat just behind him. The car and I were on course to be on the rostrum, but a three-hour race is a long time and much can happen and often does! I knew Ron had a pit stop in the offing and, sure enough, at the halfway point he stopped to refuel. My car was getting faster as the fuel was used up and Ron's car would now carry a heavy fuel load once again, which would slow the car. He was still in the pits as I came past on the next lap. I noted the Mazda of Basil van Rooyen and Peter Gough exiting the pits behind me.

Peter was catching me through the back section, so I held an inside line to let him through. As he went past and into a corner in front of me, I noticed a spray of liquid from under his car and as he lifted to brake, a flame shot out of the exhaust at the rear of the car. The whole car expanded like a balloon and with a mighty explosion, the bonnet and boot shot skywards from the car, which spun to a halt in front of me.

As I passed, I could see it was a blazing inferno inside with Peter trying to get out. I stopped the Alfa at the side of the track, jumped out and ran back as fast as I could. I saw Peter tumble from the Mazda. Marshals running from the corner with extinguishers got to him before I did. Stopping in mid-stride, I could see from where I was that Peter was badly burnt, the plastic peak of his helmet had melted and stuck to the skin on his face, but he was in the hands of people trained to handle these situations and I turned and ran back to my car. I was leading on index and intended to keep that position.

As I accelerated back onto the track, I tried to comprehend what had caused the car to explode. It had all happened very quickly, so I mentally checked to make sure my fire proofs were covering all the body parts they were designed to cover. Flags were being waved everywhere, emergency vehicles were on the track speeding to the scene, and the pace of the race slowed accordingly. Halfway through the third hour a tropical storm hit the circuit with strong winds and heavy rain; cars were sent spinning everywhere on their slick tyres. Rivers of water were running across the track, so I took the opportunity to signal my pit that I would be in for fuel. I ducked in and out again. Nevertheless, I finished with the index prize in spite of the torrential rain and Peter's mishap. The coveted trophy was mine: I was the first Rhodesian on index against all the works teams and international opposition. Peter Gough was taken to hospital in critical condition. What had happened was when the Mazda was in the pits for a driver change and refuelling, the tank cap had not closed properly, causing fuel to slop out of the tank and into the boot. The spray of liquid I had observed under the car was petrol finding its way through any opening in the floor of the car, which was highly volatile as it mixed with the tumbling air under the vehicle that was ignited by the flame from the exhaust. The day was very hot and humid, and Peter had opted not to wear his fireproof underwear, which contributed to some of his burns. In the end, he was very lucky to have been wearing a good pair of sunglasses, which probably saved his eyesight when the peak of his helmet melted onto his face.

On the way home we popped into the hospital to see how he was, but the report was not good. I am pleased to say that over time he recovered and is still racing today. He was always a gentleman and a fine race driver. That morning in the Bulawayo paper on the front page was a photo of me and Jody Scheckter, who was driving the other works Mazda, ploughing through one of the rivers running across the track during the cloudburst.

Ron told me after the race that he could not believe his eyes when I jumped ahead of him at the start. Because his car was so heavily laden with fuel, he said he felt as if he was driving with the handbrake on. After that race, he christened me 'Tricky Dickey' because of the strategy I had used to win the index of performance.

The next race was scheduled to be held at the Pietermaritzburg circuit in Natal, South Africa. I asked a friend to tow the Alfa there; he ended up having an accident en route, flipping the Alfa and trailer right over the roof of our Falcon V8 tow car. As luck would have it, the tow hitch broke, and there was no damage to the Falcon. The GTV and trailer, on the other hand, landed upside down in the middle of the road, squashing the roof level with the seats. All I could do was load it onto the stock car trailer and drive it back to the shop, where I left it until after the Christmas festivities.

I would enjoy Christmas and New Year first and decide what to do later. I spent a quiet time around Salisbury by myself reliving memories of Britt and Europe, keeping the festive season contained within the walls of my home. Being all alone in my lovely penthouse was what I needed more than anything, a time to reflect and think. It was a necessity for me to get my life back on track and to find a purpose and direction. The quiet and aloneness of this reflective period allowed my feelings of aimlessness to escape. A quiet contentment took their place, which in turn instilled within me a sense of excitement and anticipation for the future. I wasn't sure what the future held, but I convinced myself to look on the New Year as a fresh start.

New Year's Day dawned crisp and clear and the new me drove our truck out to the New Year's Day Autocross being held on the old Marlborough circuit at Duikers Leap. My friend Twiggy, who was a good deal overweight and always noisy and boisterous, was shouting about being the autocross champion, to which I commented: if I had a car, I would show him the way round. The fool offered me a drive in his wife's Christmas present, a brand new MG 1100 with less than one hundred miles on the clock. He was supposed to be going for a long run to bed it in for her. Of course, I accepted the challenge, along with a fifty-pound wager for the winner's wallet. I went out for a practice run and was very impressed with the little car. I pulverized him by a good four seconds and won the autocross outright. He paid up and I put the money behind the bar at Sable's Motor Club for all to enjoy.

On opening the national newspaper the next morning, there was Sheila's MG 1100, her pride and joy on two wheels, smack bang in the middle of the front page. The caption read, 'Dick Mawson obliterates opposition in New Year Autocross'. I don't think Twiggy's marriage ever recovered after that; about a year later he and Sheila were divorced. Sheila got the house and Twiggy got the MG. I don't know who got the kids! After New Year it was my brother's birthday. My mother, who was laying out the cold buffet, brought out a large trifle and Twiggy, being the glutton he was, picked the bowl up and said, 'I'm going to eat this all by myself,' as he raised it towards his mouth. I swear to this day I only gave it a little help! The next moment his face was buried up to his ears in the trifle. There were two cherries where his eyes should have been and a line of little silver balls where the mouth was. He stood there horrified as the custard, cream, silver balls and cherries slid slowly down his face. I took off like a scalded cat while the whole room, including my mother, collapsed with laughter.

Twiggy took it in good spirit, even though, for months afterwards every time he walked into the motor club, the members would ask if he had had any trifle lately. Whenever he was around, I had ice creams or whatever other foodstuffs he could find hurled at me from every direction. I'm glad to say I was never hit.

Chapter seventeen
Hectic lifestyle

RON phoned me halfway through the year and asked me what I knew about the Ford FVC motor. He told me that Dennis Joubert in Cape Town was selling his B16 Chevron in bits and pieces and what did I think? Fortunately, I knew the motor well, having built several overseas.

Ron needed someone who knew what they were looking at as far as the car was concerned. If he managed to sell his Renault, he asked, would I be prepared to go with him to the Cape to look at the Chevron? I said that I would go; and as it happened, Ron sold the Renault the next day. The following week, early on a Monday morning, we left on the nineteen hundred mile trip to Cape Town. The Cape Motor Club had asked us to pick up a Trike, a three-wheeled motorcycle from the film studios in Johannesburg and to tow it to Cape Town, where they wanted it for their motor show. In return, they would foot our petrol and hotel bill to the Cape.

We arrived in Johannesburg at lunchtime the next day and went to the film studios at Kyalami to fetch the Trike, which had been used in the film 'Leather Lip,' the story of a surfer who won the surfing championship and, of course, the girl who was the bonus, or was she?

The Trike was fitted with a flat-six Corvair motor and had been very professionally made. We also picked up about six hundred posters of the Trike. We stopped in Rosebank for petrol, cigarettes for Ron, cool drinks, and toasted chicken sandwiches for the road, and off we went for the twelve hundred mile drive to Cape Town. The chicken sandwiches must have been off, because about an hour down the road, I had to ask Ron to stop at the next service station. When we had not passed one twenty minutes later, I was in big trouble, and, as it turned out, so was Ron. Around the next bend a service station mercifully came into sight and we were saved.

The car had barely reached a standstill when I was out and running for the Gents, pulling my pants down as I ran. Into the single cubicle I turned, flicked the door shut and sat on the throne in one panic-stricken motion. Ron, who had caught up with me, put his hand out as the door was slamming shut and got three fingers wedged between the door and the frame. I could hear his screams of pain, but by that time I was past caring as a stream was pouring out of me like a running tap. I felt a lot better after that, and as I came out, Ron was nowhere in sight. I wondered what had happened to him.

I heard a train whistle blowing, followed by some cussing from the direction of the train tracks. I spotted Ron through the bush, squatting next to the railway line with the Blue Train on a slow meander rolling past his bare bottom. Passengers were leaning out of the windows observing the sights as their train trundled slowly through the centre of the richest gold fields in the world with the deepest mines and richest deposits. The passengers would have been enjoying an on-board commentary on all this history.

The Blue Train is a luxury train that runs from the Rand to Cape Town, and I don't think the sight of Ron's behind was on their itinerary. He seemed completely oblivious to the driver or the passengers hanging out of the windows getting a look at the gold fields, darkest Africa and Ron's bare behind for the first time. Ron shouted for me to bring some paper, which I did. I needed to go again, and by the time I got out, Ron was back in the truck.

'You stupid bastard, look at my fingers!' he shouted as he held them up; they were turning a nasty shade of black. When I suggested we stick a needle under his nails to release the pressure of the blood pooling underneath them, he groaned, 'Have you gone stark raving bonkers? These nails have been with me since birth, and nobody is going to stick a stuffing needle anywhere near them'.

'If you don't release the pressure now, you're not going to get any sleep for the next few days,' I cautioned, 'but be it on your own head'.

We continued on our way to Bloemfontein where we were stopping for the night. After half an hour, Ron's fingers were throbbing and too sore for him to drive, so I took over while he cradled his ever-worsening hand in his lap.

In Bloemfontein, Ron went into the hotel armed with all the information on the room Dennis had booked for us while a crowd had gathered around the Trike outside, which had been recognised from the newly released movie. One of the youngsters asked if I had any posters. Of course we did, said I, and added, 'They are five rand each'. By the time Ron came back, I had three hundred rand, in those days around one hundred and fifty pounds, in my pocket. When I showed him the money, he laughed and said I should wake early and sell some more.

We carried the bags up to the hotel room and as Ron was first in, he grabbed the large double bed, leaving me the three-quarter bed tucked into an alcove. I had a bath and Ron had a couple of brandies to take away the pain in his hand. I climbed into bed; it was bitterly cold, but I had two blankets and an eiderdown as well as the counterpane, so I was snug. When Ron pulled back his bed, he found himself faced with a sheet and a thin blanket. I have never heard anyone complain so bitterly to the night porter, who, unfortunately, did not have keys to the linen store, and the hotel was full so he was unable to strip a bed. Eventually, Ron went to bed dressed in a T-shirt, two jerseys, tracksuit pants and three pairs of socks. Even then the chattering of his teeth kept me awake for half an hour. His fingers kept him up most of the night, and he awoke to find them quite badly swollen.

The following morning we bought some painkillers from the

chemist and while parked, I sold another two hundred rands' worth of posters. We drove into Cape Town in the early evening after having sold another hundred rands' worth of posters at service stations and cafés along the way. These posters were a lucrative business. The Trike on the back of the car attracted all the attention, and I must admit the posters were very nice. At Sea Point a crowd gathered around the Trike, which prompted this poster salesman back into action again. In total, we had made nearly a thousand rand from sales; it was like printing money!

We secured the truck and Trike in the car park of the Elizabeth Hotel, and it wasn't long before Dennis from the Cape Motor Club came to settle our petrol and hotel bills. The weather was perfect, and as the sun set, Dennis pointed to a black line on the horizon and told us we were in for some filthy weather the next day. As it turned out, the storm arrived just after midnight, when I awoke to a huge clap of thunder. The curtains were parallel to the ceiling and the wind was howling into the room. I closed the French doors to our balcony and went back to bed. Ron was fast asleep having taken two sleeping pills.

The next morning we had a lovely breakfast on the terrace and although Ron's fingers were feeling a lot better, it was obvious he was going to lose those nails. We dropped the Trike at the motor show and then went off to view the car. The Chevron B16 was masterminded by Dereck Bennett of Chevron cars and had made its début at the 1969 Nürburgring 500km race, which it won in the hands of Brian Redman. It was a very pretty coupé and was very fast with its Cosworth motor. The car did suffer from under-steer due to not enough rear down-force. This problem was later solved by adding two orange-box rear spoilers.

I had gone through most of the parts by lunchtime but was apprehensive about a car like that in Rhodesia. Who could it be raced against? Ron had to make the decision. I could see he had fallen in love with the car and so I was not surprised when a deal was struck. We loaded everything into the van, hitched the trailer and car behind, and headed back to the hotel to bathe and change before our long return trip the following day.

We did some shopping in the morning and hit the road after an early lunch, arriving at the Marino Inn in Colesburg rather late that night.

As we filled up at the garage, the thermometer read minus eight degrees. Not only was it very cold, but we were dead beat. There were two single beds in the chalet we had rented for the night and a small two-bar heater, which switched on for ten seconds and off for twenty. After five minutes of trying to warm up my sheets, I gave up and handed the heater to Ron, who had just come out of a hot bath. He jumped into bed and straight back out again as the cold sheets hit his body. As it was after two in the morning, and I didn't figure on anyone else booking in for the night, I went across to the next chalet, stripped the beds and carried the blankets and counterpanes back to ours. Ron was under his sheet and blanket, which reminded me of a tepee.

'This 'f---ing heater is more off than it's on,' he complained bitterly.

He peeked out and saw my extra blankets. 'Where did you find those?' he asked.

'They fell from the sky,' I replied.

He had on all of his warm jerseys, tracksuit bottoms and three pairs of socks (for the second time on the trip) as well as his fireproof balaclava.

'You look like an out-of-work race driver,' I said. With that, I snuggled under the blankets.

We made an early start next morning, after having had a quick breakfast to fortify us for the long drive home. We had not gone more than a couple of miles when steam began to pour from the bonnet. We were in the middle of the desolate Karoo; the temp outside had dropped to below minus eight; and the bloody car was boiling its head off. Obviously, the water in the radiator had frozen solid overnight with the consequence that the water in the engine block, which was in a similar state, had turned to liquid once more from the heat of the running engine. With nowhere to go, it had boiled away.

I whipped off the top radiator hose, knowing I could fill the block from there. The hot water and steam would eventually melt the ice in the radiator, and we would be on our way once more. Ron fetched the water from the back of the truck and as he returned I could hear him chortling to himself. He deposited the plastic container onto the mudguard, setting it down with a loud bang as I realised that the water in the container was frozen solid.

'Ice for your Scotch,' he commented.

This was the last straw, and I was rolling on the ground with laughter. Once my mirth had abated a little, I told Ron if he wanted to move the van and his precious race car, he would need to get me some water somewhere, perhaps the nearest river.

'That request could only come from Mawson,' he replied disparagingly.

'We are in the middle of a stuffing desert and he sends me off to look for a bloody river'.

I looked out over the Karoo, a combination of suddenly rising hills with arid plains between. The region is covered in fynbos and Karoo scrub, on which large flocks of sheep feast. When they grow fat and are slaughtered, they are famous for the delicious taste of their flesh. Once the exclusive home to the Khoi and the San people, or Karoo Bushmen as most people know them, the Karoo remained relatively untouched for tens of thousands of years. The area was considered uninhabitable – by the Bantu, Dutch and the British. However, following the establishment of the first early settler outposts, and then the building of the railway, it has been steadily occupied. Ron was right; I could not see a patch of green anywhere. 'You'll have to walk back to the hotel then,' I said.

'It's bloody miles' he remarked through chattering teeth.

I remembered that Dennis had given us some Glycol to use in the

Chevron radiator, and it was somewhere in the back of the truck. I mentioned this and Ron disappeared like a mole, rummaging through spares and body parts for the car, which were piled to the roof, returning a few moments later with the container of Glycol. I filled the block, reconnected the hose and started the motor. The car had been facing east and the rising sun had begun to melt the iced-up water in the radiator. The warmed-up Glycol from the block melted what ice was left in the radiator, and as the water and Glycol started to mix and circulate, everything was working again as it should. We managed to arrive home the next day without further incident.

For the next week at the motor club, all we heard from Ron was about his fingers, and how I had almost let him freeze to death on the way there and on the way home. Ron had a Cockney way of telling a story, which was always hilarious and had the whole club in stitches.

After repairing the Alfa, I raced and rallied her for the rest of the year. Ron got the Chevron on the track but I got the impression it was a little bit too much for him, and he was never comfortable in the car. Stock cars were coming to Salisbury and I was asked by the organisers to prepare one. I drove my Alfa around the small oval track, which had no banking. I actually thought a low-powered group two-rally car, or even a mini would be ideal for this event.

On the opening night, I went to see what was in the offing. I got to drive my brother Clive's Chrysler V8 and was able to look at the performance of the various cars. Before the meeting started, the local heroes could put their road cars on the oval, so I borrowed a Mini 1275 S with stage-two mods, which consisted of a camshaft and a cylinder head we had modified to Group Two specification, complemented by a 45 Webber side-draught carburettor, branch exhaust manifold and competition exhaust. I completed my two laps without mishap, setting an outright lap record for the track, three seconds faster than anyone had ever gone around before.

I was right. A Mini would be ideal on the oval, as with foot flat all the way around, the car would go where the front wheels were pointing. Why had no one else thought about a small front-wheel drive car, I wondered? Two weeks later, it was time for my Mini to compete and prove my theory. We put a balloon on the roof and offered a crate of beer to anyone bursting the balloon by flipping the Mini, which meant to turn it over by contact in the corners. Flip it! No one could catch it to flip it!

I qualified on pole, much to the surprise of my friend the commentator, and at the drop of the flag left them all in the dust. I could hold the Mini virtually flat all the way round the oval. My only danger came when lapping the back markers. Two races that first night resulted in two wins and a lap record. Not a bad night considering I got paid for all three and appearance money as well. In the two years I raced the Mini, no one ever popped the balloon, and it was a great favourite with the crowd because of its size.

I had become well known around town, thanks to my successes on the track and my guest appearances on Ron's TV shows. Wherever I went in town, people would nudge their companion, who, if they did not know me, knew the cars. Consequently, I lost sight of who I was. As I look back at that time in my life, I realised I had become someone I did not like at all.

Clive had crashed the E-type. He struck a culvert upon leaving the Mt Hamden Flying Club after numerous chiboolies (beers), damaging the suspension and underside of the sports car quite badly. He was not in a financial position to repair it, consequently M&M took it over with a view to repairing it in slack moments. He had just bought a house and his wife, Paddy, was pregnant at the time, so he had more than his fair share of commitments. The lads in the panel shop repaired the damage in any spare time they had, and upon completion, I took the car for a spin. Driving past the track, I decided to do a few laps and was surprised at how quick it was. As I had someone desperate to buy the Alfa, I sold it and raced the E-type for the rest of the year.

The brakes on the Jag, however, were atrocious and after two laps it was like trying to press a solid wall, and after four, there were no brakes at all. I ordered some special pads from the UK, which improved the longevity of the brakes but did not improve the stopping. The Jag was immense fun to drive and a lot of speed could be scrubbed off by throwing the car sideways into a four-wheel drift, not very healthy for tyre wear but effective for slowing the car down. I won every race I entered with that car.

When my friend Malcolm Swindon mentioned that he was organising a drag strip at the Marlborough track, I knew that the Jag, which was very quick off the line without too much wheel spin, would be a winner. We had put a stopwatch on the big Mustangs and knew that their problem was too much wheel spin. Our E-type was like a high-velocity bullet from the start line but was heavy, and we needed to shed a few pounds. To rid it of its weight, we removed everything from inside as well as bonnet and boot lid and all glass, including the windscreen. The car was now two seconds quicker down the drag strip.

All the South African dragsters and rails were coming for the meeting, but they would be in their own class, being kitted out just for dragging, with massive superchargers and special drag tyres. In practice and qualifying, we were the second fastest to Derek Henderson, who was driving the Ex Sam Tingles LDS 2.7 Climax, a Formula 1 car.

Clive and I were driving the Jag and he had the first run. First and reverse gears are very close on an E-type; the cars were revving and when the lights turned to green, the one car shot forward but Clive shot backwards like a bat out of hell. He had accidentally selected reverse. It was very lucky no one was standing directly behind the car. Race officials and marshals scattered everywhere. It is an easy mistake to make in an E-type, but one that is not easily forgotten by motor club members, and Clive got ragged mercilessly for years afterwards. We won the road car section of the drags by a couple of seconds.

The following year was 1972 and I ran a V6 Capri with a Cosworth spec engine, brake and suspension mods. On the road there was not a Capri that could live with her, and on the track she was blisteringly fast and a perfect lady.

The lease had expired on our Marlborough track where I had cut my teeth. The City Council had given us a lump of bush on the Arcturus Road to clear and build a new track, but first we had to design the new layout. As the South African Grand Prix had just been and gone, Graham Hill flew up to give his input on the design of our track, gleaned from years of F1 racing. We held a big party for him one evening at the motor club, during which I could see him looking at me, trying to put a place to the face. I caught his eye and lifting my right trouser leg pointed to my foot; I mouthed, 'Brands Hatch'.

He clicked immediately and burst into laughter. 'Hello, old chap,' Graham addressed me from five feet away, causing half the motor club to turn and stare. 'Glad to see you're back on two pins again'. I had not told anyone about many of my exploits in Europe; I knew they wouldn't believe them, and that would have pissed me off.

Graham was famous for his humour and had us all in stitches as he relayed the story of the foot and I had my leg pulled for many a year after that. I can safely say, however, that I have the only foot in the world that was carried across the pits at Brands Hatch by a world champion.

Graham came across afterwards with Taffy, and I got to buy him a drink and had the pleasure of a brief chat. What a perfect gentleman and all-round nice guy! I asked him to pass on my regards to my two friends at Lotus Cars. He had forgotten about the diff I had built for them and praised me, saying that it had lasted twice as long as any factory-assembled unit. As it had cost them nothing to boot, he bought me a drink in recompense.

'If you want to race, come and help build the new track,' was the word that went out and help we did. Most of the members spent weekends with picnic lunches building or clearing the site. Ron was a builder by trade and a damned fine one at that, so he was put in charge of all the building. I was his foreman, which was just as well because, left to me, the buildings would have fallen down immediately after the foundations were laid, I certainly didn't inherit any of my Dad's prowess as a builder. Ron knew what was potting, and once work was finished at the end of the day, we would all wander back to the motor club, where we would be joined by the girls at an early evening braai.

Everyone was pretty worn out by about 9 o' clock, and an early start back at the track the next morning necessitated some sleep. This arrangement endured pretty much every weekend until the track was completed. It was a team effort. The Vintage Car Club oldies were as actively involved as we were, and although their vehicles were a few years past racing, the enthusiasm they imparted to us youngsters will never be forgotten. Their stories of racing and rallying 'in the old days,' as they called it, kept us spellbound.

Chapter eighteen
In love again

A T this point I took a step back to look at myself and, though I did not like what I saw, I chose not to change, I found it hard to resist all the beautiful girls giving me the come-on. I believed I could have any girl who took my fancy, and it is fair to say I made the most of everything on offer with no regrets on either side. My best friend Ron often remarked he had never seen me with the same girl twice and all of them 'crackers'.

I had over two hundred and fifty trophies from racing and my life was, I am sure, what most men dream of. I was living in Shangri-La feeling like a young god who could do no wrong. Upon reflection, I realised that I was a self-centred big deal, a conceited, self-opinionated arsehole. I was not a nice person to know.

On Friday nights I drove stock cars in Salisbury, taking a flight after the meeting was finished to go to Bulawayo in order to drive there the following night. On such a Friday evening, I was called up to the stewards' office, situated at the top of the grandstand right next to the public clubhouse, for an inquiry into a racing incident.

As I passed the windows on this particular evening, I looked in at the band playing – they were friends of mine – and noticed two go-go dancers, dancing seductively next to the stage. I became rooted to the floor with my heart in overdrive because of what I saw. One of the dancers was the spitting image of my Britt. I could almost swear she was dressed in the very same hot pants combination Britt had worn on the day she walked across the Dunlop Bridge at Le Mans. Memories came flooding back as I stared at her in disbelief, my heart beating fiercely in my chest. When the music stopped, she looked straight at me and smiled. Her likeness to Britt was uncanny.

The tannoy announced my name again, snapping me out of my trance. I blew her a kiss, (she laughed and blew one back) and continued on my way to see the stewards. I decided then to come back and meet that little madam later on.

Unfortunately, there were problems with the car that night, which meant it had to be repaired in the workshop before the mechanics left for Bulawayo, so I didn't get to go back to the club house as planned. On the red-eye flight to Bulawayo later that night I could not get the image of the girl out of my head. She had brought memories of my Britt flooding back, and I knew I had to see this girl again somehow, somewhere. No girl had had such an effect on me since Britt had died. During the return flight home on Sunday evening, I picked up a newspaper from the pocket in front of my seat and, lo and behold, there was a photograph of her. She was a contestant in the Junior Miss Rhodesia Pageant and her name was Penny Brown.

Unusual for me, I went to the motor club off Jameson Avenue on the Monday after work and could not believe the sight that greeted me. There she was, Penny Brown, looking even more gorgeous than before. My insides turned to jelly as she smiled at me. She was with my mate, Brian, from the band. I already knew her name from the newspapers and that she had just turned seventeen.

'Hello, Brian; hello, Penny,' I said with a casual air I did not feel.

A look of surprise flashed across her face. She was obviously puzzled. 'How do you know my name?' she asked.

'I make it my business to know the names of all the beautiful girls in Salisbury,' I remarked with nonchalance. 'And you are without doubt, the most beautiful girl I have met in a long time'. She seemed a little flustered at my remarks and the fact that I knew her name.

Brian moved down a stool and intimated for me to sit next to Penny. I didn't need a second invitation; I was next to her in a flash.

She excused herself to go to the Ladies. 'Penny asked me to bring her here tonight to meet you,' Brian said. 'I told her you only come here on Wednesday and Friday, but she was insistent'.

'You're quite right' I replied. 'As a rule, those are the nights I would normally be here'.

'She even wanted to fly down to Bulawayo to see you over the weekend,' Brian added.

I felt quite pleased at that snippet of information, but the conversation came to a halt as Penny approached the bar. I turned as she walked into the room and again, I could not believe how much like Britt she was, the exception being she was a younger version with hazel eyes instead of blue.

My intuition told me as she sat down that she was the girl I had been searching for since the death of my beloved Britt, I hoped she would live up to my expectations. I had been with Britt for such a short time, but our relationship had been so perfect and I had really believed her to be my soul mate. An eerie feeling was washing over me as I observed this young girl who I had just been introduced to. Was she to be my second soul mate? As it had been with Britt, so it would be with Penny, and I had this feeling inside that said, 'This is right'. The chemistry between the two of us was magical, something I had been searching for in the partners I had dated after Britt and had never found in any of them. That first evening in the club bar flew by, and by the end of it, I think she had told me everything about herself.

I was experiencing the same special feelings with this girl as I had experienced with Britt: the feeling of being at ease with her and a sense that we belonged together. Excitement welled up inside me, and I determined there and then that nothing and no one would take it away from me this time. That first evening with Penny was almost like a re-enactment of my first few hours with Britt when we had wandered around Le Mans getting to know each other.

Liking turned into intense infatuation almost instantly as the minutes slipped by. I asked if I could take her home. She replied with a huge grin that of course I could. On the ride to her home, she asked me if I would take her to a photo-modelling session the next evening. This time, I was the one to reply that of course I would. I walked Penny to her door, her father answered, courtesies were exchanged, and as it was getting late, I made my excuses and left.

The following evening was rather boring for me but dinner afterwards was great. I held her hand and told her a bit more about myself. After kissing her goodnight, I made up my mind that if it had anything to do with me, she would be my recompense for the loss of Britt. She seemed forlorn when I told her I was flying to Johannesburg the next day for a race at Kyalami. I landed in Jo'burg just after lunch the next day and bought her a gold mesh bracelet from my friend Diane. As soon as the bracelet was safely locked in my bedroom, it was off to the track for the race meeting.

After landing at the airport on my return, I walked to my car to find a beautiful girl next to it. It was Penny! Before taking her home that night, I took her out for a meal and presented her with the bracelet. She was so thrilled.

The next morning, this cheeky woman phoned me and said, 'That bracelet you bought me is solid gold!'

'That's good news,' I responded dryly, 'the salesman told me it was pewter.'

'I have never owned anything so beautiful in my life,' she exclaimed with excitement in her voice.

'I have. Twice,' I said, thinking of my gorgeous Britt and now of my equally gorgeous Penny. On my next trip away, I bought her a solid gold cross and chain, for which I obtained a valuation certificate to save her the trouble of having it valued.

Penny was such a beautiful, simple, uncomplicated person, and I soon grew to love her very much. She was shy and lacked Britt's self-confidence but that would right itself with time; after all, I was twelve plus years her senior, and Ron was old enough to be her father. Who would have thought that this very special person would become my wife eleven months later, albeit to the surprise of half of Rhodesia? Ron was worried as he had now seen me with the same girl more than twice. I even told his wife, Maggie, I was going to marry Penny.

I went with Penny to the finals of the Junior Miss Rhodesia Pageant, where, much to my indignation, she was crowned runner-up. I thought she really deserved to win. It was the first time Penny had done ramp and photographic modelling, so she was very pleased with the result, and I guess that's what mattered. If she was happy, I was happy. After the show, I spoke to the judges, who explained that in the final analysis it was her height, or lack of it, that had weighed against her, even though she was quite tall at five feet seven inches. I couldn't have cared less. I was completely besotted with her and she was fated to become my reason for living.

The Kyalami Nine-Hour Endurance Race was coming up, and I had promised Pen I would take her if her father would permit, which he did. We flew to Johannesburg and booked into the Carlton Hotel, leaving immediately for the track. After practice we headed to a good seafood restaurant in Jeppe Street called Norman's Grill, which belonged to a good friend of mine. He fell instantly in love with Penny and was at great pains to tell her so, which she found quite embarrassing as he was old enough to be her grandfather. She was very young and not that worldly, especially in comparison to the old flirtatious codgers she was seated with.

We had a date to meet Ron at the track early the next morning, so an early retirement was on the cards for that night. The rest of the evening is once again mine to remember. The race itself was good and Penny thoroughly enjoyed watching from the pits with all the international drivers. It gave her a taste of what my life had been like in Europe. We left early, not only to miss the crowds, but to enjoy more of Norman's prawns.

When I arrived back at work on Monday, I found an invitation to a cocktail party waiting for me from Shell, the sponsors of much of my racing career. The guest of honour was to be Douglas Bader, whose biography had been given to me by Mom when I first lost my leg. Penny was committed to doing a modelling assignment, so I went unaccompanied. It was a very nice affair and I felt honoured when this great man found time to come and talk with me.

He spent twenty minutes listening to my story with great interest, and remarked that I should write about it some day as he had thought it very interesting and had been impressed by my achievements. He handed me his card with an invitation to call him if I was ever in the UK. A couple of weeks later, I received a letter from Douglas through Shell in Rhodesia. In his letter, he reiterated that it had been interesting to talk with me, and if I was ever in London, he would like to continue our conversation. I framed the letter and hung it in my office alongside my diplomas. Ron saw it one Friday when we were having a drink in the workshop and was impressed that Douglas Bader had taken the time to write to me.

My brother Clive had left me to join Exide Electric, an auto electrical specialist company, as a director. He saw a more stable future there than with us. Your own business has its ups and downs and at times there seem to be more downs than ups. It is not an easy thing to control, but if you stick it out and ride roughshod over the bumpy bits, the rewards are there in the end. I had employed a couple of auto electricians to take Clive's place, bringing my workforce to ten, all of whom were of the highest calibre.

Thomas, our driver and deliveryman, fancied himself as a bit of a racer, like his boss. Most delivery bikes around town were Honda 50s complete with a box for carrying goods behind the passenger seat. In keeping with our image as speed merchants, our delivery bike was a Suzuki Stinger – a small twin cylinder with competition fairing to go with our racing image. At our next meeting, a race had been scheduled for delivery bikes and we entered Thomas. His animated face was a sight for sore eyes when he showed us his racing outfit sourced from who knows where: boots, a blue boiler suit and touring gloves, all police issue. I didn't want to know and was not going to be the one to ask where he had obtained this racing gear.

At practice the week before the race, he was strutting around the pits like a world champion and one could have sworn he was a friend of Mike Hailwood's or a frontrunner in the TT races. We nicknamed him 'Aggo,' which the commentators picked up on, and after naming a couple of other competitors, it began to sound like an international event. He went around the track slowly, per my instructions, and was riding well but agitating to go faster. I had warned him against it, with the threat of dismissal if he disobeyed. He was like a hound chasing a fox and could not understand my reasoning, which was to keep everyone from knowing how fast our combination was until race day, when it would be too late for anyone to do anything about it.

Race weekend dawned and we arrived at the workshop at seven o' clock in the morning to find Thomas waiting impatiently for us, fully dressed for the race. One would have thought he had a ride on a works Honda. He was so excited he was shaking. We put the numbers on the bike and on the side of his helmet, after which he refused point blank to take it off his head. We loaded the bike and off to the circuit we went. Practice went well and I gave Thomas permission to open the bike up if he wanted, but with the threat that if he dropped it, he would pay for the damages. He qualified on pole by a large margin, and his bragging in the pit enclosure was something to be heard. I can still see the smile on his face to this day. Thomas ran away with victory by half a lap. He won a large floating trophy and a small replica, which was his to keep.

In the weeks that followed, he had numerous admirers around, and he would recount his various laps with graphic interpretations and peals of laughter. There was always lots of 'AGH-AGH' as the tale of the win was spun.

Thomas went on leave, taking both trophies with him to show his relatives and friends, and I was surprised to see him back after a week but looking very ill. He told me the inganga (witch doctor) had put a spell on him for committing adultery, and he was going to die. I told him not to believe such rubbish and that he was too much of an educated man to be taken in by the inganga's nonsense.

He had brought the floating trophy back and asked if he could extend his leave to put his affairs in order. I told him to go and think on what I had said and come back when he was better. A few days later, as I turned the corner to get to our workshop, his wife and family members were waiting for me. I knew without being told that Thomas was dead. Such is the power of witchcraft and superstition in Africa.

Probably without exception, the culture of all African tribes is saturated with ancestral worship and a high level of superstition that no amount of logic can dislodge, even for an educated man. According to Zulu mythology there exists a dwarf-like water sprite considered to be a mischievous and evil spirit that can become invisible by swallowing a pebble. It is known as a tokoloshe and is called upon by malevolent people to cause trouble for others. At its least harmful, a tokoloshe can be used to scare children, but its power extends to bringing illness and even death to the victim. The way to get rid of him is to call in the inganga, who has the power to banish it – at a cost of course. The tokoloshe emerges after dark to wreak havoc and is also renowned for raping women and biting off the toes of sleeping people.

According to legend, one way to keep the tokoloshe at bay is to put a brick beneath each leg of the bed. When entering an African's dwelling you would often notice the legs of the beds are all up on bricks and it was impossible to convince any believer of the absurdity of this. I have an idea that this myth was created by an inganga who, desperate to sell bricks, also had an appetite for toes and the fairer sex. By cleverly promoting a belief in the tokoloshe I am positive he became the top brick salesman in his company.

In Rhodesia at that time, it was expected of employers to bury their employees, and after Thomas's family had arranged the funeral with me, they left for home. It was a sad day for all of us and after work we went to the motor club to hold a wake in his honour. Most of the members knew Thomas because he usually returned their cars after repair, and he was well liked. The wake turned into quite a party and a sizeable collection was taken for his family.

Motor racing still filled most of my life. I was racing at least nine times a month, though stock cars were getting to be more of a drag than a pleasure, as my true love was track racing and, of course, my Penny. One Friday at the Glames track in Salisbury, the car floor was slippery with petrol. I looked around to find the cause of the petrol leak and found a pipe, which had come adrift from the gravity feed 5-litre tank mounted on the crash bars. The motor cut out, and as I unclasped my seat belt to reach back and reattach the pipe, I was hit from behind by another car. I was pushed into the fence at racing speed, and had I been strapped in, I would have been fine, but with no belts, my body was hurled into the crash bars alongside my seat.

I felt a searing pain in my right rib cage and could not breathe. It hurt like hell, but my surgeon Mr Nangle had said once, 'If you can't feel it, it's serious'. On that basis I convinced myself I was not badly hurt.

The race had been stopped, and marshals and medics arrived at the car as I slumped over the wheel, in and out of consciousness, but still able to hear snatches of conversation. A medic entered the car through the space that normally held the windscreen and pulled me back into the seat. I heard myself groaning in pain as I slipped back to that silent dark world where the pain abated. I had to be taken out through the windscreen, which took about half an hour, but once I had been placed on a body board, I felt more comfortable. I was given morphine for the pain before transportation to the hospital.

I was also hitched to an oxygen tank as it had been ascertained

I had a number of broken ribs and a collapsed lung. Being heavily sedated for the pain, I remember very little of the incident. When I eventually came to, I noticed that although the pain was still severe, my breathing had become easier because my lung had been re-inflated in the ambulance. I had broken six ribs and had to spend a couple of days in hospital.

Just before six the next morning I spotted a copy of the *Herald*. I had once again made the front page of the *Herald* with a picture of me being lifted through the windscreen aperture of a stock car. The headline read, 'Driver Critically Injured in Stock Car Crash…Race-car Driver Dick Mawson…blah, blah blah'. Oh dear God, my mother! I asked the nurse to bring me a phone and dialled Mom's number to assure her I was fine. Twenty minutes later she walked in with her usual 'Oh, Dee,' followed almost immediately by Ken and my Pen. Apparently, Ken had read the account in the paper and had immediately woken Penny, who had begged to be brought to me, even though it was practically the crack of dawn. Before I knew it, I had a room full of visitors.

Everyone left when the doctor on duty began to make his rounds, and once they had been convinced I was not about to not die on them. Mom told me later that my face had been grey and contorted with pain. I was heavily strapped, and if I sneezed or laughed, the pain was unbearable. I was allowed out on the Sunday morning and arrived home to find my Penny had been dropped off by her dad. I was well looked after by my two girls and come Monday morning, Mom did her damnedest to stop me going to work. I was just as determined to go and only got my way after lengthy arguments, a hard-fought battle, and lots of promises. I was not physically able to do much, as anyone who has had rib injuries will confirm. I felt as if I was suffocating and needed to take deep breaths, but when I did, it was extremely painful.

Although I heal fast and have a high pain threshold, I decided to be sensible for a change and give racing a miss the following week. Also, my two girls were being very nasty to me and issued the direst of ultimatums if I didn't co-operate. I could see that every word was meant, so I gave in gracefully. Two weeks later I was back at stock cars again on pole, although I was heavily padded and looking like the Michelin Man. The whole exercise was painful but not unbearable, and though I normally slipped in and out of the car with ease, this time it took a few minutes to load myself into the hot seat and out again. That night I won both heats, but I paid for it with a pain in my chest that persisted until the following Wednesday.

By Friday, however, the pain had abated and once again I was on pole. The race started, and by lap four I had built up a sizeable lead. Red lights came on around the circuit to indicate an accident somewhere and an immediate stop by all competitors was expected to prevent possible injury to a driver. I halted in the middle of the track, when an almighty bang from behind sent me and my car flying through the air. My head snapped back with the sudden impact, breaking the padded headrest, and my helmet hit a retaining bar on the driver's safety cell with such force that the helmet had a serious split in it from its impact with the bar.

One of the drivers in a Citroen travelling at full speed had hit me from behind and claimed later he had not seen the red flashing lights, indicating a stop to the race. It transpired he had been involved in the crash that had brought the race to a stop in the first place. My car apparently shot into the air like a cork from a champagne bottle, straight into the crash barriers lining the track.

My helmet was badly cracked where it had hit the bar, and I am sure, if it had been any other helmet, I would not be here today. I was transported to hospital again, but this time I could not phone Mom as I was in a quiet, dark place away from the pain, where at least I was spared the familiar exclamation of, 'Oh, Dee,' as my mother walked into the ward. My Penny had come with me in the ambulance and burst into tears when Mom arrived. I had been unconscious since my head hit the bar, and she was scared I was going to die. I had eight stitches, a bald patch and a nose that wouldn't stop bleeding – courtesy of the idiot in the Citroen.

I don't really remember much of the next week. I sustained a severe concussion and cracked some of the old and some new ribs to boot. I also had safety belt bruises in unmentionable places. I was connected to an assortment of bells and whistles, completely oblivious to what was going on around me. The RMSA found the driver of the Citroen guilty of dangerous driving and banned him from racing for six months.

I always felt guilty about the burdens my mother had to bear as a result of all my dreadful accidents. It was more than any mother should have to go through, but an overwhelming inner urge drove me ever forward with the insatiable desire to excel in everything I did.

I was out of hospital within a few days but was not allowed to drive for a month, which was just as well because I kept having dizzy spells and would pass out and drop to the floor, which was most embarrassing. Severe headaches plagued me twenty-four hours a day as well as frequent heavy nosebleeds, and a constant nagging pain in my rib cage. The worst part of the whole experience was 'No nookies' which was really exasperating.

I saw Dr Pockroy after ten days and he advised me to lay off motor sport for at least a year to allow healing to take place. There was a danger that if my body took any more beatings I could haemorrhage internally and that would be the end of me. My ribs and head were very sore, and I had to concede that if I carried on the way I had done in the last month, I would die. Memories of my F1 hydroplane came to mind and I thought maybe I needed to look into playing 'tiddlywinks' as the alternative sport that Mom had always encouraged me to take up.

I now had two women nagging me, one for each ear, but my consolation was Penny. That most gorgeous girl of mine had consented to marry me. I think if I had not been involved with her, my decision would have been different. The helmet was returned to my supplier in SA, and by return they sent me a brand new helmet. My injuries needed time to heal, and I was also in dire need of a break from it all so I could relax and recuperate fully.

Penny and I went to Beira for a few days, and Carlos Brito gave us the penthouse suite in his new Dom Carlos Hotel, all expenses 'on the house'. We ate prawns and lobster for breakfast, lunch and dinner, and I came away from there feeling reborn, thanks largely to Penny, who was easy to be with and with whom I could relax.

For the first time in ages we had free weekends to do with what we liked, and many of them were spent at the lake water skiing and enjoying family and friends. On one memorable occasion with Penny on board, we flew in a Cessna 180 hired from the local flying club to Bumi Hills on the shores of Lake Kariba for lunch. We buzzed the hotel as a signal for them to arrange transport for us from the airfield. Flying over the lake, the pilot banked the aircraft over an island where I noticed elephants walking from island to island. He flew in low so Penny could see the amazing spectacle beneath us. She was fascinated and delighted to be able to watch the elephants walking on the lake bottom, with just their trunks sticking out of the water like snorkels. To add to the phenomenon playing out beneath us, a big bull that was watching the cows come onto the island stood on his back legs and trumpeted so loudly the sound was clearly heard above the noise of the engine. We banked around the island and flew back towards the hotel, buzzing the strip to clear any duiker or other small antelope that might be grazing there.

We had a lovely lunch of 'kapenta' (a small sardine type fish), followed by fillets of Kariba bream with chips. There was a variety of game dishes available on the menu, including crocodile steaks and elephant trunk but I doubt they could have surpassed the taste of the bream and kapenta. In view of the flight home, we had to be satisfied with orange squash or lemonade as opposed to any form of alcohol, but no one really minded. Wild animals congregated around the dining boma, begging for scraps. Penny's favourite was a very large elephant, completely wild, which had taken a shine to her. He devoured the bread rolls in double quick time and was aggravating for more. Upon request, the waiter brought her a loaf of brown bread, which she fed him, not wanting to offend the big fellow. The bread seemed to pacify him before he moved on to see what the next table had to offer. The antics of the various animals fascinated my Penny. We took off with plenty of time to spare for a landing before dark, as none of us on board were night-rated pilots.

I had made up my mind to spend the rest of my life with Penny and, fortunately for me, she was in complete agreement. I was in the process of negotiating a partnership in a dealership, which would mean a move away from Salisbury to Bulawayo, a distance of three hundred miles.

Penny would have to be part of it, as I was not prepared to leave her in Salisbury. I sold the Mini stock car to Ed Hubbard, the man offering me the partnership in the Jaguar and BMC franchise in Bulawayo. Ed ran the car sales side of the business, and it would be up to me to run the workshop, spares and fuel outlets. I had already been carrying out many of his repairs in my Salisbury workshops, but since these workshops were too small, it seemed like a good idea.

Ed had walked out of Chile in South America, followed closely by the relevant authorities, and was a flamboyant, larger-than-life character, keen to get into motor racing. He thought the world of Penny and me, and we both liked him. Little did I know what an accomplished con man he was, and that he had escaped jail in Chile by the skin of his teeth. For all that he was a likeable character. I flew to Bulawayo to look at Sager Motors and decided to accept Ed's invitation to join him.

Pen's father was in hospital dying of lung cancer, and we both wondered what was the best way to approach her parents on the subject of her coming to Bulawayo with me. It's strange the way fate sometimes intervenes; we were about to approach her folks with a very elaborate story detailing the reasons why she should come to Bulawayo with me when my Penny discovered she was pregnant. The news delighted my mother and brought a grin to her face that reminded me of a Cheshire cat. I suppose she thought this turn of events might quench the competitive fire that burned inside me, and I would be transformed into a family man, complete with slippers, pipe, Scotch and soda, as well as a spaniel at my feet.

So a wedding was on the cards before our move and we set about planning the event. With Ken in hospital, Mom, with my future mother-in law's permission, set about organising our wedding, which was to be the event of the century if she had anything to do with it. We were married by my good friend Earl Davies, who had been in the Royal Rhodesian Air Force (RRAF) during the Second World War with our Prime Minister Ian Smith in 237 and 130 Squadrons.

My best man was my best friend, Ron Lupson, who, as the wedding march rang out, looked back to where Penny was walking towards us on her father's arm and said to me, 'You want to see what's coming down the aisle for you, my friend. She's gorgeous!'

A few seconds later she was standing next to me. Ronnie was right; Penny took my breath away and was, without a doubt, the most beautiful bride I had ever seen. Taking her hand in mine, I gazed at this beautiful woman who was to be my wife. She was dressed in a peach-coloured creation, her head adorned in a summery, wide-brimmed hat. Her mom had done her proud, and I could see the look of pride in Ken's eyes as he handed his youngest daughter into my keeping.

As we left the church, I turned, looking directly at Penny, and said: 'You are the most beautiful bride this world has ever seen. I am a lucky man. Thank you for wanting to be my wife; I promise you I will be the best husband in the world to you'. She squeezed my hand and whispered in my ear, 'Dick, I love you so very much and will try to make you a good wife'.

Our reception was held in the garden of our lovely home on Jameson Avenue, and the big marquees Mom had arranged for the guests were filled to capacity with not only personal friends but with workshop and hotel staff as well. We had wanted an open wedding and that's what it was: a very happy and wonderful way for us to start our married life together. We did not go on a honeymoon as I was closing down the business and shipping the equipment to Bulawayo. Instead, we stayed in the Presidential Suite at Meikles Hotel, and after the weekend moved to the Penthouse Suite at the Jameson Hotel.

The move progressed smoothly and by the end of the month, we had relocated, although Penny felt very lost in a new town where she knew no one. I bought her a black Labrador puppy for company. She christened the dog 'Judy', and she also brought her miniature Maltese poodle 'Suzy' from Salisbury.

My Pen found herself occupied most of the day with the dogs and setting up our new home. It must have been very difficult for a young eighteen-year-old to be thrown into the company of thirty and forty-year olds, and looking back, I think she handled it all very well. During this time, I had several meetings with the Chev Dealer Team, after which I agreed to purchase a Chev Firenza Can Am, probably one of the fastest saloon cars in the world at the time. All I could think of was Mom's face when she learnt of my latest acquisition, but I now had my Penny to hide behind.

At the time I was swollen-headed, full of my own self-importance and thought myself to be a big deal, but my day of reckoning was fast approaching. Every Friday Penny flew back to Salisbury to be with her dad, who was sinking fast. When Rhodesia's annual Rhodes and Founders weekend came up, we finally got around to taking our honeymoon. We stayed at the Polana Mar Hotel in Lourenço Marques, where we were able to spend time with Penny's sister and husband, who lived there. Afterwards, we travelled to Johannesburg where we had made a reservation for the Honeymoon Suite at the Carlton Hotel.

Naturally, we booked a table at Norman's Grill for dinner, and he was so thrilled at the news that we had tied the knot, he wouldn't hear of us paying for a thing.

I took Penny to meet a friend of mine, Diana Bomberg, to choose an engagement ring from the selection in her jewellery shop. With her eye on Penny's bump, Diana commented wryly that an engagement ring was 'a bit late in the day'. Penny looked at various rings, but I could see she had her eye on one that was rather expensive. She asked me which one I would choose, and I pointed out a small, insignificant ring at the back of the case, which was the cheapest one on display. Her face dropped, I leant across, picked up her obvious favourite and slipped it on her finger. Her eyes lit up and I asked her if she would be my wife. We were already married, but it seemed to be the right thing to do.

Penny became flustered and blushed even more furiously when customers in the shop stopped to applaud. My friend, the manager at the Carlton, who was in on the whole thing, came across with a magnum of champagne, compliments of the hotel. It was like the loaves and fishes all over again as we shared the bottle with all who were there in the shop. I hugged her and whispered she could keep the ring if she ever wanted a divorce. I am lucky she chose to kick the fibreglass shin as the other one would have been rather painful.

We arrived back in Bulawayo to find the newspapers all abuzz with the fact that one of the fastest cars in the world (my latest acquisition) was on its way to Rhodesia. Although Mom had seen the photos and the write-ups, she had resigned herself to the fact that I had to live out my own destiny, and it was up to Penny and me to fulfil it.

I had taken a six-month break to allow all my injuries to heal and now it was high time to race again. I was racing a Camaro Z28 and a Corvette Stingray for Auto Auctions in the Formula R races. It was all like a dream and it reminded me so much of my first year in Europe. I felt like the young god the Africans perceived me to be, that god who had fallen from the sky all those years ago. Everything I touched seemed to turn to gold. We had bought a lovely new house in Burnside, and Penny seemed a lot happier when she befriended a young couple who had moved in next door. The Salisbury crowd came to Bulawayo once a month to race at the Falls Road Circuit, and the usual Friday night party would run into the wee hours, leaving our house looking like a bomb site the next morning, with bodies and empty bottles lying in every conceivable nook and cranny.

At one racing event, I was driving the Corvette in a sports car race when I saw Ron coming up behind me in his Chevron. In his wisdom, he had decided to go around the outside of my car and got onto the marbles (small balls of rubber from the racing slicks) outside the racing line. He lost control in a big way when he hit the right front of my Corvette, spinning his Chevron off into the bush on the outside of the track. I ran from my car to find Ron sitting in a daze; I unfastened his seat belts and pulled him from the car. Taking off his helmet, I asked if he was alright and he asked what had happened.

'I don't know, Ron. You hit the front of my car and the last I saw, you were airborne and heading into the bush.'

Debris was scattered all over the place and he was lucky that he had not hit any of the hefty trees that dotted the track side or the drainage ditch about ten feet in front of where his car had stopped. The incident shook Ron up and on his return to Salisbury, he sold the car to my friend and co-driver, Isaac Codron.

As a replacement, Ron decided to buy a Capri Perana V8 from Basil Green in Johannesburg and asked me to go with him to view the car. I flew Pen up to Salisbury to see her dad on the Thursday, and early the next day Ron and I arrived in Jo'burg. We tested the car at Kyalami on Saturday. Even though the power from the 302 V8 was more than he had been used to, Ron felt more at home in it than he had been in the Chevron and the deal was done.

The following week Mom phoned to tell me my dad was in hospital in a coma, from which he was not expected to recover. Penny and I returned to Salisbury to see both our dads, and I knew in my heart that for me, it was time to say goodbye to mine. I held Dad's hand but there was no response. He looked terrible; his stomach was huge and his pallor was very yellow. He was a chronic alcoholic and I knew he would not survive. I leant across and whispered in his ear that he was the best dad in the whole world, that I loved him dearly and was there to say goodbye. I will swear to this day I felt a slight tightening of his grip on my hand.

Having said my goodbye, we left and went from there to Ken who was also not looking so good. He could still communicate but he knew that his time was close, and he clung to his daughter as we said goodbye. Penny was very upset and burst into tears, believing she would probably never see him alive again.

With both our dads in critical condition, the effect on my Penny was evident. Ken had begged her to leave some cigarettes with him when we left, which she did, feeling they could do no further harm than had already been done. His days were definitely numbered. I knew I would never see him again and so did he because as he held me close, he asked me to 'look after my girl'. I assured him that was my intention. As we flew home that night, we were both quiet, reflecting on the two men we had come to see, and wondering when the calls would come to inform us of their deaths.

We did not have long to wait. My call came the following Thursday. I did not go up for the funeral as I had said my goodbyes. Dad's ashes were scattered in Lake Mac; it was late autumn in the year 1973 when my dear dad left us.

Ed and I decided to put on an invitational 24-hour race at the Falls Road Circuit as an advertising campaign for the company. The race was to be for standard road cars on road tyres and with limited modifications to engines. As far as brakes and suspension were concerned, anything would be allowed. The Rhodesia Motor Sport Association put together some rules and agreed to oversee the event.

There were fourteen cars entered, each with a minimum of two drivers per car. I chose a late model 1800 SSS Datsun from Ed's stock and brought it across to the workshop to prepare. Ed loaned Ron an Opel GT from stock, and Ron's mechanics arrived a few days before the race to prepare the car. There was a mixture of Renaults, Cortinas, Mini Coopers, GSM Darts, Alfas, Opels and Datsuns.

The race started at noon on Saturday and restaurants, nightclubs, various fair-type stalls and snack bars were laid on for spectators to frequent if they got bored with the race. All the proceeds from the event were to go to a local charity.

We returned to the pits every two hours for a change of driver, refuelling, and tyre changes if needed. Caravans had been parked at the back of the pits for our use, so that Penny and the girls could keep us well fed (although, thinking back, I never did get the Lobster Thermador I ordered before the event). We were able to rest and catch forty winks in the caravans, and I even managed to get a little bit of what I fancied during one break – with my Pen, of course.

The Datsun was by far the quickest car and a comfortable drive. It did exactly what we asked of it, and as we sped on through the afternoon and night, we built up a formidable lead. I started my next stint all bright-eyed and bushy-tailed at three in the morning, but nearly finished as a mangled wreck.

While going through the esses, there was a loud bang from the front of the car, and something shot into the air. The left front dropped into the tarmac and the car started to roll. I threw the wheel to the left and felt the car lift off the tar; it spun like a top into the trees at the side of the track where it came to a stop. I jumped out only to find the left front wheel had broken. I tried to drive the car but the front dug in and I knew I was going nowhere. I waited forty minutes in vain to be rescued and decided to walk back to the pits. When I saw the truck coming belatedly around the inner road, I ran to meet it.

I was fuming and asked where the hell they had been. It was only because the control tower had been doing a lap count that anyone realised I had been missing for the last twenty minutes. Had I been trapped in the car and injured, I could have bled to death. No one had missed me! Panic from my crew had set in only when they realised I hadn't been seen in a while, and they dispatched the truck to find me. Someone had eventually woken up to the fact that their car was not clocking up laps on the circuit.

I changed the tyre, and as I left to re-join what was left of the race, I shouted that I wanted the other three wheels changed at the next stop. When I next passed the pit, I noticed the crew milling around. I double-dipped the lights and sped off into the darkness. Ed had obviously been kicking a few asses. Arriving for my scheduled stop, I waited till the car was back on the circuit before I started to kick ass myself. We had lost more than an hour to our closest rivals being driven by Ron Lupson and his two co-drivers. I didn't think there was any way we could catch them.

As luck would have it, the Opel came into the pits with a broken front suspension, which required a lengthy repair, allowing us to regain the lead. At about seven-thirty that morning the car began to misfire. We replaced everything and though I racked my brains, I could think of nothing which might be causing the problem. The Opel was slowly but surely closing the gap between us because of the time we had lost in the pits, so in the end I decided to take the chance and run the car as she was.

With an hour to go, we were overtaken and had to eat their dust. I was a faster, more experienced driver than Ed, so I took over the driver's seat. On my second lap out the misfire disappeared as if by magic, and the car leapt into life. I began reeling the Opel in, and as it crossed the line at midday to win, I was only 200 yards behind. Another lap and I would have had them, but it was not to be. We could not have planned a better finish. Braai fires were lit to cater to the crowds, who had steadily filled the track during the course of the morning with most people staying on for the prize-giving. When the trophy was presented to Ron and his two Amigos, I asked him where he had found the inganga to put a hex on our car. I was the MC for the event and Penny handed out the prizes. Once we had completed our tasks, we relaxed and enjoyed the revelry, which went on late into the night.

If nothing else, Ed Hubbard was a very good marketer and salesman. He had his sales staff moving through the crowd offering discounts on various cars and giving potential customers an on-the-spot valuation of their cars. His sales manager had brought ninety percent of the stock to the track on the Friday evening before the event, and quite a few had been sold during the race, which, of course, was what it was all about. The next morning the newspapers reported the despairs and triumphs of the race, and there was a rather large photo of the 'Three Amigos' standing on their car with 'Auto Auctions' plastered all over it – priceless free advertising for our company.

Chapter nineteen
The 'Little Chev'

THE next weekend Penny flew to Salisbury to see her dad, and I went to Kyalami to collect and race the Little Chev. The car was not at the track as I had expected it to be and a bit of a confrontation ensued between me and Monty Brett, the Chev Dealer Team Manager.

'Why is my car not here for me to qualify for the race?' I asked him in annoyance.

'Well, although we received notification that the money was on its way, it hasn't actually been received as of this moment,' was his reply.

'It just so happens that I have confirmation from the bank that the money was transferred on Tuesday as well as a confirmation from GM that they had received the money,' I responded angrily. 'If my car is not at this track by the time I return from my hotel with proof the money has been paid, you can consider the deal cancelled, and I shall have no hesitation in suing you for damages and costs,' I continued in rage.

I went to Kyalami Ranch where I was staying and got on the phone to Barclays, Botswana. They assured me that the money had been transferred the previous Tuesday and sent me a telex to that effect with reference numbers, etc. I took the telex to the track and together with my own confirmation from GM I had received in Bulawayo, I shoved it under Monty's nose and was quickly informed that my car was on its way.

It transpired that the money had indeed arrived on the Tuesday, but the accountant had noted the transfer without telling anyone, and then sent me confirmation of receipt. There were only fifteen minutes of qualifying time left by the time the Little Chev was delivered to the track, and by the time I got onto the track, there was five minutes to spare. I had never driven the car before, and it was five years since I had driven anything as powerful, apart from a few laps in Ron's Capri a few weeks previously.

I tapped her on the bonnet and said under my breath, 'You'll have to be tolerant with me, my girl'.

As I drove to get some heat into the tyres and other components, the first lap gave me some idea of the apexes to the corners. The last lap flag was out as I crossed the finish line, so this would have to be my qualifier, for which I managed a creditable fourth place on the grid behind Basil van Rooyen in the works Chev Can Am, and two Basil Green V8 Capris in the hands of South Africa champions.

I had nearly lost the car twice on my qualifying lap and decided it would be prudent to spend the first five laps of the race getting to know her. Thereafter, I could boot it and see where I ended up. Not in the catch fences, I hoped. We got to the track early, and once I had checked the car through and adjusted the seat and pedals to suit me, I felt much more confident about the race that lay ahead. I took my place on the second row of the grid after warming the car up on the stands. At the drop of the flag, I accelerated away cautiously and dropped in behind the two Capris.

Basil van Rooyen, who was on pole in the other Can Am, led into the first corner and I held steady in fourth place. Probably because the tyres were still cold, Basil slid off the track, just clipping the dirt with his left rear tyre but didn't lose the lead. He was leaving the three of us racing behind him and the rest of the field in the dust. I knew my Chev had the ability to be up there with him; it was the driver who didn't know the car that worried me.

By lap five, I had settled down and felt comfortable in the car, so I purposefully and confidently hit the apex at Leeukop very late. I came out on the inside of the two Capris with my foot flat on the accelerator.

The Little Chev shot past them in a power drift, leaving two black stripes from the rear tyres. The handling and power of the car exceeded any expectation I had, and I felt a thrill run through my body. My Little Chev excited me like no other car had done before, and I knew then that this was be the beginning of a lifelong love affair. By the time I hit the next corner I was fifty yards in front of my nearest competition, but Basil had disappeared into the distance. I set off in hot pursuit, though still driving with care as I had only driven seven laps in the car. As I came out of Leeuwkop on the next lap, I realised I was catching up with Basil at a rate of knots and my first thought was that he had slowed down to wait for me – as if!

As I shot past him to go into the lead just after the corner before the pits, I noticed the tyre on his left rear was flat, and he was entering the pit lane to have it replaced. I was now well in the lead, my usual position, with the Capris nowhere in sight, and that was how the race finished. A win first time out in a fantastic little car, a gorgeous wife at home and a prosperous business: what more could anyone ask for? I thought this had to be the best year of my life. Just as well I didn't know it was actually destined to be one of my worst. At the time, of course, I was elated and learnt later when I phoned Penny, that if Ken (my father-in-law) and she had shouted any louder, while listening to race commentary on the radio, I would have heard them eight hundred miles away on my slowing down lap. Ken had been allowed out of hospital for the weekend and, surprisingly, he sounded full of beans and told me how proud he was to have me as a son-in-law, and that he hoped to see me soon. It was a hope that would not be fulfilled; that was the last time I spoke with him.

The crowd was on its feet, clapping and cheering. I don't think they expected a one-legged driver from Rhodesia to blow away their champions. At that particular moment I cannot begin to describe my feelings; it belongs only to those who have achieved the pinnacle of their ambitions. I had been racing for sixteen years, and this was by far the most prestigious race I had won. I would never forget, of course, the seven wins I had with *Skeeter,* my beloved boat, and the first time I took her out; nor indeed my index win in the international three hour at Bulawayo. These days would be etched in my memory in indelible ink forever. Similarly long-lived would be the debt I owed my parents for their support and advice in all things pertaining to my endeavours – to be the best at whatever I attempted.

South Africa Mirror cameras were pointed in my direction with eager newsmen poking microphones in my face; it appeared everyone wanted my attention. Ironically, before the race, if my name had been mentioned, nobody would have shown the slightest bit of interest. I felt like a true celebrity as autograph hunters queued by the pit door, clamouring for my attention.

It was a bit of an anti-climax for me in a way. I was disappointed the race was over before I had had the chance to really get to know the car, and I couldn't wait to get behind the controls again. It was her sheer brute power and impeccable handling that had my adrenalin flowing, and I knew it would be a long time before we parted company. I spent a half hour signing autographs before I could get into the changing room to take off my overalls and have a welcome shower.

I bumped into Basil as he came out of the changing rooms, and he told me his car had picked up a puncture on the first lap when he slid off the track, and he had battled a deflating tyre from then until it started shredding. The fact that he'd driven so far with an ailing car was a reflection of his ability as a driver and the quality of the car he had developed.

I could not wait to get back to the hotel to phone my beloved Penny. When I got through to her it sounded like half of Rhodesia was at the house, and there was so much noise I could hardly hear her speak. It was made twice as bad because she was crying while trying to speak over the noise in the background.

I left the car at a friend's workshop, planning to return to

Johannesburg the following weekend to acquaint myself with my 'new baby' and to spend a couple of hours at Kyalami driving round the track and setting up the car to suit me. The newspapers in Johannesburg printed such banner headlines as 'Sparkling Début' and 'Rhodesian's Surprise Début'. I was very proud of my achievement, I must say, and I flew home to Rhodesia to find the newspapers there had also given my win a lot of coverage. It had been a different story before I left to collect the Can Am, when I hadn't been given much publicity at all, except the mention that 'a Little Chev should be arriving in Rhodesia shortly'. I had phoned Brian at the *Herald* before I left for South Africa, but he had not bothered to return my call. Now it was a different story, and he flew to Bulawayo for a full story and some photos.

The following weekend I took a flight to Johannesburg on Thursday evening, after I had put Penny on a plane to Salisbury. We had use of the track for the Friday, and my good friend Percy Trehare from Champion Spark Plugs was waiting for me. He could read a spark plug from a motor and tell you what the motor had for breakfast. He was, to put it bluntly, brilliant. The best lap time I had achieved the week before was one minute thirty-seven point eight seconds. Before long I was circulating at one minute thirty-two point two seconds, which I was very happy with, especially considering that the tyres were very used. Basil Green's Perana, fitted with a Gurney Weslake motor, had circulated Kyalami at a lap time of one minute thirty-five seconds, as did the Cologne Capri with Jochen Mass at the wheel. We were nearly two seconds a lap up on them. These were without doubt two of the fastest production racing saloon cars in the world in 1973. I knew there would be another second to be gained with new tyres, and to that end, I ordered a couple of sets from Mrs Mac at Dunlop in preparation for the upcoming nine-hour race.

On the home front at this time, I noticed that my beautiful wife was eating more than usual and her thickening waistline was becoming evident. She had a little bump where before she had had a flat stomach.

It was, of course, Richard Junior beginning to show. My Penny was even more beautiful and glowed with her pregnancy, so much so that heads turned to admire her wherever we went.

Mom came down from Salisbury to see us and the new house – in that order, I hope. When we collected her from the airport, she burst into tears and hugged me close. 'I notice from the press that my famous son has been doing rather well in the tiddlywinks championships,' she said with a twinkle in her eye. The tiddlywinks championship was, of course, the joke between us, but I had the distinct feeling she was very proud of me. We had to wait while she collected 'something' from the cargo section, and I expected the 'something' to be for our new house. She walked out with this baby giraffe on a lead. No, sorry, it was a pedigree Afghan puppy, which Mom knew I had always wanted. He was a beautiful golden colour, very aristocratic in appearance with legs that appeared far too long for his head and body. We christened him 'Khayam'.

Penny, Mom and I spent three lovely days together, and Mom had the chance to get to know her daughter-in-law a little better. It was my greatest wish that these two women, who meant the most to me in the world, would get along. Sadly, not all our wishes are fulfilled this side of eternity. My unspoken assessment of the relationship that existed between my mother and my wife in the unfolding years was that perhaps my mother, who to all intents and purposes had been the Alpha female in my life, may have found it difficult to finally cut the apron strings and hand over her crown to another woman. I believe the strong bond that had existed between us throughout the years was caused in part by the extreme trials, tribulations and victories she had shared with me. Also, I had always dated sophisticated women of the world, and to my mother, Penny must have seemed like a mere child in need of her guidance and wisdom. Penny vehemently rejected any help my mother offered, and I think she resented the implication that she needed any help in the first place. Such are the misunderstandings of the good old generation gap. It is also possible that Penny harboured an element of jealousy because of the bond my mother and I shared.

Whatever the underlying causes, their relationship, though falling far short of what I had hoped for, settled into one of an unspoken truce. They tolerated one another with politeness and decorum out of love and respect for me, and for the children yet to be born. For all that, I like to believe and choose to believe, there were moments of genuine affection bubbling under the surface between them. How can mere man ever hope to understand the foibles and contradictions of a woman? Who can live with them? Who can live without them?

Newspaper reports were printed about my invitation to drive the nine-hour race at Kyalami as part of the Chev dealer team, which included the SA rally champion, Jan Hettema. He had rallied a Little Chev that year and had won the SA championship. Jan had raced in the nine-hour many times with great success, and I knew I could not have found a better co-driver. He was particularly quick and consistent during the night hours, and that would complement my own skills.

Chapter twenty
Into the fire

THE Little Chev in 1973 was the fastest production saloon race car in the world, and I am proud to say that I won more races with my Can Am than any other driver – living or dead. I had another race coming up in South Africa, but after that was over and done with, I would be bringing the car back to Rhodesia with me. She needed a thorough going over in preparation for the upcoming nine-hour endurance race, and there were a number of modifications I wanted to make, such as larger ducts for brake cooling, a bigger fuel tank, and a re-spray in our company colours. I also wanted to record a time on the Falls Road Circuit so that any modifications or developments on the car could be compared with the Kyalami times. I saw Penny off to Salisbury and left for Johannesburg, feeling really excited and exhilarated at the prospect of driving such a fast car again.

Basil was to make an attempt to break the one hundred mile an hour lap in a saloon car at the Rand autumn trophy race meeting. It would be a feat which no other saloon car had come close to achieving on the Kyalami circuit. The Little Chev was the only saloon car with anywhere near the times required to lap Kyalami at this speed. He made the attempt on a clear track but was eight tenths of a second away from the magical ton. So it was decided to use me to slingshot Basil into the kink before the pits. He followed me at full speed through the esses, and I hit the apex very late into Leeukop, with the result that I came out of the corner on the inside under full power with Basil so close behind me it would have been difficult to push a cigarette paper between us. I kept on the inside going into the kink, and Basil, with full throttle, slipped out of the slipstream to pass me on the outside and up over the crest to cross the finish line two tenths short of the magical time. As far as I know that was the quickest time a saloon car ever went around Kyalami in the early seventies. Soon after that, South Africa had petrol restrictions and all racing came to an end.

Meanwhile, the two Little Chevs were on the front row of the grid for the next race at Kyalami, and an exciting centre-spread picture was published of the two cars dicing together in *Car Magazine*. We were off the line like a couple of hares with a pack of hounds after us, and by the time we got to the kink, just before the pits, no cars could be seen in our rear view mirrors or any other mirror. We raced lap after lap glued together, and there was really nothing in it, but two-thirds of the way through the race, my car began to fill with smoke and I had to drop back. All gauges showed everything to be fine, except for the ammeter, which was flicking around madly. A short time later I was having trouble seeing out of the windscreen because the smoke was so thick, and Basil was disappearing into the distance. By the smell I knew it to be an electrical fire. Suddenly the ammeter melted out of the dash and dropped to the floor as flames shot out of the dashboard.

I had a couple of laps to go and was still in second place. Nothing was going to stop me from finishing: not the flame licking the Nomex glove on my left hand, nor the large hole where the ammeter used to be, or the robust flame melting the steering wheel. I removed the glove from my right hand and stuffed it into the hole in the dash, which dampened the flame a little, but my hand was getting scorched with no fireproofing to protect it. I was getting into trouble as a result of the thick acrid smoke filling the interior of the car. The burning Nomex glove shot out of the dash, got stuck on the roll bar, and set the roof lining ablaze, wherever I looked I could see flames. I removed the left glove and stuffed it into the flames emanating from the dash, the windscreen was covered in black soot and was useless for any sort of vision of the track. The finish line was so close now. By looking out of the driver's window and keeping as close as possible to the inside of the track I was able to finish the race. I crossed the line with smoke billowing out of the window and pulled right across the pit lane and braked to a stop.

The flames seemed to be everywhere; I hit my six-point safety harness release, and opened the door to climb out over the roll bar when the pit marshal arrived. I thought he would give me a hand to extricate myself from the bowels of the inferno, but instead he hit the button on the extinguisher he was carrying. I shouted 'NO' but my voice was lost under the Bell helmet and balaclava I was wearing. In an instant I was turned into the abominable snowman, covered from head to foot in white foam as was the entire interior of my car. Another marshal arrived at the passenger side, wrenched open the door, and proceeded to cover me and the interior of the car with the same white powder. I was in more danger of choking to death on the foam and powder from the extinguishers than from the fire and smoke!

The first marshal was by now trying to lift a gasping driver – being me – out of the white snow field they had just created. Once I considered myself safe enough from an onslaught by the marshals, I was able to survey the scene. It looked like something out of the Swiss Alps with white foam and powder everywhere. I removed my Bell helmet and balaclava and then examined the damage to my hands, which were burnt and sore. A doctor looked at the burns on my hands and offered to dress them. I told him I would shower first as the foam or the powder from the extinguishers was stinging and aggravating the burnt flesh, which was creating more pain for me than the burns themselves. I assured him I would see him immediately after my shower.

I left the car in the care of my mechanics, who were removing it from the pit lane. I went under the shower fully dressed, including helmet and balaclava. As the water poured over me, I washed my helmet and balaclava, peeled off the fireproof overalls, flameproof underwear, driving boots and socks. The burns I had sustained stung like hell as the water washed away the foam and powder which had come to me courtesy of the Kyalami marshals.

I went to the doctor's rooms once I was squeaky clean, and he applied Burnol cream and bandaged my hands. It was the back of them that had sustained the most damage, but they looked far worse than they actually were. The laundry service at the hotel soon had my racing suit and accessories looking like new again, and after I had stripped the helmet, given it a good wash in the bath, and assembled it again, it was fine. I flew home the next day, and by the time I saw Penny, the bandages had started to turn yellow with the discharge from the burns, which meant I was in big 'kak' for not telling her about the incident on the phone. Before I knew it, I was whipped off to the hospital to have the burns redressed. The skin from the back of my left hand came off with the bandage. It was painful but as I said, it looked worse than it actually was because the flesh underneath the scorched surface was healthy and only slightly scorched.

When she saw the damage, the look on her face told me I was in danger of being hauled off to a plastic surgeon for skin grafts. Any and all protests I made to let things just 'be', fell on deaf ears; and first thing the following Monday morning I was taken kicking and shouting to my doctor, who managed to assure my wife I was not about to die. He prescribed some penicillin gauze to stop infection and to keep the burns moist.

The car had arrived in Bulawayo on Sunday afternoon. The mechanics stripped all the upholstery, seats, dash and roof lining from the car as well as the window screen, which had cracked from the heat. On Monday morning I had the car brought to the wash bay where I turned the fire hose on full blast into the interior. If I thought I had been exposed to an inordinate amount of foam at the time of the fire, it was a minuscule amount compared to the approximately two tons I washed out of the car. I made out a list of the spares I would need, and the order was placed before ten o' clock that morning. We went through the car mechanically; all the burnt components were removed and replaced and the shell re-sprayed – and we were ready to rock and roll at the Falls Road Circuit. The repairs had taken two weeks, and I was looking forward to this test.

I got the car down to a one minute thirty-nine point two second lap, which was two seconds quicker than the speed the Cologne Capri had achieved in the hands of Jochen Mass. My Penny wanted a ride in this fantastic car, so I buckled her in securely and drove around the track at a more sedate speed. She asked me to go faster so I accelerated out of the top corner in a power drift and down the straight. I usually went through the kink flat at a hundred and forty miles an hour, but I had my pregnant Penny on board so I lifted and feathered through there at a hundred and twenty miles per hour. There was a loud bang as I hit the apex of the corner, and something shot up from the left front, which dug into the tarmac as the car dropped. I felt the back of the car lift and knew it was going to flip boot over bonnet if I didn't take some action to rectify the situation instantly.

An experienced driver is, in a sense, one with the machine under him. It's as if he feels everything through the seat of his pants. The result is that as soon as a tricky situation arises, he is already compensating by utilizing either the throttle or the steering wheel. As I felt the front digging in and the rear lifting, I turned the wheel hard left. This reaction lifted the left front out of the tarmac, spun the car in the opposite direction. After a couple of gyrations the car came to a stop on the outside of the track.

As the drama unfolded, Penny stayed very calm. I leapt out of the car as quickly as I could and ran around to open the passenger door. 'Are you alright?' I asked with measured calmness.

'I feel a little dazed,' she replied, 'but I wasn't afraid because I knew you'd get us out of this in one piece'.

I undid the safety belts and helped her out of the car. 'I can see help is on its way, so sit on the car boot until it gets here and I'll wait with you.'

Help arrived and I eased her into the car. 'Take Penny back to the pits and keep an eye on her until I get there,' I instructed the driver. 'I just want to see what damage has been done to the car, and ascertain what the hell happened.' What had happened was simply that a wheel had broken. Apart from that there was no other damage.

When I got back to the pits, I took Penny to hospital, with the worry that the seat belts across her stomach or the shock to her system may have caused damage to either her or the baby or both. The doctor at the hospital conducted some tests to ascertain possible injury and insisted she stay in overnight for observation.

'Don't worry,' I said as I kissed her goodbye. 'Everything will be just fine and I'll see you in the morning, my love. Have a good rest.'

'We don't have a phone yet,' she reminded me. 'How will I be able to get in touch with you if I need to?'

'Don't worry' I replied reassuringly, 'I'll give the hospital John Love's telephone number in case of any emergency'. John Love was a good friend and neighbour of ours as well as the South African and Rhodesian F1 champion who lived just round the corner. I was bathing the next morning before leaving for the hospital, when I was interrupted by a knock on the door. It was John with the news that Penny had given birth to a baby boy. It was 12 September 1973 and I had a son.

The words were barely out of his mouth when I jumped into my car, still wet from my bath, desperately trying to dress myself as I drove. I was struck by the tiny being, my son, lying in an incubator next to Penny's bed. Tears rolled down her cheeks as I tried to console her. To take her mind off what had happened, I suggested she phone her dad to tell him he had a grandson. Through her tears she spoke to Ken and promised that this baby, his first grandson, would be named after him. She also promised to send him photographs of our son just as soon as she was out of hospital. Mr Kibble, the specialist in charge of our new baby boy, frightened me when he explained the dangers surrounding the life of such a premature child. He was so very small, his lungs were not properly developed, and if he survived, he would have to stay in hospital for at least two months. All at once, the most meaningful realities of life began to dawn on me. I knew in a flash of recognition that Penny and this small bundle fighting for life inside the incubator were the most important things in my world.

Feelings of guilt and remorse swept through me. I was responsible for my wife and child's safety, and the ignorance of youth had allowed me to let her in the car, but it was with the exuberance of youth that she got in. If we could go back and change our mistakes, I wonder what path our lives would take. It would certainly be very different from the ones we have lived.

We had no option but to leave our son in hospital when Penny was discharged. I drove her there every morning to be with him and had to literally drag her away in the evenings.

There were problems that had to be overcome, and when Penny flew of necessity up to Salisbury to see her dad, I made a promise that I would take good care of him while she was away. I kept that promise, but because he was out of any physical reach, with oxygen and food tubes going into his tiny body, I felt helpless and could do no more than sit with him. Penny told me on the phone from her dad's bedside how thrilled he was with the photographs of his grandson, and I was pleased that at least he'd had the chance to see him. When I picked Penny up at the airport on her return, the only thing on her mind was to get to the hospital to be with her son.

His most urgent problem was under-developed lungs, which failed four or five times a day, preventing him from breathing. At such times alarms would go off, alerting the nurses of his need for immediate resuscitation. Mr Kibble could not be sure how much damage, if any, his tiny brain was sustaining every time this happened.

I had no alternative but to be in Johannesburg if I wanted to qualify for the international nine-hour endurance race, and I insisted Penny come with me. I realised she was in desperate need of a break, even if she didn't, and if anything happened to Kenneth, I reasoned, she would need me to be by her side.

Mr Kibble had stressed to us that there was very little anyone could do apart from pray. Our prayer life was well under control and from the beginning, many hours had been spent on our knees. We were allowed a few precious moments to hold and hug our baby before we left for the airport, and although I felt very uneasy about leaving him, I knew there was nothing to be gained by staying.

When we arrived in Johannesburg, Penny insisted we phone the hospital immediately, and the day brightened considerably when we were given the good news that he was still with us. At Kyalami, where we parked behind our pit, I was besieged by autograph hunters. Penny thought it a huge joke that anyone would want her husband's autograph and with that, she produced pen and paper from her handbag and asked me if I would give her my autograph as well. I pulled her aside and whispered meaningfully in her ear, 'I'll give you a proper autograph in front of all these people if you're not careful'.

'Oh yes, please,' she replied, little wench that she was! The trip had relaxed her and she seemed sparkling and vivacious once again.

With a glint of devilry in my eyes, I said to the autograph seekers, 'Do you realise that this girl I am with is an international film actress from Rhodesia?'

It was my turn to laugh, when looking flustered and completely out of her depth, she was soon surrounded by people waving books wanting her autograph. When she eventually found her way to me, I put my arms around her and pulled her into the security area at the rear of the pits. We would need the memory of this light enjoyable moment later in the day when we were faced with devastating news from home.

A nine-hour race is a long stretch, so when I qualified the car in one minute thirty-six point eight seconds, I was happy. I had revved the motor to six thousand five hundred revs per minute instead of the maximum seven thousand eight hundred, in order to save wear and tear on the brakes and motor. I only used the brakes heavily three times around the circuit, allowing them plenty of time to cool before the next application.

Back at the hotel after that day's racing was done, we had a message to phone the hospital. Our sense of foreboding, which hung over us as I phoned home, was well founded. Dr Kibble regretfully told me our son had passed away two hours before.

I tried to console my Penny, who was stricken with grief. That night the two of us lay in the darkened room sharing our heartbreak and mourning the loss of our child. I phoned a funeral parlour in Bulawayo to make arrangements for his body to be removed from the hospital and to set in motion arrangements for his funeral to be held the following Thursday.

Although I desperately needed a good night's sleep in preparation for the race the next day, unsurprisingly, in view of the tragic circumstances, it was not to be. It turned out to be a very long night with little sleep for either of us. All we wanted to do was to get home to be with our son, and the last thing I felt like doing was to take part in a motor race. My heart was no longer in it. But I had a commitment to fulfil, and there was nothing to be gained from being at home. There was no longer anything we could do for our baby. Although I had lost interest in the race, I knew once I sat in the seat and put the visor down, a calmness would descend, and my mind and body would become one with the car.

I would normally start and finish an endurance race, but because of the circumstances, I was trying to organise an immediate flight home upon completion of my drive. Consequently, I was not driving at the time of the accident. The decision whether or not to leave for

Bulawayo earlier than planned was taken from me when the car left the track on lap eighteen with the oil coolers ripped off in the process. I was not fated to drive in that nine-hour race.

My thoughts turned to home where my dead son awaited us, and we were free and could depart for home to be with him. Nothing was available that night, but the first flight out the following morning had two seats available for us.

After we landed, at Penny's insistence, we went straight to the funeral parlour to see our child, who was dressed in a white smock in his small white coffin. He looked like a little angel. Someone had placed a long-stemmed red rose in his hand.

He had fought so valiantly to stay with us, but we knew he was now safe in the arms of Jesus and an aura of peace seemed to surround him.

Within the confines of the chapel, we looked down at our son in his coffin. He was no longer vulnerable to the hurts of this world, and I felt humility and love stirring from within me. I realised there would be nothing I would not give, apart from Penny, to have him back with us. Penny was sobbing uncontrollably, and she turned away as I said my goodbye alone to my little boy.

My Penny was inconsolable and totally devastated at the loss of her son. When we got home, she broke down at the sight of the nursery she had been preparing for our baby. It really was beautiful, decorated with little racing cars and figures dressed in blue and white livery. A large picture of me with the Little Chev hung on one wall and the mobile above the cot consisted of little Chev Can Am's, all made by Penny.

Every morning I dropped her at the funeral home where she would stay with our son until I collected her after work.

On the day of the funeral, the coffin seemed so dwarfed by the size of the chapel. Five of us were in attendance, and although the chapel was almost empty, I felt a deep peace and tranquillity there, a very special and spiritual experience.

Kenneth was cremated and we decided to scatter his ashes at the racetrack because we spent so much time there testing and racing. I could think of no better place for him to be close to us.

Chapter twenty-one
Grief's aftermath

B**UT** there was never again to be an 'us' at the Falls Road Circuit because Penny never set foot inside it again. She retreated into a world of her own to mourn the loss of her baby, and if she spoke a dozen words to me in that time, it was a lot. I went into the nursery one day after I got home from work to find it stripped bare of everything except a chair in which she would sit for hours alone with the memory of her son. Penny went into a deep depression, and I blamed myself for not having had the common sense to refuse her a ride in a full-blown race car. I can only say in my defence that I was young and stupid, but for all that I believe I will one day have to give an account of myself.

I sent Penny home for a few days to be with her parents in the hope that Ken could cheer her up. But he was a very sick man. She gave her father another picture of his grandson taken with us before we left for Kyalami. He placed the photograph on his bedside table in the hospital and even though our baby was dead, he proudly presented him to staff and visitors as his first grandson. I thank God that He had brought Penny and I together, as it was this togetherness that pulled us through.

The year had started as being the most fantastic one of my life but had now disintegrated into the worst, and there was more to come. That bloody year 1973 took me to a pinnacle in my life, and then dropped me and my Penny into the entrance to hell.

As I had not been driving at the time of the accident, I stripped the motor to ascertain if it had run without oil when the coolers were ripped off. Fortunately, the motor was fine so I rebuilt it, and at the same time fitted it with a different cam and bigger valves, which proved to make her much more responsive. My Little Chev was ready to run once more. One of my mechanics volunteered to get into the boot and come with me on a lap around the track at racing speed. At my signal, he lifted the boot lid with its wing on it as high as he could, which proved, as I suspected, that the wing was purely for decorative purposes. The boot had to be lifted just over a foot before the air stream flowing over the roof hit the wing, giving the benefit of some down force.

Mom bought Penny a top-of-the-line Singer sewing machine in the hope it would give her some interest in life once again. I bought the cabinet to house it in, along with whatever other sewing equipment she needed. The machine just sat there day after day, untouched and probably unnoticed, while Penny continued to deeply grieve over the loss of her son and the imminent death of her father. She was nineteen years old and the tragedies of these two events were too much for her to handle. Nothing anyone did or said could alleviate the depth of her despair and sadness.

A characteristic I had always found so appealing about her was that even when she was angry or sad, I could always coax a grin from her, however reluctant. But during her time of mourning nothing worked. She seemed immune to anything I said or did behind the wall she had built around herself.

It was heartbreaking for me to watch someone I loved hurting so much, and I didn't know which way to turn. I persuaded her to take riding lessons and flew her home every weekend to be close to her dad, which helped for a while; but it all came to an end when Ken died. Penny was in Salisbury when he died and stayed on for the funeral with her two sisters and brother, who had flown in from different parts of the world. I was unable to be there due to other unavoidable commitments. My Penny had been very close to her dad, and his death really finished off the year for her. In the process she had become a completely different girl to the one I had married in May.

My heart ached for her when I reflected on all the things that had happened in a few short months. A move to a strange town had forced her away from her home and the friends she loved, and she had lost a son and a father, as well as a father-in-law. Marriage to me had been chucked in along the way, which brought her a home of her own to look after – all in all, quite a lot for a young girl to cope with and adjust to in a six-month period.

A number of fights between her and my mom did not help matters, and I had to mediate between the two of them on more than one occasion. I knew with certainty that in order for her to get well and regain her equilibrium, I would need to take her back to her home in Salisbury. It only began to dawn on me in later years how miserably I had failed Penny during this period of her life. I was twelve years older than Penny and had not fully understood what she was going through. I had not recognised or compensated for the enormity of the things that had been thrown at her within the space of a few months. The only miserable compensation I could make was to apologise to her from a truly contrite heart.

Ed Hubbard, my partner, was giving me a few problems at the time, which needed to be resolved. He thought nothing of taking my mechanics away from whatever work of mine they were doing to work on one of his race cars. I had a major set-to with him on one occasion, after which he realised he was in the wrong, apologised and everything went back on track, leaving me more time to once again concentrate on Penny's happiness. Following that episode, on a Thursday morning two weeks later, I arrived at work to find the CID (Criminal Investigation Department) crawling all over the place and going through papers in my office.

'What the hell do you think you are doing?' I demanded.

'Looking for evidence' was their calm reply.

Ed and Auto Auctions had been double and triple discounting their cars. I informed the officers that my business was a separate entity from the one belonging to Ed, and I produced the legal agreement drawn up between the two firms at the start of business. I also invited them to investigate any dealings I had with Auto Auctions and instructed my secretary, Mrs Smith, to work with the police to that end. The CID found no evidence to prove I was involved in any Auto Auctions business apart from the workshop, and politely withdrew.

However, Ed and his wife Ursula were arrested, and it seemed certain the whole business was about to implode. Auto Auctions was in partnership with my own company and held the lease on Sager Motors, which we owned jointly. I closed the doors early that Friday and motored to Salisbury to chat with my lawyer. Ever tried to get an Afghan hound into a Corvette Stingray, together with the wife's luggage and two other dogs?

I decided to be sensible and buy a more practical vehicle. The Corvette belonged to Auto Auctions anyway, and I knew I would not be able to use it much longer. Did I buy a nice sensible station wagon? Of course not – I bought a Porsche 911.

I had also hired a security company to babysit my business while I was away with strict instructions that all the paper clips were to remain where I had left them. During court proceedings on Monday morning, Ed was bound over, while Ursula was released on bail. I spoke to her briefly, but she had no idea what lay in store for them except to say if they were found guilty, they would obviously have to face the consequences.

Penny had fallen in love with the Porsche, and I suspected the possibility existed that I could be dumped in exchange for a two-litre German car. All she had to get before I would let her loose in it was her driving license. I would have given her the world if I thought it would have cured her depression. The opportunity to return to Salisbury had come out of the blue, and I didn't need to think twice about moving my Penny back. Perhaps I would rediscover and recapture the young lady I had married. It was nearly Christmas, a time to reflect on a year I would never forget, not only for its ups and its downs but also for the devastation it brought to two lives.

I was surprised to learn that the bank was laying claim to my Little Chev, but they withdrew once I had proved ownership with documents from GM, together with the import permit for the car. Even so, as fraud was involved, the matter still had to go through the courts, and the bank would be responsible for storing the vehicle to my satisfaction until the case was heard. I phoned my lawyer in Salisbury, who advised me to document and record everything I was temporarily leaving behind, and to lodge the documents with the court. This state of affairs happened to suit me because, in the short term, I did not have a place to store my car in Salisbury. I lodged the said documents with the court, and, after the removals, had all our belongings safely packed in a van. We were ready to return home to Salisbury.

In fact, we did not have a home any more, either in Salisbury or Bulawayo. I had bought the house from one of Ed's companies, and at this point it had not yet been registered in my name. The company concerned was now in the hands of the administrators and would probably go into liquidation. I could have kicked myself up hill and down dale. It was my big-headed stupidity that had caused Penny to lose not only our baby but her new house and our business as well. Added to that, my Penny was still lost inside herself, somewhere in a place I could not reach. But, heaven be praised, we were still together; she was and always would be 'my Pen', and we were going home to Salisbury come February. Penny was very happy about that and I was glad to see the end of 1973.

We moved into a rented house in Helensvale, and one of the first things I did was to organise my little Aries, born on 28 March 1954, a surprise twentieth birthday party, to which I invited all her friends as well as some of mine. Penny seemed happier, especially as I spent as much time as I could with her. Although she was not fully recovered, I could see a vast improvement. We had been on the lookout for a home of our own and about four months into the year, Penny had seen and fallen in love with a new house on the market situated on two acres of land on the slopes of Rolfe Valley. On a Friday evening, we drove to said house on Salisbury Drive to supposedly look it over once again. I hadn't told her of the deposit I had already paid on the house. On our arrival I handed her the keys to the front door on the veranda and said, 'Your new house'.

'We can't afford it after the losses at Auto Auctions,' she replied with uncertainty in her voice.

'You let me worry about that side of things,' I replied. 'It's a beautiful home perfectly suited to the gorgeous woman who's going to live in it'. I knew she was thrilled, but there still remained an aura of sadness about her, which I couldn't seem to penetrate no matter what I did. We moved in the following week and Penny busied herself getting her home in order.

She began to perk up a little bit and, wonder of wonders, developed a keen interest in sewing, which I greatly encouraged by buying her an overlocker as an accessory to the sewing machine Mom had bought her. The baby outfits and track suits she produced became very much in demand and before long she had built up quite a clientele, eager to buy her creations. She became the haute couture of Salisbury and loved every minute of it. My mother and Penny seemed to be getting on a lot better, and Mom taught her to knit, with the result that matinee jackets in all sizes and colours were being produced by the dozen.

On Saturday afternoons it became a regular event for all the would-be 'Yves Saint Laurents' to congregate at our house to show off their latest creations to one another. It was not really my scene and, wanting a hobby of sorts, I had a fish tank built between the kitchen and dining room, which was an open plan. It was eight feet long by four feet high, and I stocked it with the most beautiful tropical fish I could find. I hoped it would serve as a therapeutic remedy and give my Penny another interest to help take her mind off the loss of our son.

Pen's first big drama unfolded when she realised the angelfish were eating the smaller fish, so we traded the angels in for a friendlier non-carnivorous breed. The second big drama resulted from her endeavours to be kind. One particularly cold night she turned up the thermostat in the tank to make the water more comfortable for the fish. By morning they were nicely poached and floating on the top of the water. At the sight of them she screamed for me to come. I surveyed the massacre that met my eyes and in an effort to calm her down, blamed a faulty thermostat for the destruction. I attended to a mass burial in the back yard and phoned Leslie's Tropical Fish to arrange a restocking of Penny's tank. With that done, the thermostat was left to its own devices, and Pen left any attempt at a bouillabaisse to me!

I went to Bulawayo to collect the Chev, which the law courts had released, along with other assets seized by the liquidator. All the spares as well as the spare rims and tyres had mysteriously disappeared, and I called on the bank to admit liability before I took possession of the car. They denied anything was missing, and the next morning I met with bank officials so we could go through the car with a fine-tooth comb together. We ended up with two full pages of missing parts.

Fortunately, when the bank had taken possession of the car, I had drawn up a document signed by me and co-signed by bank officials, which listed exactly all the accessories that were with the car at the time. The document was registered and held by the court, so there was no way they could squirm out of it, the bank supposedly being the only body with access to the car. The cost to the bank for the replacement of all accessories was an amount of four thousand five hundred rand. As the car, including all spares, had cost me six thousand rand (the exchange rate rand to pound being two to one), I was on the right side for a change. At least something was going in the right direction.

Chapter twenty-two
On two wheels

ONE Saturday afternoon I went to the motor club to find a bunch of motorcyclists leaving for a ride out along the bush trails. This was just what the doctor ordered, I thought to myself: it would get me out of the house while the fashion show was in progress. It meant little to me that the trail riders were South African Champions: the likes of Keith, Dave, Robbie and Gary Peterson, along with Ophie Howard and a few more to boot. They were all friends of mine, and they could show me how it was done, although what these men had forgotten about motorcycle control was more than I could ever hope to learn.

I secured a second hand 250 Honda Elsinore, which was a full race machine, not really ideal for trail riding, but learn I did – the hard way. Riding it was akin to riding an F1; the front tyre would have lasted forever, as it never touched the ground until sixth gear was selected. I was told by a number of people on that day of the difficulties I would face, and the consensus was, 'You can't ride that bike on a trail ride'.

Oh no! There was that word – 'can't' again. It was difficult, but not impossible and I eventually proved them all wrong, though I endured some spectacular crashes in the learning. I had so much fun that I felt the pain was worth it.

I did not have the proper riding gear on my first major ride with the big guns, consequently, I arrived back at the motor club in a sorry state. I managed to hide from Penny the limp and the loss of a fair amount of skin from around my person until near bedtime. She walked into the bathroom as I lay in the bath naked with nowhere to hide. She was extremely angry when she saw my bruises and grazes from head to toe. I was in the dog box once again. My new toy was confiscated forthwith until, as she put it, I learnt to ride it properly. All the protests and excuses I made fell on deaf ears.

After a long sob story and a promise not to ride like a lunatic, I was allowed to straddle my new acquisition once more. I became a rider with decorum who waved my fellow riders through and ended up eating everyone's dust; it was driving me mad. I had to get the bulletproof riding gear to enable me to speed recklessly down the road and laugh at the consequences. No motorcycling gear was available for purchase at that time in Rhodesia, so Ron and I took a quick trip to Johannesburg where I bought a set of SIDI Moto Cross boots, the best that could be bought, along with gloves and other items of protective clothing. I was now ready for anything the trail could throw at me. In my new gear, I felt indestructible. Feeling indestructible, however, can lead to being overconfident, which in turn often results in being knocked back down the ladder very quickly by the powers who map out our destinies.

The following Saturday the 'indestructible motorcycle rider' roared out of the motor club with his brand new indestructible Sidi Boots and Kevlar protection around the more vulnerable spots, looking every inch a professional and off into the Sekei Tribal Trust Land (TTL). At about 4:30 that afternoon I was riding through some vlei (open rocky moist grass with a few trees) when the indestructible left foot encased in boot struck a large rock hidden in the grass. The bridge of my foot struck the rock and was trapped between the rock and the motorcycle foot peg.

I managed to stay on the bike as it shot into the air on impact with the rock. I managed to recover from the disaster and land normally. I continued the ride and didn't feel any pain until I tried to stand on my left foot to cross a small river.

I felt a sharp pain akin to being stabbed with a blunt knife, and I could feel broken bone grating together. I was forced to sit back in the saddle to negotiate the river crossing. When I stopped on the other side and tried to put my foot down, the pain was so severe I nearly passed out. I realised I had badly damaged the bridge of my foot inside its indestructible boot when it had been caught between the rock and the foot peg of the bike. Unfortunately for me, the indestructible part of the boot only protected the toes so the bridge of my foot and the leather of the boot had taken the full impact. My friend Roger Mumford rode me out of Sekei TTL to a main road and left me to ride to the hospital alone, a distance of twenty miles.

As I was removing my helmet and face mask in front of the hospital doors, the receptionist came out to tell me to move the bike. I explained the situation, and she arranged for a porter to park the bike for me and sat me in a wheelchair as my foot was throbbing and bloody sore. A doctor arrived to examine my foot, turning it gently in different directions, but the pain was so severe I couldn't stop from crying out.

'We'll have to cut that boot off and get you up to X-ray,' he told me.

'Over my dead body,' I replied. The thought of my shiny new indestructible Sidi boot being cut to shreds with a scalpel was inconceivable.

The doctor transferred his attention to my right ankle and tried to move it around from side to side. This time there was obviously no pain but, being a solid ankle, the whole leg below the knee ended up in his hands, complete with indestructible Sidi boot.

'That one is indestructible,' I laughed. He just looked at me and shook his head: no sense of humour, some of these medical men.

The pain nearly rendered me unconscious, but by the time he arrived back in the room armed with scalpels and other dangerous looking weapons, I had managed to remove the boot intact, by myself. My forehead was bathed in sweat, and the foot had ballooned to twice its size and was throbbing like a toothache from hell. X-rays revealed that the bridge of my foot was broken in numerous places, so it was a plaster cast and painkillers for me. It was deemed expedient for me to stay in hospital overnight but after much argument, an agreement was reached for my wife to take me home.

Although Penny drove her Porsche all over Rolfe Valley and Chisipite, she had never ventured into town because she did not have a driving license. I knew coming to fetch me would be a huge challenge for her: one she would not take kindly to. On phoning, the silent treatment on the other end of the phone said it all, but in the end she was able to arrange for my best friend, Ron, to come with her. Thoughtfully, she brought my crutches. I had thought it prudent some time before to buy my own set of crutches as in the long run it would be cheaper than continually having to hire them. It seemed that it had become the normal course of events for me to walk into the motor club at 12:30 in the afternoon only to return home at eight that night on crutches, and I am sure Penny had come to view them as permanent fixtures.

My shares had reached rock bottom with my wife. Ron and I had to wait for her to go out before, armed with an angle grinder, we modified the cast so I could continue to drive. I think she would have cheerfully throttled me if she had seen what we were doing. The angle grinder was in my hands throughout the covert operation because, if anyone was going to cut off my other foot, I would prefer it to be me.

The following Saturday I attempted to ride the bike, but soon realised I wasn't doing my broken bones any favours when I painfully tried to start the bike, so I was forced to give up. Also, I would have to change the gears by hand instead of foot, which would have made riding in the bush almost an impossibility. For that weekend at least, I resigned myself to being CCABW (chief cook and bottle washer) to the local girls at their sewing circle in my home.

On the home front, Mom was helping Penny with her sewing and had taught her some crochet stitches, as well as assisting her in establishing a garden. The two of them were getting along much better in their shared interests, which was a relief to me. Penny enjoyed choosing the flowers, trees and shrubs for her garden, and it was not long before what had once been two acres of bush was transformed into beautiful beds of flowers and a lush green lawn. She and Mom had laboured hard but the results were well worth it. They were very proud of their creation, as I was of them.

My business partner Ed's trial came up in mid-1974, and he and Ursula were both jailed with deportation orders against them at the end of the sentences. My business liaison with Ed had cost me a lot of money and the pay-out I received from the company was peanuts. I chose to be philosophical about it and put it down to experience. These things happen in life and, on the bright side, there were now four of us to consider.

Oh, yes – I did say four. Penny had discovered she was pregnant with twins! Her happiness shone brightly around her whole being in a radiant, maternal glow. It became evident to me that we needed a tow car as well as something a bit bigger than the Porsche so, with Pen's permission, I sold it and bought an S-type Jag.

Mom had been given an invitation through the hotel to attend the opening of the Montclair Casino in Inyanga, and Penny and I accompanied her. I entered and won the trout fishing contest on Loch Moodie, the local trout fishing dam, much to the chagrin and raised eyebrows of all the retired colonels and majors from around the district.

I do confess to baiting the hook with flying ants instead of those coloured feathered hooks designed to float invitingly on top of the water. After spending the day before in interminable rain and casting said feathered hooks under the noses of the rising trout with absolutely no success, I had decided flying ants were the answer, and they were. There were millions of them down by the loch, flying from their nests after the overnight rain. The military gentlemen would have frowned deeply upon my modus operandi had they known. In trout fishing circles it is frowned upon to catch the trout with anything except the manmade trout fly in competition, but the trout virtually queued up to take the bait once I had changed to the flying ants. It was a very enjoyable weekend. I was the first-ever winner of the trout fishing competition at the hotel from their newly stocked dam, though I have a feeling my name will be struck from the roll of honour if any of them ever read about the flying ants.

Our new race circuit had been graded and compacted, and the tar was about to be laid. Once this had been done, the club members were scheduled to come back to the site to erect toilet blocks and install water and sewage systems. Ron had done most of the building on the site and asked me to meet him early one morning before the other volunteers arrived. I found him at the entrance to the clubhouse toilets and showers with a wet cement plaque on the wall on which he asked me to press my hand. When I did, he proceeded to write 'DICK MAWSON'S S--- HOUSE' next to my hand print.

Taffy, who happened to be in the vicinity, was a little taken aback at this frame of reference on our new toilet block. He made Ron change the 'S... house' to read 'Ablution Block,' insisting we retain a sense of propriety for the sake of visiting wives and dignitaries. Ron objected that it would not have the same ring to it, and I thought the change a bit posh myself, but Taffy was insistent and got his way in the end.

My plaster was due to come off in a week but feeling my foot had healed enough already and impatient to go on a trail ride, I removed it myself. I slipped my indestructible boot gingerly over the injury, got someone to help me kick start the bike, and I was off with other riders on what proved to be a very wet ride towards Mazoe.

All the rivers and streams were so swollen and running so fast that it became impossible to continue with the ride. We were soaked to the skin and got washed out wherever we rode. The bike started to misfire, and I decided to leave it at a friend's house where I phoned Pen to come and collect me. My foot was throbbing like hell as I hobbled out to the car when Penny arrived, and after taking off my boot, I found it had swollen considerably. She voiced her opinion of how stupid she thought me to be, riding the bike so soon after the doctor had removed the plaster. I didn't respond to her statement at the time because she was unaware that I had removed it myself. I knew in my heart of hearts that 'Murphy's Law' would come into play, and the truth would come out somewhere along the line, and I would once again be in big 'kak'. But then I often think it's better to seek forgiveness than to ask permission. Being stupid, I didn't seek it at the time.

The next morning, dressed in shorts and slops, Penny drove me to fetch the bike from our friend's house. I attempted a couple of kick-starts, but it was so painful I decided Penny could tow me with the Jag until I could jump start it. With what I thought was a brainwave, I pushed the bike to the road, put it into second gear, pulled in the clutch and held onto the door pillar of the Jag with my free hand. At about 40 mph I let go of the car, opened the throttle wide, feeling sure the bike was flooded, and released the clutch.

The bike fired immediately and took off like a Saturn V rocket heading for the moon. I became detached from the bike, which was airborne somewhere above the roof of the Jaguar. I was plummeting to earth at one hundred and twenty feet per second while travelling forwards at around forty miles per hour and crashed into the tarmac on all fours. Skidding along the abrasive surface, I felt my leg come off and, because I was in shorts and slops, felt a sore burning sensation from the body parts in touch with the road. From my wrists to my elbows and from my knee down to my shin, the pain increased in intensity the further I slid. As I was coming to a stop, I rolled onto my back and lay there looking up at the beautiful blue Rhodesian sky and wishing I could find a hole to crawl into. There was blood gushing from multiple abrasions everywhere.

Penny had stopped the car and started to get out. I saw that two African gentlemen were running to help when they suddenly stopped in their tracks. I knew what they were seeing! Lying in the middle of the road, there was a leg; further down the road lay a body on its back minus a leg with blood gushing from legs and arms. I saw them turn from the scene and run in the opposite direction.

Penny arrived at my side sounding just like Mom with the cry of, 'Oh, Dick, just look at you what have you done!' Then she burst out crying. My injuries were very sore by this time. I am the one who feels the pain; I should be the one crying, I thought to myself before speaking up. 'Pen, you'll have me crying in a minute. Be a love and get some towels from Brett's house before I bleed to death'.

She left and emerged from the house with an armful of towels, which I bound around my knees and forearms to stem the flow of blood while Penny went to fetch the car. I tried to put my leg on, but it was impossible because of gravel ingrained in the raw flesh.

The bike had landed on a tree, which had broken its eventual fall to the ground. A gentleman came out of his house to see if we were alright and, at my request, kindly agreed to look after the bike until I could fetch it. Penny drove me to hospital. The most painful procedure was having the gravel picked from the open wounds, which took a couple of hours.

The hospital released me, lending me a fold-up wheelchair because my stump was so swollen and weeping it was impossible to wear my leg. At home, Pen settled me on the bed and made us a lovely lunch, which I felt I did not deserve in view of the unnecessary drama I had created.

I was dreading going to sleep that night as I knew I would wake up to a lot of pain. As it turned out, things were not initially as I had anticipated, but when the effects of the painkillers wore off I knew all about it. I could hardly complain as my injuries had been self-inflicted. If one does a stupid thing without the proper equipment, then expect to suffer. Would I ever learn? The answer to that question is 'no', and to this day, I still think little of hopping on a bike dressed only in shorts and slops.

On Tuesday we went to hospital for more dressings, and as luck would have it, the doctor who had set my broken foot was on duty. I had to confess to having removed the plaster myself in order to ride the bike. I looked around at my Penny, but she avoided looking at me, and the old saying, 'Picture, no sound,' came to mind. Thereafter, she subjected me to three days of silence before she let rip, and then I had a picture of 'cross girl with plenty sound'. I deserved it, but what could I do? I was too sore to fight or protest and, in any case, I am a lover not a fighter. I was in the wrong and I needed to hear it from Pen. She had every right to scold me as I was not being fair to her and I needed to change.

In truth, I was in a hell of a state. I had lost my leg at eleven; badly damaged my good hip at sixteen; suffered severe concussion, a collapsed lung and multiple broken ribs at thirty-one; smashed the bridge of my good foot at the age of thirty-three; and now this accident. I had very little skin left on the underside of both my arms and legs; there was little of my body left intact, but like all things hurtful in life, the pain eventually subsides, and the sun begins to shine again. Your wife forgives you and loves you again and, wonder of wonders, the lovemaking is better than it had been with everything in perfect working order. I had taken a bit of a hammering, and it became a matter of urgency for my stump to heal so I could walk again and get out of the damned wheelchair. Fortunately, I mend fast and two weeks later I was up and about, though I did promise Penny there would be no more 'Mr Indestructible'.

As soon as I was able, we called to thank the gentleman who had so kindly looked after my bike and to arrange to remove it from his premises. I had a quiet ride with a friend in the vlei behind his house, but I rode with extreme caution, mostly in third gear, knowing if I arrived home with so much as a new scratch, I would be in BIG trouble.

Third gear on an Elsinore is akin to flat-out on the Greeves my friend was riding. He got carried away, thinking his bike was faster than mine, and lying flat on the tank, he did not see the looming fence. It is important when riding in the bush, to look out for fence posts, which are normally strung with barbed wire to keep cattle straying from the African homesteads. To hit barbed wire on a motorbike at speed could tear a rider to pieces or even kill him.

I was pointing forward for him to look up but he was having none of it, and as I braked to a halt, I watched him hit the fence at about fifty miles per hour. He was lucky that it was only fencing wire he ran into and not barbed wire. The fence gradually absorbed the speed of the bike, like a longbow being drawn, and then it shot him and the bike back the way they had come at a speed of roughly a hundred miles per hour and a good ten feet in the air. I saw bike and rider hit the deck about twenty yards behind me and winced at what sounded like very painful contact being made between ground and man. The whole incident happened before my eyes in slow motion, reducing me to helpless laughter.

When I eventually arrived alongside the stupid human lying on the ground emitting cries of pain, he asked me what had happened. When I was finally able to tell him through my mirth, he became quite indignant and asked why the hell I hadn't warned him about the fence. On reaching his bike I packed up laughing once again. It was now about eighteen inches shorter as a result of its accident and looked ridiculous lying mangled in the mud on the ground. I have never been able to work out how I was supposed to convey to him the existence of the fence when, at the time, I had come to a halt and he was at full throttle heading away from me.

He came off lightly with no broken bones, just painful bruising and torn ligaments, which left him limping around for the next six weeks. I believe he sold the bike soon after having a costly front-end repair done.

As I was determined to finish a trail ride without afterwards walking on crutches, some of us decided on a ride to the Sekei Tribal

Trust Land, which involved crossing the Mackabusi River. Since there had been a lot of rain, the river was swollen and flowing swiftly, and three bikes became bogged down on a sandbank.

I decided to cross the river by jumping the bank slightly downstream of them, which involved a five-foot drop from the riverbank into the water. I theorized the bike would land in the middle of the river, and I would be able to negotiate the bank on the other side with relative ease. The best laid plans of mice and men can sometimes come to nought!

I executed the whole manoeuvre perfectly, or so I thought, and it would have worked, except the bike landed in ten-foot-deep water, which put a spoke in the works, and together we sank to the bottom of the river. I hadn't taken into account that when the river ran normally, it was a good seven feet lower than it was on that day. I kicked off the bottom and swam to the bank with difficulty as my water-logged clothing and helmet weighed me down. The three bikers who had been stuck on the sandbank had in the meantime extricated themselves, and after they had managed to control their mirth at my misfortune, they came across to give me some help.

I stripped off all my clothes down to my underpants and hung them on a tree to dry, and with a rope borrowed from one of the other riders, I dived down to find the bike. The water was very muddy so I only managed to locate it on my third attempt. I attached the rope and with the help of the others dragged it to dry land. They left me to continue their ride. It took me so long to get the bike restarted, I knew I would have no way of catching them. It is dangerous to ride alone in the African bush as one can fall at any time and incur an injury, so I turned back and motored to the club to await the return of my co-riders. On the bright side, I arrived home that night without crutches, dressings or a limp. Penny checked me all over, and I mean all over, for damage to her property, and I got a fantastic reward for being a good boy.

The next weekend there were four South African motorcycle

champions on the ride so I knew the pace would be fast. A couple of hours into the ride we sped up a rocky hill and ducked into a forest on the way down. The bikes were doing around eighty miles per hour over the ridge, and then we braked, slowing the bikes to around forty miles per hour to run downhill through trees to a river at the bottom. When running downhill, it is wise to use the rear brake as use of the front brake in the soft earth can lock the front wheel, resulting in the rider being thrown over the handlebars into the trees and rocks on the way down, with disastrous results. It all sounds easy and would have been if my throttle hadn't stuck fully open, and for some reason I had no rear brake. I found myself heading for destruction. My only thought at the impending disaster was how cross my Penny would be if I came home damaged or in a casket.

I knew to touch the front brake at that speed, running downhill, would have high-sided the bike into the trees, smashing me and the bike to pieces in the process. I flew down the hill past all the champions at such an alarming speed it seemed they were standing still. How I missed trees and rocks in my downward flight I will never know. I was going so fast I did not have time to look down to see why the foot brake had failed. I only knew if I hit something or came off the bike, it would be the end of me, and my Penny would end up shouting at a corpse.

The hill flattened out as I flew on to what I believed was my certain destruction, and then the bike launched itself off the riverbank. At the speed I was going it flew almost right across the river. I thought fleetingly of bailing out but I did not have time to act on my thoughts. The trail leading out of the river was a fraction of a second away, and I somehow managed to line up the bike so perfectly that it shot out of the river. The bike rose into the air like a Polaris missile launch from a nuclear sub, with water pouring from the frame and rider.

With the forward momentum and luck on my side, I managed to land the bike on its back wheel. As the front wheel touched the ground, I was able to gently apply the front brakes, which loaded the front forks and added weight to the front wheel, thus slowing the bike. The jammed throttle had released as I landed (probably the jolt on landing) and the bike was halfway up the hill on the opposite side of the river before it was travelling slowly enough for me to safely look down at the brake pedal. It was then I noticed that my right foot was missing, or was it? I looked again. It was there but the toe was pointing towards the rear of the bike.

I laid the bike down in sheer exhaustion. Adrenalin was coursing unabated through my veins, but I was relieved to be alive, though how I didn't know. My guardian angel must surely have been working overtime, and I wondered if he was paid danger money for looking after me. As I lay there in the dust and gravel, I gave a prayer of thanks to whoever had got me through the ordeal I had just encountered, and by so doing had undoubtedly saved me and my marriage in the process.

I lifted my head to see the other trail riders stopped and every last one of them was doubled over in laughter. They were rolling on the ground laughing, their bikes and bodies lying where they had fallen as they vented their hilarity at my misfortune.

I was finished; if I had tried to stand, I would have fallen over. I lay there with every fibre of my being trying to recover from my ordeal. It took an age for their mirth to abate, but I was glad of the respite as it allowed me time to compose myself. Once they finished laughing at my misfortunes, they arrived en masse and turned me over to remove my helmet, as I just did not have the energy to take it off myself. I was exhausted and could have lain there for the rest of the day quite easily.

I looked at these motorcycle champions and knew I had to say something stupid: 'So why were you all going so slowly down that hill?'

Their response to my question is unprintable and not suitable for those of a more delicate disposition. They propped me up against a tree and twisted my foot to face the right way. I realised that coming up the hill I must have struck a rock with the right foot with such force that the foot had been rotated 180 degrees, keeping me from applying the rear brake. Discussing the incident over a beer back at the motor club, they were all adamant that the speed at which they were descending the hill was as fast as they could go with any safety.

They had watched open-mouthed as this future world champion/ maniac flew past them and were impressed by the speed and his ability to control the bucking machine under him – with help from above, I might add. I was just glad to get home to Penny in one piece and none the worse for wear apart from a few bruises, which she found acceptable.

The bikers planned a long run for the following week to the Shavanoia River and back to Domboshawa through Tribal Trust Lands where insurgents were known to be operating. We all armed ourselves for the run and I made sure my FN Browning (semi-automatic pistol) was ready for action. With four grenades besides, we felt prepared for whatever we might encounter. We set off early on a lovely fast trail ride to the river. Nearing Domboshawa, we had to slow down because of the difficult terrain. Domboshawa is the nearest thing to a mountain Salisbury has. It is famous for its large open-mouth cave adorned with bushman paintings.

The weather had become misty with light rain, so we stopped to dry off and look at the paintings. The trail ran along an eighteen-inch ledge the length of the mountain; it was strewn with rocks and coverts, and the mountain sloped away at seventy degrees to the left and right of the rider. I had ridden the ledge many times before so knew from experience it had to be taken at a steady speed of twenty-five miles per hour and a good strategy was to look fifty yards ahead at all times. The mountain sloped away to the left for about ten feet and then there was a drop of about two hundred feet onto rocks below.

My house was quite near Domboshawa. Feeling wet and cold and being a non-smoker I decided to go home for a shower and change of clothes. I left a few minutes ahead of the other riders, who were still smoking the remnants of their cigarettes. My right leg slipped off the wet foot-peg and the toe of the boot wedged itself under a boulder pulling my leg off. I could not stop as I had no leg to put down on the right, and if I lay the bike down, it would slide down the mountain and drop over the edge, followed by me. When I saw a covert looming up out of the mist, I decided to lay the bike down there so bike and rider would slide into trees and bushes instead of dropping over the edge. I knew the other riders would be along any minute and all would be well.

About five minutes later I heard the bikes coming along the ledge, but then they stopped and I couldn't hear another thing. I propped myself up on a rock and shouted in their direction, but a gusty wind was blowing my shouts away from them. I got no response. Now and again I could hear sounds coming from their direction, but obviously they could not hear me and I did not know what was going on.

I was told afterwards that as they were riding along the ledge, the lead bike spotted my leg with the toe wedged under the boulder standing there all by itself. Presuming I had gone over the edge, they had brought their bikes to a halt as, obviously, they all had right legs they could put down on the slope of the mountain. The rock face was wet and slippery so great caution had to be exercised at all times. After parking their bikes alongside some rocks, they went back to the place from which they guessed I had fallen. Ropes were triangulated and one of the riders was lowered down to the misty edge to have a look, but through the mist and rain, visibility was not ideal. The rider was hoisted back up and it was decided that two of them would attempt a drive around to the base of the cliff to find me. The leader would in the meantime find a phone to alert the emergency services of my fall. Thank God that decision was made.

As I heard the bike approaching, I stood on one leg holding onto a tree in the middle of the ledge. The rider came out of the mist and rain and braked to a sudden halt when he saw me. He removed his helmet and goggles revealing an ashen face as he exclaimed, 'Bloody hell, Dick, we all thought you were dead and when I saw you standing here I thought you were a ghost'.

We turned his bike in the covert and he rode back to tell the others that the funeral was off. They arrived about half an hour later after having a hell of a job turning his bike around on the narrow, slippery ledge. I reattached my leg and being once more transformed into a state of wholeness, we left for home.

Not one of the bikes had any form of lights, which made travelling difficult because by this time it was getting quite dark. We were all soaked to the skin and stopped at my house, which fortunately boasted three full bathrooms, making the whole operation of bathing quicker and easier. I lent my companions dry clothes, and by this time Penny had rustled up hot coffee and sandwiches, which were wolfed down by all with great gusto.

Once they were dried and fed, Penny and I gave them a lift back to the motor club. As the guys were coming back the next day to collect their bikes, we laid on a braai in appreciation for the help they had given me. The topic of conversation, naturally, became my assumed fall over the ledge at Dombashawa, and as the night wore on and more alcohol was consumed, the course of events became more and more elaborate; the heroes got more heroic and increased in number. Eventually, the beer turned the story into an international rescue of note.

I was offered a new Yamaha 125DT and as I had a keen buyer for the Honda, I picked up my new toy and rode it back to the workshop. I pulled it to pieces, fitting a new barrel, which took a bigger piston, resulting in the increase of fifty ccs from a one two five to a one seven five. I modified the ports in the barrel and the windows on the pistons, fitting the new parts into the bike. I ran her in and was myself surprised at her rocket-like performance. I couldn't wait for the next trail ride, which turned out to be for the following week at Goromonzi.

My beautiful pregnant wife was eating a lot more than usual and losing her model figure again, but she didn't mind and neither did I because on the whole she was fine, bless her, and very involved with knitting, sewing, entertaining friends and, in general, fussing around her house. She was slowly but surely returning to her old self again. I told her excitedly all about the new bike, but I realised her interest was, at best, feigned. I teased her that I would probably not need the crutches any more, and if she knew anyone who needed them, she could sell them. I don't know what it is about my girls, but she gave me 'the look', just like the one my mother had always given me. Basically 'the look' meant 'yeah, right'.

The planned ride to Goromonzi that weekend was cancelled due to consistent rain, so I took the bike into the vlei down the road from our house, just to play. I came home a couple of hours later drenched to the skin but all in one piece. I was dying to get my new bike out on a trail ride, and the following weekend there was a foot-up (you are not allowed to put your foot down on the ground) trail ride that my good friend Robby Rushforth was organising. He was also a national champion in many categories relating to motorcycling and race cars.

A special bike is used by the experts for foot-up trails, but someone who is a competent rider can use a normal bike, and on that basis I entered. A long piece of tape marked out the course to be followed through rivers and over rocks and boulders. I did well for all of the first thirty feet before I hit the first boulder and went headlong over the handlebars as the bike came to a dead stop. One of my middle fingers was pointing in an odd direction, but helpers pulled it as straight as they could get it and taped it to my index finger with insulating tape. That incident ended my trial riding for the day and convinced me to announce my permanent retirement from the sport of foot-up trails.

I told Penny I had hurt my finger falling on some rocks, but one or two of my friends often took delight in getting me into trouble on the home front, and this occasion was to be no exception. The truth came out when, at prize giving held the following Wednesday night at the motor club, I was awarded the booby prize for the shortest run with the most damage. Of course the story told had become very exaggerated (as usual), but I was in the dog box with my wife for telling porkies (fibs). I told my Penny I had fallen on rocks; I just omitted to tell her it was off the bike and onto some rocks.

Needless to say, I got whisked off to hospital the next day so the doctor could check out the injury. The verdict was a broken finger, which I could have told him myself. His advice was to break the finger again so it could be properly straightened. I asked him if he was mad and told him I was quite happy with the finger just as it was, but to satisfy my wife, I agreed to a splint.

We had been invited to a wedding on the day of the next trail ride but as hard as I tried to juggle things, I just could not participate in both the events. So, wedding it was to keep the peace. Penny and I danced a lot that night, and my leg became painful as a result of the woollen stump sock and a nylon sheath rucking up and chaffing the stump.

We were seated at a corner table at the back of the room with a wall on one side and a curtain on the other. As a rule, I am not in the habit of sitting down at a table and ripping off my leg, but this was a case of necessity. I slipped my trouser leg up to remove the leg and smooth out the socks when around the corner of the table I heard a small gasp, and saw an equally small boy run back to his mother at the next table. He returned later with his mother, who told me that for the last half hour her son had been trying to pull his leg off 'like the man at the other table'. On the point of giving up, he had insisted his mother accompany him to see this unique man. She knew who I was and apologised for the interruption and embarrassment.

I was quite used to children asking me all sorts of questions about my leg and often allowed them to poke sticks into the vent hole that let water in and out when I went swimming. I slipped up my trouser leg and removed the leg for the benefit of the little boy. The look of astonishment on his face was priceless. He left the table tugging on his leg and looking puzzled when it did not come off in his hands like mine had done. His father, who was a customer of mine, told me when he came in to have some work done on his car that he was sure his son's right leg was now half an inch longer than the left because he spent so much time tugging away in an attempt to detach it.

Some of the bikers and I were going to Ruwa, which was a little 'warm', as in potentially dangerous from the point of view of insurgents. I got a sit-rep (situation report) from the army, which told me they were active in the area. On that basis I decided to carry a gun to be on the safe side. It was a fast ride and any guerrilla would have had to be a superb shot with his AK47 to have hit any one of us. I was pleased with my bike, which handled much better than the old one and was as light as a feather to throw around.

We had come across a few army patrols and were stopped at one point in an area with rocky terrain. Alan, who was an excellent rider, was showing off his new bike but avoiding disasters by the skin of his teeth. In the end, he ran the bike up a steep slope at great speed, using a boulder to launch himself ten feet into the air and disappeared out of sight. There was a long silence followed by an almighty crash.

The rest of us motored to the top of the slope to find that instead of a slope running down the other side as we might have expected, there was a chasm into which bike and rider had dropped, landing on rocks forty feet below. Two riders got down the face of the chasm with the aid of ropes to find Alan alive but badly hurt. I shot back to where we had seen the last Army patrol and they called in a chopper and medic from the New Sarum Air Base.

Fifteen minutes later the Alouette arrived and Alan was strapped onto a body board and winched into the helicopter to be transported to hospital. We left the bike where it was. It was in pieces; the frame had broken in two from the impact of the crash. Alan's injuries were serious. His back had been fractured in a number of places and he was in hospital for a couple of months. I never did see him ride trail bikes again after that, and his bike was eventually retrieved in bits. I must admit when I saw him lying there on the rocks, the thought crossed my mind, 'What the hell are you doing this for if it's so dangerous?' But half a mile down the road with the throttle wide open and adrenalin coursing through my veins, the thought vanished on the wind.

We had a big braai at the house the following weekend and after a few beers, the bikes came out. Dangerous, after beer. Our house was built on a large two-acre plot so there was room enough to reach good speeds. The lawn was terraced, and to make it competitive, we tied ribbons onto a pole. As a bike was jumped from the terrace, the highest ribbon attainable was to be snatched by the rider; the one with the highest ribbon was the winner. It was great fun but with too many beers and no helmets or protective clothing, it was lunacy. I snatched a ribbon and landed on the front wheel, one hand on the bars and one holding the ribbon. Unfortunately, the front end let go and the front wheel slid away on the slippery grass. The bike went into a three hundred and sixty degree flip, throwing me face first into the ground, smashing my cheekbone and damaging my good foot. The beer anaesthetised the pain, for the time being anyway, but by midnight I had Penny take me to hospital. My face was so badly swollen it had become lopsided, and I could no longer walk on my sore and throbbing foot.

I was in trouble once again with my Penny in her 'picture, no sound' mode with seemingly little compassion for me. Could I blame her? No, she was married to an idiot who was trying to self-destruct. I had broken my cheek and jawbone as well as fracturing my ankle. On the way home in the wee hours I made her a promise: 'No more motorbike heroics'.

I don't know if she understood my mumbling, my jaw was wired, sore and swollen, to say nothing of my very painful foot. Again, my injuries were self-inflicted, and I couldn't help but laugh at myself. What a prick – would I never learn? I must really have an excellent guardian angel, and if I ever I get into heaven, I will thank him profusely because, for most of my life, it seems, he has needed to work exceedingly hard to save me from myself.

When I was settled into bed with every single part of me hurting like hell, I turned and whispered in my wife's ear, 'I suppose a bonk would be out of the question'.

She burst out laughing. 'Would you like me on top or underneath?' I don't think I could have raised a smile, never mind anything else; in fact, I knew I couldn't. But the phrase stuck with us throughout our marriage and broke the ice on many occasions.

It was Wednesday before I could get up and about; my body couldn't take much more punishment. I was sore in places I didn't know I had, and I was peeing blood. It took me twenty minutes to get out of bed. What a wreck! My Penny had heard what I said in the car after leaving hospital, and asked me if I had meant it. I replied that I didn't say things I didn't mean, and she would see a changed me in future and I meant it. I realised with clarity that my constant urge to prove myself better than my peers put me on a self-destruct course, and I had to stop that from happening, otherwise I would not be around when my twins arrived. I hung up my Sidi boots with the firm decision they would only be worn for a social run down to the local river to play.

I could have killed for a Rhodesian T-bone steak and chips, but my Penny cooked some stewing steak and vegetables instead and popped the results in the blender so I could drink it through a straw. Until my jaw was healed and the wire removed, a liquid diet would have to suffice.

The day my jaw was unwired I shot down to a friend's restaurant, 'Da Guido', and he cooked me a T-bone steak so large and delicious that I battled to finish it. Upon my arrival home, my Penny, bless her, had also cooked the largest T-bone steak she could find for my dinner. I managed to eat only half of it as by this time my jaw was really very achy. I confessed unwillingly to my lady that I had been to Guido's for lunch, and two Rhodesian T-bones in one day were more than I could handle. I polished off the other half for lunch the next day. I took heed of Penny's admonition regarding the stupidity of ignoring the fact that I could injure myself permanently if I carried on the way I had been. There was even the likelihood of ending up a cripple for life (echoes of Mom). With the memory of Alan's severe injuries playing on my mind, that was the last time I ever hurt myself badly in a motorbike accident (touch wood). All future rides became decidedly more sedate, and apart from the odd roasty (gravel burn) I sustained from time to time, that was the end of my self-inflicted injuries.

I was aware of the damage my body had sustained externally and had begun to feel the internal effects of the damage as well. I already had one leg missing and the other pinned at the hip, so was somewhat reluctant to add any more missing or damaged limbs to the current list. Besides, I had something wondrous to look forward to – the birth of my twins.

Chapter twenty-three
A destructive storm

FOR the time being, my days consisted of helping at the hotel and running my garage. Justin, who we had initially employed at the age of sixteen, was now my manager and virtually ran the hotel by himself, which took a lot of weight off Mom's shoulders. We ran a very popular three-course lunch every day with a choice of three different main meals and often had the honour of our Prime Minister Ian Smith's patronage, together with his cabinet ministers, whose lunches would often linger on into the afternoon. Justin supplied them with endless cups of tea and coffee as required, and messengers would scramble back and forth laden with documents from the government offices situated only half a block away.

We spent the weekends at Lake Mac relaxing, entertaining and enjoying the beautiful Rhodesian weather as we cruised around in our twenty-foot cabin cruiser.

The summer blended into autumn. Donnybrook Park, our new race track, was open but because of petrol restrictions, racing was unfortunately curtailed.

I kept my promise to Penny and only used the bike socially and even reached the stage where my body had healed so perfectly, I felt confident enough to hang my crutches in the garage out of the way. I felt blessed with good health, love, and living with my gorgeous wife.

Ron and I took a trip to Johannesburg to collect some updated spares for the Can Am and to pick up a racing Gordini I had bought. We packed everything into the Renault, loaded the Renault onto the trailer and began the long journey home. Rhodesians at that time were always short of forex (foreign exchange) and found devious ways of bringing goods into the country without having to apply for an import permit, which would require an explanation of where the forex had come from. To avoid the question, we declared that all the parts we were bringing through were used and not for resale. On our arrival at Beit Bridge, the customs controller called us into his office after officials had inspected the vehicle and its contents to ask us about certain items.

We went into long detailed explanations about them being used parts and even attempted to bluff him into believing that the brand new racing slicks on board, which we had covered in mud, were so old they had no tread left. The controller smiled with studied patience and said to us: 'You are Dick Mawson, and you are Ron Lupson. I am Barrie Smith, a member of the Bog-Wheelers Motorcycle Scramblers Club. Those tyres you claim are worn out are brand new racing slicks, you have a new Chev motor covered by used Renault suspension, and you have a cooler bag full of seafood, which you describe as snacks for the journey'.

He was bang on with everything he said. What could we do? We were about to lose the whole lot. He turned to us and said, 'I know you are not bringing the spares through for resale or profit, but I am handing you a warning, which it is incumbent upon me to do. When you see me in the motor club, you can buy me a beer. Now bugger off before I change my mind.'

Ron and I expressed eternal gratitude and scurried out of his office like a couple of scalded meerkats. The Rhodesian customs officials, black or white, were a great bunch of guys, who would many a time turn a blind eye to the illegal manner in which goods were brought into the country.

Upon my return to Salisbury, I built up the motor I had brought through the border for the Can Am and was thrilled when she gave me five hundred and eight horsepower on the dyno. I had gone to fifteen-inch wheels and bigger brakes and had adjustable racing rose joints on the front suspension which made it all fully adjustable. With all this new gear fitted, I took the Can Am to the Bulawayo track and, by the end of the afternoon, had achieved a time five seconds quicker than any other saloon car had ever been around there. I had achieved this time with an old set of tyres fitted to the car, which John Love had given me from his F1, so I was well pleased. I felt I could beat anything the mighty South Africans threw at me once motor racing in Rhodesia got back on track. Because I wanted to keep the new set-up for the real competition I would have to deal with in the future, I refitted the old gear, which was more than enough to deal with any Rhodesian opposition I might encounter in the meantime.

Some good news I heard while in Bulawayo was that Andy Quinn had built a replica of my Chev. I didn't view the Perana as opposition but another Chev might well prove to be, maybe I would need my new set-up after all. When it was ready to race, we got a bit of feedback in terms of the times it was achieving, and I became excited at the prospect of finally having someone to really race against.

Andy had finished the car and entered it in a Salisbury race at the Donnybrook circuit. He arrived there early on the Friday to do some testing and to make any final adjustments. I arrived at the circuit a little after three to find Andy's Chev on its trailer with the whole front of the car written off. Andy himself was in a critical condition in Salisbury Hospital. Donnybrook was a twisty circuit and a heavy car like the Chev required the driver to have a lot of upper body strength to handle it. Because Andy was a little fellow who was having difficulty switching direction in time to apex the corners, he had removed his shoulder straps from his safety harness so he could move the top of his body closer to the steering wheel. Apparently, his throttle jammed open as he was about to brake for the esses. He did not have a 'kill' switch, which is essential in a race car with that amount of power, and he had ploughed into a six-foot earth wall at over a hundred miles per hour.

His injuries would not have been so severe if he had been fully belted in, but with no shoulder belts, the top half of his body was thrown forward, his chest hit the steering wheel and the right side of his skull was opened up on impact with the windscreen pillar.

He was lucky he did not die then and there. As it was, he spent over a year in hospital. His car was scrap, and so ended what I had hoped to be another car to play with on the Rhodesian circuits.

Four individual clubs – Vintage, Volvo, Mashonaland and MG – combined to make up the Sables Motor Club. Our clubhouse was on Jameson Avenue. The main committee of the motor club had a three-day visit to Leopard's Rock Hotel to get members to intermingle socially at this lovely hotel in the Vumba Mountains overlooking Mozambique.

We all left the clubhouse in convoy at about nine that Friday morning and, needless to say, the journey evolved into a road race among a few of us to see who could get to our destination first. My Penny slept all the way, in spite of the fact that we travelled at great speed, and we were settled on the lawn enjoying tea and scones by the time the second car arrived. I had booked the Princess Margaret suite, so named as Princess Margaret had occupied the suite on her 1949 visit to Rhodesia. The suite was situated in front of the hotel, looking out towards Gorongoza in Mozambique.

Once the majority of guests had arrived, we had a lovely buffet lunch of pâté on toast, Inyanga brown trout, cheese and biscuits. Members arrived during the course of the afternoon in dribs and drabs, and at 4.30pm we attended a cocktail party, which had been laid on for us by the hotel. From there we went into dinner.

Many of us were up early the next morning to take a walk along the escarpment, followed by a leisurely breakfast on the front lawn. Planned entertainment for the day included a walk to the top of Leopard's Rock behind the hotel and a golfing challenge. I had never played in a golf competition before and was a hacker. I had borrowed a two and an eight iron, along with a sand wedge and putter from a mate.

Ron, on the other hand, had borrowed a set of fancy clubs from his MD. The putter was crooked at the bottom and the driver was called 'Big Bertha' – very intimidating but the trick was to know how to use them. His kit also included a very fancy cart, umbrella, towels, and yellow dusters to dry and polish his balls – I think the right terminology to use should be 'golf balls'.

Ron blasted a ball off the tee using Big Bertha, and the ball reached a speed of a thousand miles per hour in a second. This ballistic missile hit a tree to the left of the fairway, screamed back over our heads and disappeared into thick bush behind us, the first of many lost balls! Everyone on the first tee ducked.

'Good shot,' I cried, 'if we were playing the other way!'

I don't know if the ball was ever found, but Ron persisted with Big Bertha, with the result that I won all nine holes. He never got the chance to dust or polish any golf ball with his yellow duster because every ball he hit he lost. This was an expensive weekend for him, and I won every hole by default. Penny spent the whole morning on the front lawn feeding herself and the twins copious amounts of toasted sandwiches, cream scones and tea – very sensible young lady, my Pen.

The next day Ron bought some cheap golf balls off his caddy. I couldn't resist remarking, 'You are probably buying back all the balls you lost yesterday!' He didn't smile at my humour.

We played the second nine holes that morning and by the seventeenth, Ron had again lost all his balls. I very magnanimously lent him two of mine so he could finish the course. I knew he was bound to lose them on the last two holes but what the heck, I had won every one from him up to that point and as the last two holes were the most difficult on the course, his record for the game would be eighteen holes, eighteen balls! The seventeenth hole was about three hundred feet below the tee in a natural bowl surrounded by forest. Ron hit both balls into the trees while I whacked mine high in the air with an eight iron. The ball arced in a beautiful curve and then – do I need to say

The gods who fell from the sky

how and where it landed? A hole in one is rarely achieved, except by the likes of golfers of the calibre of Gary Player and Nicky Price.

'Jammy sod,' was the comment made by my fellow competitor.

I couldn't resist rubbing it in. On the way down to the hole I said to Ron: 'I think I'll be packing up motor sport to take up golf. Obviously I was born to play the game'.

Ron's comments are unprintable and he refused to play the last hole because all the motor club members who weren't playing had congregated there to watch the players finish. He had lost his two remaining balls at the seventeenth anyway.

After the game, we had a lovely buffet lunch and a quiet trip back home. The prize giving was held at the motor sports clubhouse on the following Wednesday, and there was no one more surprised than me to learn I was the overall winner, having won every hole from my friend Ronald John.

Ron was the Master of Ceremonies as usual, and he announced that not only was I 'Tricky Dickey' on the race track, but that I was a ringer at golf as well, and he had definite proof I had been tutored by Mark McNulty and Nicky Price. I replied that as in racing and life, 'The winner takes it all,' and staggered off the stage with my huge trophy, which was all of three inches high and too small to be inscribed. I am very proud of it though, as it is without doubt the only golf trophy I will ever win. Many of the Vintage Car Club members were excellent golfers and could easily have beaten any one of us, but they had not entered the competition in the spirit of the weekend. They had elected instead to leave the golf to the motor racers, and go to Leopard's Rock for cream teas or to take their vintage cars on a good run around the Vumba.

A few weeks later a crowd of us decided a camping trip to Kariba was just what everyone needed. I loaded my trail bike onto the boat, hitched the boat to the car, and after obtaining a sit-rep, we were off for our weekend. We found a great campsite at Chirara right near the water, and planned to eat at the Cutty Sark and Kariba Breezes hotels on the lake shoreline. The first night out we had only been asleep a couple of hours when we heard a commotion outside our tent, and I discovered a rather large hippo with her head in the rubbish bin looking for titbits. Penny took one look at this animal and retired to the car for the rest of the night.

We awoke early to a beautiful dawn and were on the lake at first light. The hotel kitchen had packed a breakfast hamper, a picnic basket for lunch, and plenty of cold soft drinks to sustain us. We filled our faces with the delicious fare and spent the rest of the morning playing around the islands and inlets chasing crocs from the sandbanks and annoying a mother hippo with calf. The calf would swim up to the boat for the titbits on offer, not intimidated in the least by these bearers of scrumptious delights but, for mother hippo, it was a different matter altogether. She was keeping a close eye on her calf and did not view the antics being played out before her in a good light. She kept calling out to her mate in great consternation presumably instructing him to intervene by charging the boat. When he did, we turned the boat away from him and headed for deep water from where we watched dad escort his errant child back to an anxiously waiting mom.

By two in the afternoon the weather started turning. I could see a tropical storm brewing over the Matusadona Mountain range, and I headed for shore and berthed the boat inside the harbour at Kariba Breezes Hotel. A dark grey line of cloud edged the top of the mountains surrounding Kariba and ominous rumbles of thunder could be heard in the distance, accompanied by vivid flashes of lightning which lit up the ever darkening sky. Driven by the freshening wind, foamy white horses were beginning to appear on the top of the waves, lapping the shore with ever greater intensity.

Penny was getting cold and went to the room of a friend for a hot bath while I went back to the campsite to batten down the tent. I arrived to find our tent lying flat on the ground, the wind having whipped out all the pegs. Fortunately, all our belongings were locked in the car. The wind was by that time picking up serious strength, and I could see a huge storm approaching from the south. I wound the canvas of the tent around the centre poles, tying it tightly with rope, and drove back to the hotel. I rounded up all the able-bodied men, and we went down to the harbour where the waves were crashing over the top of the twelve-foot high harbour wall. With the wind howling, we loaded my boat onto the trailer, and I towed her up to the trailer park and left her in a corner sheltered from the wind.

Satisfied that the boat was safe, I returned to the hotel to find my Pen standing on the balcony watching the approaching storm as it swept across the lake. I put my arm around my beautiful wife, and she cuddled into me while we watched the ferocity of the storm sweeping towards us. For those who do not know Kariba, it is a man-made inland lake, one hundred and sixty miles long by sixty miles wide and as dangerous as an ocean if measures are not taken to respect it as such. The waves had grown to at least fifteen feet in height, crashing over the harbour wall, and I knew there was big trouble brewing.

I returned to the harbour to help with the boats that had broken free from their moorings and were in the process of being destroyed as they were pounded against the rocks. The harbour was full of crafts that had outrun the storm but with no space left on the beach to berth them. A number of us got together to sink the boats because they would be safer on the bottom of the dam rather than on the surface, where they faced being smashed to pieces on the rocks. We had sunk about fifty boats when the harbour wall gave way and the full force of the storm hit us.

Realising their boats would be safer on the open water rather than risk being damaged moored to a harbour wall, a number of big boat owners queuing to berth, decided to drop their wives and children ashore before turning into the storm. I paused momentarily to watch them disappear into the veil of driving rain and the mountainous waves being whipped up by howling gale-force winds. I saluted their bravery before turning away, knowing what a great deal of courage and skill it would take to negotiate and rise above those frighteningly monstrous walls of water in order to steer their crafts to the safety of calmer waters where they could wait out the storm.

The full force of the storm really hit about ten minutes later with driving rain so intense it obscured any view of the hotel, and the music from the balcony was drowned out in the uproar. Another large part of the harbour wall collapsed before we finally departed, drenched to the bone, to join wives and girlfriends in the safety of the hotel. The storm lasted a little more than an hour before it abated. Devastation of great magnitude surrounded us, but as the night had closed in, we went to bed leaving everything as it was until the morning. Penny and I shared a room in the hotel with friends that night.

The next morning, the scene of destruction facing us all was not as bad as it had first appeared. I borrowed a generator, compressor and water pump from CMED (the government motor workshops where I had served my time as a motor mechanic), as well as some grader tubes to demonstrate to boat owners how to raise their boats off the bottom of the lake. Grader tubes were stuffed inside the cabin or under the decking and blown up with the compressor until the boat was semi-floating, at which point we were able to drag it onto the beach where water was removed with the water pump. Once the boats were floating again, the plugs had to be removed from the engines, distributors dried, oil changed on four strokes and the motor spun over without spark plugs to blow out any water.

In the aftermath of the storm most of them were back on the water by lunchtime, none the worse for wear. But out on the lake could be seen many that had not fared so well. Boats were drifting upside down; others were partially submerged and were kept afloat only by their buoyancy tanks, which saved them from sinking to the bottom of the lake. They had broken free of their moorings, swept out into the dam by the driving wind and ferocity of the storm. The boats, which only hours before had been racing across calm waters in balmy sunshine, now looked forlorn as they bobbed up and down with the flotsam and jetsam of debris and personal belongings floating beside them.

I greatly sympathised with those whose boats had disappeared, seemingly without a trace. Armed with binoculars, owners aboard the boats of friends or good Samaritans scanned the water for their lost property. I heard later that some boats were found floating up to twenty-five miles from their moorings while the remains of others were found smashed to pieces on the rocks.

Only a small portion of the harbour wall was left standing but apart from that, the damage was limited, including to my tent, which was as I had left it, wrapped around a pole. Looking out towards Kariba Heights though, we could see a variety of tents stuck in the tree branches on the side of the escarpment. We packed up the campsite, and a few of us decided to go on a bike run along the power lines. All the trees and stumps had been removed to facilitate passage by power line repair vehicles.

About a mile or two into the ride we passed a herd of elephant off to our left, feeding on the branches and shrubs blown to the ground by the storm. The bulls flapped their ears in a show of protective aggression, but we sped past them unconcerned, and a little further along the road we came across a couple of rhino who were also enjoying the fruits of the storm. Travelling at a good speed over a rise, the bikes flew into the air, provoking dangerous signs of aggression from a pride of lions whose females were obviously unfamiliar with flying objects and perceived them to be a threat to their cubs. The males remained in the shade of the trees, obviously quite undaunted, and left the protection of the cubs to the females. I turned the bike in the air away from the charging females and prayed for a safe landing. The lionesses already had a good head of steam up, and I knew that any delay could result in serious damage to Penny's Dickey!

Talk about an adrenalin rush! As I landed, I immediately accelerated at full throttle away from the nearest lioness and, not looking back, concentrated on the ground ahead of me, knowing this was not the time to fall off. I fancied I could almost feel the hot breath of a lioness breathing down my back. The creepy feeling persisted that at any moment, she would drag me down and that would be that. I navigated round in a big circle so I was now heading back to the relative safety of the rhino and elephant. I glanced quickly behind me and let out a sigh of relief when I saw there was no angry momma on my tail. I motored on back to the campsite to await the return of the other riders, who, with the advent of the lions, had shot off in all directions, choosing their own individual path to safety. Fortunately, we all got back to the hotel in one piece. Needless to say, the stories in the pub that night became more exaggerated as the beer went down.

Chapter twenty-four
Double loss

THE following week Penny went into hospital, faced with the possibility of another premature birth. The twin boys were born the next day, the first of May 1975. The smaller of the two died at three hours old while my bigger son lived for seven hours. It was evening by the time I left my Pen in hospital, devastated and heavily sedated. Gary Strong, a youth pastor and personal friend, was in the hospital at the time, and I asked him to visit her and then baptise the babies, whom we named Ron and John after our good friend, Ronald John Lupson.

I was in a daze, definitely not on this planet, as I wandered aimlessly around with all sorts of questions running through my head. I could not believe the same dreadful train of events had happened to us again and the question kept screaming through my mind, 'What will I do with my Pen when I eventually get her home?' She was coming right from the loss of our first son, and now we would have to face the death of our twin boys. At the time it didn't dawn on me just how long it would take for my Penny to recover from these tragedies. It would eventually take thirty-four years for me to get the girl back that I had married.

Penny was heavily sedated at the funeral and leant heavily on my arm for support. Our sons had been together since conception and in death they stayed together sharing a single coffin, a heart-breaking sight in a church filled with flowers and loving friends, who faithfully supported us in our sorrow. I took my Penny home and she went straight to our room, crying out for the one thing neither I nor anyone else could give her. She wanted her twins alive and well and asleep in the nursery she had almost finished furnishing.

I lay in silence beside her, holding her hand, but it was as if she was not even aware of my presence. I thought about the two lives God had allowed to be taken from us. Perhaps it would have been easier for us if we had someone or something to blame for our loss, but after searching my soul, there seemed only God left to blame. Intense anger welled up inside me that would not go away, and I was to face the biggest battle of my life in trying to bring Penny back from the place in which she had imprisoned herself. I blamed myself for the loss of our first child, and now I sought a reason to blame myself for the death of the twins.

Gary Strong and his wife came to dinner to speak to us about the tragedy we had suffered, and to bring spiritual comfort to us. If they had looked into my Penny's eyes as I did, they would have seen the absence of life in them. Earl, our friend and the minister who had married us, and his wife Lorraine, came to console us as well, and to speak God's Words of Life into our tragedy. Even though he was a forceful speaker, I could see Penny did not hear a word he spoke. I continued to search my mind for possible reasons why it had happened. Perhaps riding in the boat, maybe the storm or the incident with the lions: any of these things might have affected her. I desperately needed something on which to pin the blame and so find absolution for myself.

I scattered the remains of our two little Angels at Donnybrook Race Circuit but as I had with Kenneth at the Falls Road Circuit, I did it alone. Penny refused to come with me and never again did she accompany me to a race circuit.

She simply went through the motions of living: refusing to eat, confining herself to the bedroom and taking no interest whatsoever in life. She cried for hours in her brokenness, and I was very afraid she would try to take her own life. She lost so much weight that her features became almost skeletal-like in their appearance.

I came home one day to find her beautiful nursery an empty shell. She had trashed it and thrown the resultant debris in our rubbish pit at the back of the garden. There was nothing left, she had smashed everything to smithereens and set fire to the pit; it was all just ashes blowing away on the wind. I, too, was devastated, but she locked me out, refusing to share her grief with me, and by so doing disallowed me from sharing my grief with her. This went on for months. I had to force her to eat and she barely moved from our room.

Grief is a price we often pay for love, but the frustration and anger that was building within me refused to dissipate. Why could I not find a way to unlock her broken heart and fill it with love again? Was she blind, could she not see my heart was breaking for her as well as for our twins? I looked for something, anything, which might kick-start her interest in life, but it was difficult in that she had every material thing she wanted.

In desperation, I settled on another Porsche, remembering how much she had enjoyed the last one. With great anticipation I led her outside and handed her the keys. 'Yours,' I said.

'It's nice,' she replied, giving it no more than a cursory glance before going back inside to the haven that was our bedroom. I kept the damn thing for a couple of weeks and then resold it, not that I think Penny much cared at the time or even noticed. I wished so desperately that Penny would lay bare her heart and talk to me, but she was not forthcoming, and I was left to find solace for my grief alone. I began to get angry with her because most of every day she would sit or lie on the bed in tears with a flat refusal to leave the sanctuary of our bedroom.

I sat alone in our lounge late one August evening with thoughts scrambling through my head while all the emotions of the last few months brewed and churned inside me. Turning over in my mind ways to unlock Penny's grief had brought me to breaking point. A tropical rainstorm was brewing; the wind freshened suddenly, the smell of rain becoming prevalent on the air. I watched lightning strikes run down the tall buildings in the distance. With my feelings for Penny and her dilemma overwhelming me, I got up and opened the French doors to stand on the veranda where I felt a few drops of rain from the fast approaching storm splatter on my chest.

The strength of the wind and rain intensified in a second, as it does in Africa, and it soaked me. I looked back to see our sun filter curtains flapping parallel to the lounge ceiling and then turned my face full into the wind. I screamed my anger and frustration into the face of the oncoming storm, which released me from the bottled-up feelings I had carried since the death of my twins. My anger was carried away on the wind to the edges of eternity. I had not even noticed the tears streaming down my cheeks but could taste their saltiness.

I was lost with nowhere to turn when suddenly, out of nowhere, I felt two arms encircle me and heard a soft voice speak to me above the noise of the thunder and lightning, the wind and rain, adding to the cacophony of sound, 'What are you doing, Dick, shouting at the storm? Please, come to bed. I'm all right now. I just needed time. Come, my darling'.

I turned to kiss her passionately. A feeling of relief flowed through me as I felt her come back to me at last, as her body melted into mine.

The woman I loved was now standing alongside me as my wife once again. We were soaked to the skin as the thunder rumbled, and the lightning danced in the sky, creating a symphony to heal two broken hearts. I was alone with my grief no more. My Penny had returned. I lifted her into my arms and carried her to bed. That night, as the storm raged overhead, our two bodies were as one, and out of that passionate love we shared in the intimacy of our home, my son was conceived!

Penny found a new gynaecologist to look after her, and he promised her she would carry this baby to full term and would deliver a strong healthy child. His name was Eric Simons and he later became one of the top gynaecologists in Harley Street, London. He insisted Penny have a stitch put in the neck of her uterus to help her carry the baby to full term. I wanted to do all in my power to help my Penny have the baby we both wanted so desperately. I complied with my Penny's wishes as well as her doctor's, hoping this would bring my Pen back to her old self. She virtually put herself to bed for the full nine months, such was her determination to carry and deliver a baby to full term. As a precaution, Mr Simons admitted Penny into hospital just before the baby's due date. He was taking no chances in breaking the promise he had made to her at the beginning of her pregnancy.

On a Sunday afternoon after I had driven in an autocross event, I was just about to leave the club to go to the hospital to see Penny, when my mom walked in. I had seen Penny the night before; she was comfortable and I had no cause whatsoever for concern. With no word of greeting addressed to either me or my brother, who was sitting next to me, she said, 'Penny gave birth to your son this morning'. My heart sank.

'She would like you to go and meet him,' she added.

I was out of the club and into the car in a flash and, as grubby as I was, made it to the hospital in record time. Obviously, I am not a fast runner but as quickly as I could, I arrived at her room and burst through the door. Eric Simons was there with the paediatrician, and my little son was lying in an incubator next to Penny's bed.

As I entered the room she burst into tears. 'I'm so sorry, Dick,' she said.

Those words almost stopped my heart from beating such was my fear of another death, which I knew Penny could never have survived. I looked across at the incubator, the baby was alive and moving. I went to the side of the bed and kissed her. She was visibly upset and I needed to know what was going on.

With a pounding heart I went to talk to the doctors. It transpired that Eric had been to see Pen early that morning before going to Lake McIllwaine to water ski with friends. Later in the morning she had started to haemorrhage badly, and the hospital had somehow got a message through to him to come to her side. If I am to believe Eric, he beat my best time from the Lake to Salisbury in his Jaguar, and still in his swimming costume, hurriedly donned an operating gown. He had our son out of Penny in double quick time. The attending paediatrician struggled to get the baby to breathe, as apparently he had been drowning in the womb. Thankfully, oh so thankfully, he won the battle, and our son took his first breath at midday on the 16th of May 1976. Penny and I had a real live son! Both doctors were of the firm opinion that he was fine, but the precaution needed to be taken to keep him in an incubator under observation for a few days.

I looked into Pen's eyes and saw the lingering sadness still there. In spite of the doctors' positive outlook, I was still afraid something might happen to the baby, so I stayed with my wife and son late into the night. I did not want Penny to face another possible death with no one by her side. Our baby was feeding well and had a healthy cry, but Penny was in a lot of pain from the caesarean section. Medication for pain was restricted because it was Penny's wish to breastfeed.

She eventually dropped off to sleep, and I went home to shower and climb into bed, but I was at Pen's bedside just after six the following morning, before leaving to check on breakfast at the hotel. Mom was playing with the idea of retiring, and I would take over the management as well as the running of the Whitehall. Our staff had been with us for thirty years, so the change was purely on paper.

Penny had refused to name the baby until after it was born, and I expected her to name him after her father but, to my surprise, she insisted on naming him after me.

'Why did you say sorry to me when I arrived at the hospital yesterday'? I asked.

'Because I was afraid Richard would not survive,' she replied with tears in her eyes. 'I saw him being snatched from me with blood pouring from his mouth, making him cough and splutter. There was blood everywhere'.

I felt a lump in my throat for all that my twenty-two-year-old wife had been through and for the joy of at long last being able to hold a live, healthy baby in her arms.

I was allowed to take my family home after five days, and the days that ensued became a huge learning curve for me. Penny was still very sore and understandably paranoid about Richard's survival. The first night home she was in a state of anxiety and agitation, checking on him every five minutes and fixating on the possibility of finding him dead in his cot.

To give my Penny peace of mind so that she could sleep, I took this tiny creature, the best of Penny and me, laid him in the crook of my arm and thus we slept all night – father and son. Whenever he awoke, I would hand him to my Pen, who fed him, changed his nappy and handed him straight back to me, where she felt he would be safe. This nightly procedure carried on for at least six weeks, but eventually Penny grew in confidence. I knew she was well on the road to recovery the night she first took our happy, healthy baby boy over herself.

Mom had decided she wanted to spend a few years with her family and friends in the land of her birth, so when Richard was three months old, we took her to Durban where she boarded a ship bound for England. I was very sad to see her go, but of course it had to be her choice.

Even though Penny was now the mother of a beautiful, healthy child, an aura of sadness still surrounded her. I found it difficult to get her to relax and once again to enjoy life to the full. I tried everything – short breaks to Kariba and Inyanga, house parties – anything I thought might make her happy. Richard was a beautiful little boy, perfect in every way. We could take him anywhere, and he would go to sleep in his camp cot. I sometimes even took him with me to practice when I was racing, and Pen would pack a bag with folded nappies, bottles of milk and all the other paraphernalia babies seem to need. Off we would go, father and son and the Little Chev.

Richard was never any trouble. At practice the wives of competing drivers would often compete with one another to look after him, and it was plain to see he had inherited his allure to the opposite sex from his dad! Richard obviously never came to the circuit with me on racing days as they were far too long for someone so young, and he was too small to be away from his mom for long periods of time.

Chapter twenty-five
Maturity brings strength

PEN was becoming more comfortable with our Rich and the more I got to know the two of them, the more I loved them. An aura of sadness lingered on which, strange as it may sound, endeared her to me even more. Richard came everywhere he could with me, and on Sundays when there was no motor racing on the go, we would go for a ride on the bike, with him sitting on the tank between my legs.

He would point excitedly when we spotted any duiker (a small buck) or dassies (rock rabbits), and I kept bread in my backpack so we could feed the ducks and fish at Balantyne Park. The ducks were a particular favourite of his, except when they got over enthusiastic. He would then jump into my arms and look from a safe vantage point at them fighting and squabbling over the bread at Dad's feet. I would lift him across my legs and head for home when, further into the ride, his little head would flop forward as he fell asleep. He was a beautiful child and I was totally besotted with him.

Our jaunts usually took a couple of hours, so by the time we got home, 'Lazy Bones' (Pen) would usually be awake and available to take over. She would change his nappy and put him down to continue his nap. I always cooked brunch on a Sunday, and when Rich woke he would have his bottle and we would spend the rest of the day by the pool. Most of our Sundays were spent in this way. I dearly loved my wife, my son, my life and my family. They were my reason for living and if anything hurt them, I would seek recompense.

If I could snatch a few days off, we liked to head for Kariba with the boat. It was always a pleasure and a relief to arrive at an air-conditioned hotel as parts of the Zambezi Valley are below sea level, making driving an extremely hot and uncomfortable affair. Pen would feed and change Richard, who had slept most of the way, while I put the boat in the water. With a picnic lunch from the hotel and bottles for Rich, we would leave the Marina for the coolness of the lake, stopping a couple of miles offshore to swim and wash off the dust from our trip.

Pen would dive into the water and swim back to the boat post haste, maintaining that, even if I had it in writing from the crocs themselves, she would never be convinced they would not attack in deep water. She would lay some big fluffy towels on the roof of the cabin, and off would come the bikini for that all-over tan. She was one of the most beautiful girls in this world, with or without clothes. The rocking of the boat would send Richard into a deep sleep, which left us free to make love, eat and drink, play with the hippos and calves in the bays, and generally enjoy each other as if we were on honeymoon and the only people left on this planet of ours. I felt privileged to have had the opportunity to have her all to myself to do as we pleased. It was so good to live days like these.

Tiger fish, which are plentiful in Lake Kariba, were our only other concern and it is wise to treat them with a fair amount of respect and caution. They have teeth comparable in sharpness to a small leopard, and many a fisherman has lost a finger or two while trying to remove a hook. It is advisable to divest yourself of all jewellery before entering the water in order to avoid a flash of light reflecting off a ring or a bracelet, which a tiger fish can mistake for their next dinner. It is also a must to wear a bathing costume if you are of the male gender in case Mr Tiger fish mistakes your prized possession for a little minnow. A quick snap and Bob would become your aunt instead of your uncle.

We often met and socialised with fellow boaters on the lake, but I preferred the quiet times with my little family as opposed to the normally wet weekends (a bunch of guys + plenty of beer). We would get an early morning start and head for Bumi Hills, and then up the Umi River where a well-known croc lived in one of the bays. He was known as Bismarck and was over twenty-feet long. I am probably one of the few who has seen him out on a sandbank. It was not only his length that was impressive but his breadth as well. His standing height must have been close to four feet, which is an estimation, of course, as I never met anyone brave enough to approach him with a tape measure.

We would motor for about twenty miles towards the Matusadona Mountains, viewing the herds of game on the banks of the Umi River and scores of crocodiles basking in the sun on sandbanks, with hippos wallowing happily in the water. After a morning of game viewing, we would turn and head for home, stopping off at either Tiger Bay or the Bumi Hills Hotel for lunch, a swim and a beer or two before setting out on the sixty-mile trip across the lake to our hotel. Those were good days full of fun and happiness. I felt truly blessed and thanked God for giving me the opportunity to live in such a paradise with my loved ones.

Penny's depression was up and down. She had good weeks and bad months and after a series of tests she was diagnosed with severe depression, an invisible disease that stretches a relationship to the breaking point. Depression has the power of turning a happy carefree person into a suicide case in the course of a day. It is triggered in the brain and takes over the thoughts and reasoning of a normally fit and healthy person.

I would end up helping her fight this disease with every fibre of my being for a long time. In all my second hand experience of it, I would never fully understand it and still don't. I just know what terrible repercussions it can have on an entire family, but I vowed that if it was my lot in life to carry her through, even to my own detriment, I was willing to do so without complaint. From this path I never swayed in all the years of our marriage. I was always there for her; she came first and the children next, a reality she relied on throughout her life. In the space of two years, she wrote off six cars; the insurance company refused to further insure her. Richard had been with her in two of the accidents, and it was only by the grace of God he escaped unhurt. I had no choice but to pull her driving license and refuse to buy her any more cars.

One of Penny's friends told me about a certain incident involving her. Upon questioning, Penny admitted her guilt and asked my forgiveness. I was extremely hurt and angry and let her know my feelings. She had overstepped the mark as far as our marriage was concerned, albeit under the influence of alcohol and prescription drugs, my reaction of fierce anger drove her to an attempted suicide. Fortunately, I was on hand and quick action and a stomach pump saw her recover in hospital.

Once I knew she would be fine, I left an apprehensive Penny to weigh her options after a stern talking to. I was home alone with a small boy, who kept asking for his mother. Although my pride told me to leave her, the remainder of me still loved her dearly. My thoughts strayed to the fact that you cannot learn the lessons of life if you don't make mistakes, and Penny was adamant that this had been a mistake and error of judgement that she would rue to her dying day.

After visiting Pen in hospital, Earl Davies and Gary Strong both called me on the phone, asking me to forgive her. They were very familiar with the problems she had suffered with the loss of our three babies, and they had both counselled her from time to time. I knew after listening to them that I had to forgive myself first of all, for all I had put this girl through, and I knew deep down it would only be stupid pride that might block a path to forgiveness.

I needed to be alone to think, and after farming Richard out for the night, I went to the chalet at Lake Mac where it was peaceful and quiet. I lay back and let the events of the past few years wash over me. Outside the chalet, the night seemed devoid of all sound. In the silence, I felt vulnerable to my own conscience and its persistent echo of memory. I made up my mind that night that my marriage was going to last, for better or worse, and it was up to me to make it work. Pen had asked my forgiveness and I came to the place where I was fully prepared to grant it. Little had been of real worth in my life until she came into it, and my beautiful little boy would be lost to me in some measure if I threw my marriage out of the window.

My life was all about happiness, laughter and good times and my family was part of this, but along the way come the tears of life. You need to find your equilibrium by balancing the good with the bad. Love between two people is about sharing and balancing your lives and love for one another. Out of that love come children who are an extension of that love, and so the lineage continues.

This incident was a defining moment in my life and the beginning of a change in me for the better. I felt her depression was in some ways my fault, and I determined that if it took me to the end of my days, I would make amends. I could not change the past, nor the circumstances that past had created, just as I could not change the seasons or the blowing of the wind. But it was within my power to change myself. I knew I had to learn to look at life through the eyes of my wife. I went to the hospital to talk to Pen. When I walked in, I couldn't help but notice the look of apprehension etched on her face.

I sat down on the bed, took her hand and began talking, 'There have been many girls in my life,' I said, 'but until Britt came on the scene, none of them meant anything to me. If Britt was still with me, I would not have met you, and I would have been the poorer for that. You, my love,' I continued, 'are the most important being in my life, closely followed by Richard. If we split up, I shall lose you both and I don't want that'.

At the end of my monologue, Penny was sobbing uncontrollably and in-between sobs in a soft voice, I heard her say, 'I'm so sorry, Dick! So sorry! I'll make it up to you if you'll have me back! Please, give me another chance and forgive me'.

When love is absolute between two people 'sorry' is not a word that needs to be uttered, maybe just an explanation as to 'why,' but that can come later when emotions have retreated and the soul is forgiving. I wanted my Penny back as part of our family and so did our son.

'My beautiful girl,' I responded with an ache in my throat, 'a love like ours can overcome any difficulties in its path, but it is never one sided; it requires both of us to maintain, nurture and build on the love we have. You know I don't want to lose you or Richard, so get your mind right and come home. We both miss you'.

The following day Richard and I collected a happier and less apprehensive Penny, and my son was delighted to have his mom back with him again.

On my arrival home with Pen and Richard, there was a message for me from overseas. My good friend Paul Hawkins had been killed in his Lola Chev at Aulton Park. He had been a great guy and was someone who had taught me so much about international racing, surely one of the greatest sports car drivers of the sixties and seventies.

Rhodesia had been independent for ten years and the sanctions imposed by the British and Americans were having little or no effect. They had turned this small nation into a self-sufficient paradise, and we showed a finger to the rest of the world. Rhodesia was known as the 'Jewel of Africa'. It was self-supporting in agricultural products and was the largest exporter of beef in the world. The Rhodesian dollar was at its peak, equal to US$1.45, so the currency was rated higher than the American dollar. I think that's something special, all without foreign aid. The Rhodesian Armed Forces were rated as the best counter-insurgency troops in the world. Our Air Force, although using outmoded equipment, was top rated, and the pilots were considered to be exceptionally skilled. The police force still went unarmed, except when called out on anti-insurgency patrols.

In spite of these achievements and reputations, the incidents by insurgents involving attacks on farms and missions close to our borders were escalating. The perpetrators were coming across the border, mounting an attack and scurrying back to the neighbouring country, where they thought themselves safe. We had troops in the field who were thin on the ground and by the time they reached the scene of the attack, the culprits were long gone.

Without a shadow of a doubt, Rhodesia had the best interracial relationships in the whole of Africa, if not the world. To my dying day, I will stand by that. Furthermore, the Rhodesian Army was over eighty per cent black, which should give everyone pause for thought.

Ian Smith was roundly condemned when he made his, 'I have the happiest Africans in Africa' speech. As Rhodesians, we hated the foreign press with a passion and failed to understand their vindictive attitude towards us.

The insurgent incursions were on the increase and we needed more manpower to assist the fighting men of our little country. The Rhodesian government called for volunteers, and Rhodesians rose to the challenge. Such was the volume of people willing to defend what they had that, instead of a day to process any volunteers, it took nearly a week.

I went along with Ron for a medical and an interview and applied to join the army, not really expecting to be called up, but with the mechanical qualifications and technical knowledge I had, they must have recognised that I could complement a mechanised regiment. Mawson GR was given the rank of Sergeant and put on the army payroll. I was assigned to the Armoured Cars division as a senior NCO. Ron was attached to Internal Affairs at Chikurubi Prison; the nickname 'Chikurubi Ron' seemed appropriate and stuck. I suggested to Ron that he was on the wrong side of the bars. Unfortunately, his retort was unprintable. I must take more care in future with the selection of my friends.

Though I had a busy life to keep me out of mischief with a wife who slipped in and out of depression, a hotel to help run, and my busy workshop, I found myself itching to establish myself within the Rhodesian Army. Rhodesians stood unanimous in the belief that their country was worth fighting for, and even if the war meant hanging on to our paradise for only a few more years, which is what transpired before it was given away by the Brits and Americans, I was determined to help defend my country and serve it with distinction and every ounce of my being.

I knew that it was a physical impossibility to be a part of the fire-force or to run with the Scouts, but I also knew there would be a place for me somewhere within the security forces where I could fit in and serve with distinction. I felt strongly that to serve in the Rhodesian Army was a part of my destiny, and how right that proved to be.

At the time I applied to join, I was informed that I would be under no obligation to go operational, but if I passed certain criteria, the situation could be reviewed. This offer excited me because it gave me the opportunity to prove my worth as an equal to the best in the army. Passing the army's criteria would put me onto a level playing field, which would enable me again to gauge my worth in comparison to my fellow man.

Looking back and seeing how our lives played out, the decision I made to see things through was the right one, and as a family we dealt with all the crises life threw at us and moved on. When we don't have the answers in life, we have to live with the questions in order finally to answer them.

If you have enjoyed reading my story so far, you may like to read the sequel which covers my family's move to a new country and in particular the downward spiral my Penny's life took until she reached rock bottom. I try to describe her fight against bipolar, the condition which had haunted her since the loss of our babies, her slow and arduous climb back to the top with many regressions along the way, and the family's struggle to keep Penny alive through her many suicide attempts. My friend, the mountain, continued to present me and my beloved wife with some very steep, rocky and laborious slopes to climb and conquer. And conquer them we did. I know that for a fact.

I envy no man.
My wants and desires are consumed by my search
to quench their urgencies.
In this way I discover my ability to accomplish every quest.